The Russian “House”

The Russian "House"

An Examination of Post-Soviet Russian Culture in the Times of Putin

Jason C. Vaughn

Hamilton Books

Lanham • Boulder • New York • Toronto • London

An imprint of The Rowman & Littlefield Publishing Group, Inc.
4501 Forbes Boulevard, Suite 200, Lanham, Maryland 20706
Hamilton Books Acquisitions Department (301) 459-3366

6 Tinworth Street, London SE11 5AL, United Kingdom

Printed in the United States of America
British Library Cataloguing in Publication Information Available

Library of Congress Control Number: 2018956550
ISBN: 978-0-7618-7056-2 (cloth : alk. cloth)—ISBN: 978-0-7618-7057-9 (electronic)

∞™ The paper used in this publication meets the minimum requirements of American National Standard for Information Sciences Permanence of Paper for Printed Library Materials, ANSI/NISO Z39.48-1992.

Printed in the United States of America

For the American Armed Services.
And those who have died for our country.
Fight with Honor.
In particular, thank you to my uncles Alvin and Billy.
You are my heroes.

And, of course, for T.

Contents

List of Figures

Appreciation

Thank you to all the people in Russia/Eurasia I have interviewed, taught English to, and talked with over the years, and for their often polite (and rarely impolite) opinions. Thank you to my friends and family for all the valuable support over the years. Thank you to Dr. Peter J.S. Duncan, Dr. Trevor Thomas, and Professor Martyn Rady from my graduate school, School of Slavonic and East European Studies/University College London, for all their ideas, opinions, support, and advice concerning my book(s) over many years. Lastly, but far from least, thank you to my wife for telling me when I was (and am) on the right track, and when I most definitely was (and am) not.

Research Question(s)

The primary focus here is on what Russians think about Russia. As such, how and in what context do Russians perceive their social and cultural position(s) domestically and internationally?

Secondarily, but by extension, what do Russians "want" from their leaders and political elites in the post-Soviet era? Nationalism is a hindrance, it is true, and has arguably come to the forefront, in large part due to the self-aggrandizing policies of the leaders themselves headed by second (and fourth) Russian president Vladimir Vladimirovich Putin. Are such policies giving ordinary Russians what they "want," as some of those same leaders suggest, or are such policies simply gathering popular support by perpetuating latent fears in Russian society?

As such, given the more aggressive foreign and domestic policies towards Crimea and elsewhere, and widely-publicized but aimless anti-corruption policies internally (also given the circumstances in which Russia is one of the most corruption-riddled countries on Earth), where do Russians think that Russia is "coming from" and where do they think that Russia should be "going?"

Transliteration

Russian language texts are translated and transliterated by the author and, in this book, will usually be transliterated according to the Library of Congress system, except in those cases including names and sources where another transliterated version is better known and/or more common. Here, Yeltsin will never be El'tsin, for example.

Short Summary of Purpose

This book examines Russian society as considered by the Russian people. This study recognizes the political, economic, and social structure of post-Soviet Russia in the 2010s-era given that the Russian citizenry, the ethnic, the civil and the national, still desires, and recognizes the need for, reform while still relying on a host of ideas which Russian society and culture reflexively fall back on. This book will examine categorizations as separated into five co-equal "constructs" that this book will posit to be axiomatic of Russian culture and worthy of consideration in further view of the possibility for Russia to one day become a stable and prosperous country without authoritarianism, bloodshed, militarism, or excess nationalism.

ONE

Introduction

"Aversion, fear, suspicion, and jealousy usually stem from a lack of trust and respect."

—Dmitry Pisarev, Russian writer, 1840–1868

ANALYTICAL ASSESSMENT

This publication is premised on the belief that, to understand Russia, one must attempt to independently understand the Russian people.

Although many parallels and much analysis will be made addressing the leadership and regime of the second and fourth President (and, for a short time in between, Prime Minister) Vladimir Vladimirovich Putin, understanding Russia is presupposed on understanding the Russian people, and not the Putin regime. Such examination will address the media environment and the status of civil society in Russia today. These will however be seen in the context of attempting to analyze what the Russian people think and believe and not the other way around, that is, analyzing the Russian people based only on analysis of the Putin regime and the media, political, and legal environment that that regime inspires.

In this book, I maintain and argue that Russia and the Russian people can be separated from the Putin regime.

On one hand, Russia is a country of great history and great accomplishment, despite an authoritarian present and past. The Russian people are one of the kindest, most generous, and most intelligent peoples of the world and I have little bad to say about them.

On the other hand, the Putin regime and its allies (the high-level operators, the "vory"[1] or—thieves—the associated oligarchs and liars that run the Russian state) is a debilitating drain on Russia that does not represent the true nature of the Russian people. The operators and thieves within the regime take Russia's resources at the expense of the Russian people.

When television "experts" and even some very smart observers refer to the Putin regime, Russia, and the Russian people synonymously, my blood pressure rises a bit. Furthermore, I routinely hear on-line, on television, and from "experts," about "Russian" hacking and so forth. There is nothing uniquely "Russian" about hacking, or about viruses or breaking other peoples' computer systems, these are international state-backed criminal activities done by individuals at Putin's, his regime's, and (hence) the Kremlin's behest and are attributable to no nationality. Who knows the nationality of those people that the Kremlin finds to hack America's computer systems?

Instead, I prefer the term "Kremlin" hacking, or "Kremlin" this-or-that when referring to the Putin regime's international criminal activities.

Generally-speaking, I will forward a practical,[2] as opposed to any absolute or strict ideological,[3] consideration of Russians about their country and that there is a grey area between that which Russians "want," it being some degree of the: 1) specific—the simplistic dissemination of law and order, "fighting" disorder, undeniable and often nationalistically-based, espoused by Putin and his regime, competing with the: 2) general—the perceived need for modernity, or what evolved and used to be called (in Soviet parlance when that earlier regime was faltering) openness or "glasnost," and restructuring or "perestroika."

Therein, while currently the first degree indicated (the "specific") is, by default from its own rhetoric, pro-regime, the second degree (the "general") also lends itself somewhat today to the perpetuation of simple popular support for the leadership of Russia.[4] What is often required in Russian political culture, as in all political cultures it must be said, the temporary polity for solving specific issues coexists with the permanent need for improving overall life; adversity often leads to a push to return to what "worked before," (in the Russian case, aspects of Soviet Communism) and no book as this one can fail but to notice this.

In some respects, the concepts of Russia within the contextualization as here discussed will maintain that democracy in the Russian case has both a degree of adherence to democratic precepts, and of destruction of the same, oftentimes co-existing ever so uncomfortably alongside one another.

Reasons for this book are clear. This analytical endeavor is useful in supporting those who make, develop, and otherwise establish policy operating in and on Russia based on the need to engage on the issue of how to deal with the Russian peoples' outlook on politics both independent of, and in view of, their approach to the political regime. Many times, over the course of many years, I have been asked: why, indeed, do the Russian people support the Putin regime? This book is in part my answer.

My first book was intended to understand the social constituency of this question: in detail, an exploration of how to understand the "pathways" of lies in Russian culture and society. These arguments and queries were further justified by the revelation that Russian state-supported hacking had a role to play in the 2016 American Presidential election. While somewhat peripheral concerning many of the discussions here covered in this book, significant points relevant to the Russian regime's multiple efforts to repeatedly externalize Russia's internal polity cannot be avoided herein, and this will be, as such, another argument touched upon.[5]

Back on the theory at hand, this book is a further sociological exploration of how Russians "understand" and "see" Russia, how they "perceive" Russia as a society, and how this can affect the Russian political system.

This book however does not seek to encompass all facets or every approach possible, that might indeed be infinite, yet it will use extensive and detailed research and my long study in Russia to create a unique view on how ordinary Russians respond to the predominant situation internally-focused and externally-influenced by both the Putin regime and by international actors.

Through this book, one can better understand the Russian people, how they exist, and what the future may hold, in specific in dealing with Western governments and business interests.

This book will also not be a prolonged study of the "Russian soul," or some metaphysical abstract like that. For my part, the concept of the "Russian soul" is over-used and not any different from anyone else's "soul." Too many times, I've heard from too many usually-good analysts (and I will not name names), talking about the greatness or aversions inherent or relative to the "Russian soul." I find that whole argument distasteful, more than a little laughable, and will treat it as such.

Over the course of this book, I will consider that the de facto "laissez faire" attitude (referred to at times as apathy) among the people does itself have its own limits, but by and large, motivations to change are not often constituent of generating inspiration or innovation exceeding the quasi-boundaries notable of Putin and "Putinism."

In fact, I argue here that any alleged "apathy" of the Russian people is false. Saying that they are apathetic implies that the Russian people have exposure to and access to all the means necessary to make rational decisions. Because of the Putin regime's limitations on media and civil society, the Russian people do not have all the "tools" necessary to make informed political decisions, so they vote for what they "know," that is: the Putin regime.

Also, while not indicative of society but is encouraged by "Putinism," Russian society is morally forced into a zero-sum game, where either one is the aggressor, or one is representative of the weak. I advance here that this worrisome drift from apathy to aggression (and back again) is one of the most unfortunate resulting trends in Russian society of the post-Soviet era.

Reflecting the hybrid analysis by other scholars and organizations, as to be covered, the Putin regime publicly professes a democratic ideology, but projects harsh authoritarianism when dealing with issues when authority is challenged. I also agree however that in Russia, there are many misunderstandings on what constitutes authoritarianism, and oftentimes, the terminology of democracy is misunderstood, as accurately posited by Henry E. Hale: "While there is a great deal of variety across Russian individuals in their support for democracy, we find that relatively few Russians can be called true authoritarians. [. . .] At the same time, Russians do display a greater preference for relying on strong individual leadership than is typical of Western democracies."[6]

While the Putin regime has met potentially explosive situations where there has been at least the possibility of some loss of control, particularly but not only in the Bolotnaya Square protests of 2011, at the same time, due in part to the failure to sustain any initiative, the Russian opposition has also been dissonant, divided, and, quite simply, often "talked itself into nothingness,"[7] and duly missed key possibilities for possible upheaval or revolution such as during those same events. As such, I will allege that the current state of Russia is, at least in smallest part, the fault of the Russian pro-democracy opposition and not purely on the Putin regime and the Yeltsin regime before it. No one with a government interest is absolved here of responsibility, not the regime, not the bureaucracy, and not the failed attempts of the opposition or of civil democrats.

Over the course of these chapters, three concurrent themes will be found to be dominant in Russian society. These are: Eternal Russia; Independent Russia; and Unique Russia.

Much will be discussed about these three themes but suffice it to say at this point that each theme contains an aspect of how Russians "perceive" their country and its place in the world.

The three themes are also important in that Putin's, and his regime's, policies recognize the value in those themes. The regime then associates and dedicates emphasis to those three themes, and therein lies much of his support in Russian public opinion. Although it will be of secondary importance in this book, I could argue that the key failure(s) of President Boris Yeltsin before Putin was Yeltsin's inability through his own policies to clearly emphasize a progressive polity and turn away from conservative temptations (including the choice of Putin as his successor).

In this book, I will also address relevant issues, problems, and conflicts in Russia and how Russia is dealt with internationally, while ideally keeping the Russian people interests in mind. Reviewing those who have worked parallel to my research over the years, my fellow analysts have often focused on the Putin regime, what Putin "fears" the "most" regarding the people, and how his regime ultimately could and will come to an end.

While I've maintained before[8] that Putin probably fears a so-called "color" revolution the most, a concerted lack of regime authority therein such as has occurred in other former Soviet republics and Soviet bloc countries (and I maintain that as such), the answer to the second question is yet unpredictable.

"Putinism" as an extent regime will no doubt come to an end one day. I am hopeful that "Putinism" will end when the Russian public and opposition, likely not with external help, will find the right mix of initiative and environment to turn the page on "Putinism."

Putin however is probably planning his step-down from power as a peaceful transition to a chosen successor. Furthermore, as with Putin's own predecessor, Boris Yeltsin, and Putin's continued influence notwithstanding, at least some elements of his departure could be personally defined by Putin's successor(s) and possibly not by Putin himself.

This book also asks as to where the people of Russia will be headed in the future, again in the abstract, after considering the past and present. Ever so ugly the road might be, I will cover that as well.

The future of the Russian people does predominantly lie in Europe, as opposed to lying in some Eurasian abstract; yet most importantly the future lies in defining Russia as Russia and in joining the world as a peaceable member of the "family of nations." The future, or at least to what extent we can define it, also must involve defining Russians as uniquely Russian, but who can also share in that "family of nations."

However, there is a necessity in keeping some elements of the status quo, despite whatever disappointments which are inevitable, and which often substitute for real reform that have been and continue to be undertaken by the current regime in this perpetually flawed situation. Russia will continue to be a significant force in international politics, and Russians in general, I've found, have a will to continue to consider themselves as a worldly-engaging people, if not as a superpower-leading people.

Again, regarding Russia's current trajectory, the aggressive foreign policies of Putin and his regime will likely not last beyond his personal leadership; no other political actor in Russia, at least in the foreseeable future, has both the will and initiative to attempt the types of things that Putin has done in places like Ukraine, Georgia, and Syria. When Putin disappears from the Kremlin, there will be at least some pause when Russia will look in on itself (and it may be a stark time indeed) rather than external to the world, although potential international crises that cannot wait of course will have to be dealt with as well.

Indeed, one distinctive part of Putin and "Putinism" is the degree to which the leader has promoted his own all-encompassing leadership above all his fellow political actors, who are not-infrequently portrayed informally in culture as being, as it were, inferior. Putin is the single leader, and in the atmosphere of late 2010s Russia, only he can "allow" a successor.

As a side note, given what I have said about a peaceful transition, if leadership change necessarily needs to happen suddenly for whatever reason, the succession will not be unchallenged, and a somewhat prolonged power struggle quite possibly could occur. In that situation, as covered in this book, and as they say in the movies, then "all bets are off." Nevertheless, I will stick to my analysis of the Russian people (and how they are analyzed), the regime when outstanding, and the predictions of the future will be kept to a minimum (though on very rare occasions, when appropriate, I will get out my "crystal ball" as well).

ENGAGEMENT OF THE ISSUE AT HAND

To engage on the issues explored here, I will first look at how this book originated, if you will:

The Russian people have fascinated me all my life. While growing up, I read all the classics, Tolstoy, Dostoevsky, and so on, but also I (as a young American in the Reagan era) saw the movies where the Soviets were the bad guys and I just had to know, who are these people and how can we better understand them? Over the course of doing research for this book and for my preceding publications, I've had the honor of trying to figure out the Russian people and meet a lot of great and not-so-great people along the way.

Much of the research here has further been necessitated by my work, that of providing perspective for government and military officials who are tasked with dealing with Russian foreign and military policies.

One of the primary sources of inspiration for the topic of this book came long before my analytical career truly started however, when I was working on my graduate degree(s) in Moscow with the assistance of Moscow State University. One boring evening after looking for people to interview for their opinion(s) on the second Chechen war early on in that conflict, a notable Russian friend of mine, experienced in the ways of the Caucasus and himself from a southern Russian town near Krasnodar Krai, unexpectedly told me in English, and in an alliterative way all his own, that (and here I must paraphrase because I was not keeping precise notes or any recording at the time): "Russia was, and is, as a country, like a well-kept, well-lived in, but sometimes well-abused, house."

Somewhat taken by surprise by the sudden and rather philosophical (which was not his normal countenance) comment, and because he said it completely out of the blue, I asked him what that was supposed to mean, thinking that he was "playing with my mind" after several vodkas we had just finished (in the Russian style no less, with pickles and black bread). My own thought was: how can a house, one might ask, be well-kept and well-abused? Anyway.

He related the idea not so far removed from perhaps similar Western parables where the house of a Russian family was a special place, that there was always warmth in the home, that the family would always eke through life by using some amount of a traditional modus operandi, that the Russian home was both a place of closely-held respect and of light-hearted spectacle. Of course, God had a place in every Russian home. Blood was thicker than water etc. etc.

With a subdued smile I said ok, pondering on the rather hearty (some might say mawkish) tone of the conversation, which had gone rather quickly from him and I discussing then-current Russo-American relations to that suddenly quiet contemplation of the Russian "home." As the subject only lingered over the course of another vodka or two, we moved on to topics far removed as we often did. Nevertheless, I didn't forget the analogy; having always had a deep interest in Russian "thought," it was, I must say, quite interesting to me. I succinctly never forgot it; here over the course of this publication, and in view of my research question which has itself been long contemplated and exigent, I feel I should ponder it further.

So, let's look at this Russian "house," and how we should build and treat such an edifice:

Not that I'm a great builder, my concept is something like this. In constructing a free-standing house, one normally lays a foundation first. The "foundation," the Russian people, are strong. It is solid, made of concrete, or in the older era, stone or something equally solid, and then the framework starts going up, shortly followed by the walls. The framework oftentimes is wood or metal; the walls can be brick, can be wood, can be concrete, but whatever it is, it must be part and parcel with the frame for steadying the walls, and then placed onto the top: the roof, while the walls and inner portions are simultaneously installed.

Whatever the case, walls and roof must be strong. They must withstand the elements, must age well and must provide protection from whatever else may come to endanger the structure or those who occupy it.

As so it goes, post-Soviet Russia inherited a "house" that had a decrepit unkempt structure and that held a questionable self-important "status" that some (but far from all) "residents" and "neighbors" held to be of great significance. It would be like inheriting a building of long history but nearly fit for condemnation, or something like that.

Soviet Communism had many notable modern achievements: some few economic (particularly in the first decades[9]) and some of a scientific nature, and symbols and ideas which were created in revolutionary times and nobly held by some, at least in theory, and few of these could just be overtly discounted; these are what made the Soviet Union the superpower that for a fair amount of time rivaled the United States in global influence. While realistically, for the many who studied and to some degree understood the Soviet Union, many of these rivaling achievements were illusory when compared to the strong economy of the United States, at least a few believed that the Soviet Union could in some way "win" the Cold War, whatever that meant.

Nevertheless, the "house" was a shamble; it was a different story altogether as the structure was, not to be too brazen, made of relative spit and duct tape. The decrepit and cruel nature of the Soviet idea, not to mention age, took its toll; as time went on, the "house." was rotten, dilapidated, and quite literally falling apart.

Countless lives had been lost through failed policies and intentionally-designed horrors (for instance, Ukraine's Moscow-created famine, the Holomodor,[10] and all the great amount of intelligence and humanity wasted in the Gulags.[11] dotting the Soviet artifice), all in the vain effort to keep the "party" in the "house" going for those very few at the top who supported and did not question the regime and to design and build further on those previous "achievements," such as they were.

Post–1991, Russians, the citizenry, elites, and government, undertook many years of unsure reform that, as of the mid-2010s, created some signs of renaissance in some specific ways, but the structure remains deeply flawed in others. Further signs of racism and xenophobia, and you name it, are significant.[12] All the while Russians constituting at least the ethnic and/or civil "Russian" core,[13] sought to keep an array of "constructs," by which I mean ideas and concepts, in Russian life which step back to their history, their tradition(s) and their imperial past(s).

Given all this, the most important thing that I have endeavored to do is to provide political, military, and social actors with a productive context of engaging the issue at hand; that is: of how to address, or make policy, or understand, or live in, or research, or what have you, Russian society.

METHODOLOGY

This book is separated into five "constructs" as pertaining to how ordinary Russians view each aspect of the past, present, and future of Russia. These constructs correspond to, according to my own research, what Russians think and hold most dear in considerations of their society and culture, and they represent what, how, and in what context Russians view everyday life. While I understand that other analysts and observers may disagree with the choices or approach stated here, given my own experience, I personally consider it to be the best of the choices available.

In the order this book will seek to examine them successively; they are: the "Idea of Russia," the "Respect and Spectacle of Russia," the "Skill of Russia," the "Ally, Family and Friends of Russia," and the "Money" of Russia.

Over the course of a chapter dedicated to each construct, new research, interviews, cultural, and media primary and secondary sources will be used to give a better understanding of what is Russian life in the beginning of the twenty-first century.

Specifically, my research and interviews of the Russian public across Russia over the past fifteen-plus years will be the basis for this work.

Again, it is a deeply-held position in my mind that the Putin regime is not the real Russia. The Russian people are the real Russia, and I pursue this here with purpose.

Adding to my research, and filling in the blanks when necessary, media examination and the continued review of well-conducted public opinion survey results will be used, duly produced by the likes of the Levada Centre and other such independent organizations which have long reputations for good and reliable statistical production in Russia.

According to what cleavages (young vs. old, etc.) that I could separate, I myself asked just simply: "What do you think of this?" or "What do you think of that?"

Given the five constructs organized in this book, other questions involve: "What is important for you in particular?" "What is important for Russia?" "What does the government do that helps/worries you; makes you happy/sad?" "Do you support Putin?" "What ideas do you associate/not associate with Putin?" Sometimes most importantly: "Are you Russian?" and "Why?"

Indeed: "What is the meaning of being Russian?" Many of my most outstanding and interesting responses have been in off-the-record and unthinking comments from various ordinary Russians "on the street," or in my classrooms, and I will seek to incorporate these responses as much as possible into the text here.

For a brief example, one of my adult students at the English school I worked at in late 2015 told me straight out that nothing was more important for Russia than the family and respect. Putin supported those things, he added, and he supported those ideals by just standing up to Western "pressure" (I didn't ask what kind of pressure; I wish I did) and by being the President that Russia "needed him to be," which reminded me of something from a Batman movie from some years ago. Later, he augmented and expanded on his statement: then including various components in which I will mention later in this book. However, for now I'll acknowledge his public points further with the fact that his fellow students in that same class were looking straight at me and nodding their heads in agreement.

The primary title of this book is *The Russian "House."* I've always thought that Putin's domestic policies have been opposite to the English expression, "to build a house from the ground up," meaning that you start at the bottom and work your way up. The Putin regime has, since the fall of the Soviet Union, betrayed the population and has failed to create a forum for civic and social advancement, if anything making the house as a "bunker" downwards. One characteristic of the rule of second (and fourth) President Vladimir Vladimirovich Putin has been to reinforce this structure through those "tried-and-true" means of power available to him, primarily through the normalized doctrine of enforcing order (but not law) on the Russian people.

By extension, those "means of power" unduly take advantage of the Russian peoples' senses of patriotism, nationalism, and martyrdom,[14] which I discuss here in this book by means of the three "themes" (Eternal Russia, Independent Russia, and Unique Russia). The regime's doctrine culminates, if you will, when the people (and at least a fair amount do indeed) walk into the voting booth/area and cast a vote for Putin, or his supporting parties.

What this book will not do is either attempt to abjectly criticize the ideals that ordinary Russians hold dear, nor will it attempt to be all-encompassing in examining the outlooks of said population. These are approaches which are exhausting and are to be avoided here. Also, while literature has inevitably shaped my views on modern Russia, I tend to veer away from reliance on literature-based arguments explaining Russian public opinion.[15] For instance, Dostoevsky, that author's arguments on truth and justice and against the schools of thought surrounding enlightenment of the nineteenth century, before and beyond, do provide an in-depth classicist explanation of much in Russian life and I do not deny that, however I most often try to focus on more pragmatic explanations of society in politics in Russia today.

Structurally, the five constructs of this book I have chosen because in all my travels, interviews, and conversations which I've held across Russia, this collection represents the most common points on which the Russian public and their culture often repeats, "comes back to," and/or "falls back on," if you will.

The three themes, as I will discuss, are involved in all five chapters/constructs to be covered, however some of the themes may be more appropriate in some constructs than others.

Further, there are many smaller and more personal points of which have been expressed to me. Like in other countries with other peoples, everyone has a life story. Everyone has their own "universe" or "solar system," to an extent, whereby their families and friends "revolve" around; those certain elements or ideals exist and "move through space" towards a future which is sometimes definite and certain, but oftentimes not, and so on. Yet, the Russian "people," with their own unique paradigmatic qualities, have their own views and constructs related to their country, many of which they are proud of, and which I will examine as a highly interested analyst and observer.

Again, of principal interest are Russia's interventions in parts of Ukraine and Georgia. Outside the former Soviet space, Russian ships and planes once again attempt to deploy, operate, and train in and around the more distant regions of the world, albeit not in Soviet-level strength, but with some capability. 2016 saw Russian intervention in the Syrian Civil War, in support of the Putin regime's ally, the Syrian al-Assad regime, against pro-Western Syrian rebel factions. Significantly, that year also the first deployment of Russia's only currently operating aircraft carrier,[16] the relatively-old "Admiral Kuznetsov," also to the shores of Syria.[17]

Supposedly, these operations were, as following the current Russian government policy, only meant to attack the extremist Da'esh/Islamic State forces. Independent observers[18] however understand with common sense that Putin's intention is to support Assad as an "old" ally, and this will be addressed obliquely insofar as the Russian people are concerned. Whatever the case, the complicated multi-faceted civil war in Syria, in the very center of the Middle East, has threatened global stability and has lastingly destroyed quite a lot of post-Soviet rapprochement between Russia and the West.

Also, in less capable shows of force, Russian special forces and their drones have appeared to deploy in the Egypt-Libya region;[19] Russian ships patrolled around the world; Russian planes routinely flew (and fly) across the Pacific, the Caribbean Sea, the Baltic Sea and the North Sea to what extent they can (and it is limited) until they are intercepted by NATO aircraft. As a further side note, although generally unaddressed in Russian society, Russian mercenaries have been showing up in combat arenas, most prominently in Syria under the aegis of the company name Wagner ("Vagner") where they have had mixed results in supporting official Russian forces and Assad-supporting groups.[20]

Nevertheless, focus in this book will remain on the Russian people and not on the Putin regime's global adventures, of which the Russian people are only vaguely aware.

"DEFINING" RUSSIA'S SYSTEM—ADDITIONAL FINDINGS

Through this study of the Russian people, alongside the three aspects of "Eternal Russia," et al. already mentioned in previous sections, another argument presented in this publication will focus to an extent on defining the mode under which the Russian regime exists.

It is my experience that Russia operates under a system of perpetual motion towards authoritarianism; a motion that must be broken through a better opposition, improved civil society, and independent media if Russia and the Russian people are to break out of this groupthink, if you will.

Many policy makers and/or observers misunderstand, for example, why Russians do not more actively seek to be "European," as the Ukrainians and peoples of the Baltic States do. On that question, outside the many surveys onto a more personal level, when you go to Lithuania, Latvia and Estonia, all former republics of the Soviet Union but now member states of the European Union, and you ask the peoples there if they are European, most often you hear a "full-throated" "YES! We are European." Go only a small distance to the southeast, to St. Petersburg, and you find much more apprehension of the European ideal. Russia becomes separate, not European and not Asian either, but something else; thereby uniquely "Russian."

It will also be suggested here that Putin is not entirely anti-democratic per se, especially when it does not suit him (and Putin has all the acting cues of a democrat well-rehearsed).

In contrast, although it is of little comfort to Russians when and where their human rights are abridged, having seen perhaps hundreds of his speeches and public appearances over the past seventeen-plus years, I believe that Putin has his own deluded view of the world and might even consider himself a democratic actor, in that he consumes his own rhetoric, and, on both the domestic and international scenes, he is a rational actor.

Parallel to that, there are indeed some few and rare indicators that there is some loose (undeniably very loose) democratic standard to which Putin is held to, in which October 2017 polling data from Levada Centre seems to indicate that 76 percent of Russians hold him totally or in part responsible for Russia's problems.[21]

In Russian media, and internationally more than perhaps necessary, he is not surprisingly most often portrayed in that context as a person of his time, a Russian "man," righteous in his views of Russia as a power, albeit provably not under the fictitious rule of law which he himself has implied through his actions on many occasions.

Putin in some ways reflects what Russians like about the "man in charge." As will be covered in due time, Russian people love "heart." They love someone who reflects their outlook, if not precisely their morals. They love a president that can "fly," if you will, that can fight, that can respond to them in a wholly "Russian" fashion (more on that later also) and that can secure the country from those who (looking at Western countries) seem to want to change Russia in their own ways. Russians love Russia. In some ways, the Putin portrayal is "Russia," even if gross aspects of "Putinism" are definitively not Russia in general.

Therefore, in furtherance to that, despite that portrayal-necessitated lip service, Putin is by no means a democrat, if not wholeheartedly an open authoritarian.

There is a gray area relevant here within an understanding of being a democrat in Russian society as well. This gray area is vast in Russian society, and for example, is a place where the concept of "freedom" can be understood differently.

As a concept, this reflects back on an understanding of the Russian word, Volya, in Russian socio-cultural norms: Volya is that spiritual freedom which is absolute, and which can be characterized as most often connected to "violence, pornography, obscenity and nihilism."[22] Volya is very different from rule-based understandings of freedom in Western society, which is characterized more by the Russian word, Svoboda, which means "freedom" but within a set of sociopolitical restrictions and rules. It is such as how Dostoevsky and Tolstoy had varying depictions of how "freedom" is the absence of restriction, without rules and so on, and so do the Russian people, when addressed on the question, see issues of Putin's "law and order" quite differently (and that too will be touched on throughout this book).

As has been explored inexhaustibly by numerous academics et al., and will be discussed in process here in this book, Putin lives and works in a supposedly democratic system that his regime controls ("managed democracy" or "electoral regime"[23]), that is democratic only in some aspects, services only a limited civil society, and which appeals to a default Russian worldview (although, I would argue, this is correspondingly not full "populism,"[24] as that is sometimes depicted, i.e., there is most oftentimes less of a politically-inspired call to the "common man" in Putin's polity, but, once again, more on that later). He gives short shrift to dissent and, though not always obvious, he guards the elites that support him, once referenced as the "Siloviki" but now expanded into not simply those from a background descended from the Russian intelligence services of the past, as that word has suggested. His coterie now simply reflects a hardened set of elites with skill-sets that can help themselves loot Russia and maintain the Putin regime.[25]

Putin in the context of this book is a man dedicated to taking advantage of whatever he can to keep himself and his regime "in the money" and in power as long as possible. In my own conceptual analysis, I avoid ideology and oftentimes relate Putin to being not so different from any system-abusing thief operating in such an environment, albeit with privileges far beyond any "bank-robber."

As a side note, while some analysts prefer the depiction, I also tend to avoid characterizations of Putin as head of a mafia, but only because such characterizations tend to expropriate facile portrayals of such from pop culture, i.e., seeing Putin as mafia Don figure,[26] but anyway, I digress.

Insofar as his policies take advantage of innate weaknesses of Russia given its history and culture to the benefit of him and his regime, this is corruption, full-stop. Further, I would argue that, beyond being an ambiguous "democrat," Putin cares nothing about constitutional process. Applicable here: as Daphne Skillen wrote regarding 1990s journalists in her brilliant 2017 book on freedom of speech in Russia: "Being a democrat was rather vague; it could mean no more than liking the Beatles."[27]

If given the chance, I would tend to agree with what Mikhail Zygar wrote for the Atlantic in April 2017, that Putin is, if anything, a Tsarist groupie seeking a "victorious Russian empire."[28] In this regard, the argument i.e., "What is Putin?" has the air of pointlessness that other questions like "Is Putin an intelligent person?" have, that is, the lack of any standing given the world we observe and attempt to analyze today.

Back to the argument at hand though, as a potential leadership variant, Putin's opponents, it must be said, are not so much better, as to be discussed over the course of this book. Most of the time, they make noise and achieve little of substance. Some of them labor to find instances of abuse of power and corruption, and, in the case of Alexei Navalny, sometimes find something real (of which I will talk about in due time), that not so many ordinary Russians are surprised by and, indeed, care about.

Looking at those who oppose Putin, Navalny, as will be mentioned multiple times in this book, is probably the strongest of the current set of opposition leaders. He has sought out and published videos et al. on corruption for years. The opposition leaders (in general) and their parties organize marches, sometimes large ones.[29] Yet, as to whether one of these opposition figures could lead Russia and keep the country together as a stable country if given the reins of power, questions still dog the list of Russian opposition leaders, Navalny included.

The methodology inherent to this study will hopefully shed light on many of these questions, through an original and in-depth examination of that very first question here discussed: "What do Russians think about Russia?" Indeed, the importance for today of understanding Russian culture, and these five constructs, is both apparent and undeniable.

PARALLEL ANALYTICAL PUBLICATIONS

Several parallel analytical publications must be mentioned here, reflecting other valuable studies which have been and continue to be published and which inspired my work on this book overall. There are many books, chapters, and studies that have at least touched on aspects of the work I conducted for this publication, however I will only focus on a few which guided and supplemented my work herein. Many more publications will be covered and referred to over the course of this book as necessary to review points and literature which paralleled my own.[30]

A forerunner of this book in some aspects is Ellen Carnaghan's 2007 book, *Out of Order: Russian Political Values in an Imperfect World*, in which she asks the question, much similar to my own: "but what do Russians think, and what are the sources of those attitudes?"[31] Differing from my own work, Carnaghan uses many more statistical analyses and focus groupings (as opposed to my more socio-political and cultural focus) in order to solve the question of Russians' political values, producing many valid findings along the way which are of great relevance here. Quite correctly, based on her focus groups, Carnaghan finds that: "While it is true that some of my respondents might have been convinced to curtail their new freedoms in the hope of greater social order, this reflected less a low value placed on freedom than awareness that personal freedoms can hardly be practiced in a lawless environment."[32]

As I will often reference as well, Carnaghan therefore hits on the continuing Russian social and political catch-22 of putting Putin's professed "order" on a pedestal next to, and in competition with, what could happen if the Putin regime were "softer" on political opposition, if you will.

More recently, there are many books of notable value (as of the time of this writing), and which are worthy of mentioning here: Karen Dawisha's *Putin's Kleptocracy* was a very influential publication for my first book, and we cannot forget it here, especially when we discuss how things often get missing in Russia, where property goes, and how corruption dominates Russian society.[33] Masha Gessen's *The Future is History*[34] and *A Man Without a Face,*[35] Lilia Shevtsova's *Putin's Russia,*[36] Luke Harding's *Mafia State,*[37] and (as mentioned before) Daphne Skillen's *Freedom of Speech in Russia*[38] all take quite strong looks at aspects of the malevolence inherent to the Putin regime, how it takes advantage of the Russian people, and how it's constituencies make money, and all these writers have strong arguments that are worthy of discussion.

For instance, Masha Gessen's book, *The Future is History,* follows and characterizes several Russians, one or two well-known, like assassinated reformer Boris Nemtsov's daughter, Zhanna, in their relationship(s) with power and the authorities in a valid attempt by Gessen to say that Homo Sovieticus, the "evil" characterization of Soviet people created by Soviet Communism and depicted by sociologist Yuri Levada's adherent, Lev Gudkov, still exists and is rising in the age of Putin. In partial agreement with this, noting that Homo Sovieticus was a product of its own time, I've never felt that today's Russian in general is analogously depicted by any such mindset, or at least not so bound as some observers imply by use of analysis and polling opinion data. Nevertheless, Gessen reliably and distinctly addresses many of the societal and cultural aspects which I try to discuss more in the context of overall Russian society in this book.

Indeed, while I keep my focus steady at the people, or at least I try to, most of those writers, academics, and journalists examine top-heavy issues, if you will. As such, I am equally trying to show how Putin and his regime manage to dominate "aspects" of Russian society and, by extension, those aspects as applicable to many of the small corners of Russia's sociopolitical sphere.

It must be mentioned, for those seeking a more social and historical context about the rise of Putin in the post-Soviet era and how "thoughts" of a free civil society altered into public support for aspects of authoritarianism, look no further than Arkady Ostrovsky's *The Invention of Russia: The Journey from Gorbachev's Freedom to Putin's War,*[39] which does a wonderful job of trying to explain this sociopolitical journey. Ostrovsky's work parallels my own in that both his book and this one seeks to find a "human" side to what the Russian people are thinking, where they are coming from, and where they are going. My five-aspect approach is considerably different from Ostrovsky's, however, in that I try to define a specifically more broad-scope view of the Russian people and how they "exist" and how they "view" Russia itself in a world existing on just the cusp of relative chaos.[40]

One central publication focusing on the argument presented here is Nikolay Petrov, Maria Lipman and Henry E. Hale's recent paper on the: "Three Dilemmas of Hybrid Regime Governance: Russia from Putin to Putin." In this paper, Petrov and company discuss in detail the Russian public's view of the Putin regime and its demands on the government et al. Whereas this publication focuses on how Russians view Russia relative to five archetypes of understanding, Petrov, Lipman, and Hale's work looks alternatively at managing difficulties that are presented to the Putin regime with keeping power while at the same time keeping the people happy. As they correctly say, and as they point out, the Russian government is a hybrid regime meaning that autocratic elements and democratic elements are constantly rubbing up against one another in the on-going governance of the country. Petrov and company write: "In particular, we argue that Russia's peculiar combination of authoritarian and democratic elements can be understood as emerging from a series of what we call dilemmas of hybrid regime governance. Here we focus on three: the dilemma of elections, the dilemma of mass media, and the dilemma of the state."[41]

Petrov, Lipman, and Hale's work thereby focuses more on the practical and pragmatic of the Russian regime's view of the people and the people's view of the state, instead of delving more into the collective mindset(s) and understanding(s) of the Russian people, which I find to be the more interesting. Their views of the tests that the Russian leadership endure, different as reflecting the inherent authoritarian aspect of Putin and his crew, are profound and of great substance in any study of this subject matter. Indeed, their work is of great value and will be referred to again over the course of this publication. Furthermore, Hale's solo work on public opinion research and his studies are of great use to those seeking to understand ordinary Russians' understanding of democracy and how that term and others are frequently misinterpreted.[42]

Anne L. Clunan's 2009 book on *The Social Construction of Russia's Resurgence: Aspirations, Identity, and Security Interests*[43] is also very interesting in paralleling my study of the Russian people and the social development of post-Soviet Russia. I have been inspired by her writings concerning those interests inherent to Russia's social constructs. When I was focusing on how the Russian people understood and "respected" the Putin regime, Clunan's work was always in the back of my mind, as they say.

Paul T. Christensen's 2013 chapter on "Russia as Semi-Periphery: Political Economy, the State, and Society in the Contemporary World System"[44] inspired much of my work on understanding the Respect of Russia and its categorization as a "semi-periphery" state, and I will oftentimes refer to Christensen's writing in that chapter.

Joan DeBardeleben's and Mikhail Zherebstsova's chapter on "Managerial Patronage"[45] and the "Power Vertical," and Elena Belokurova's chapter on "NGOs and Politics,"[46] gave me greater understandings on the political forces at work in relation to the Russian people and I was greatly moved by DeBardeleben's and Zherebstsova's idea of a "managerial patronage" model. Their work in Orlov oblast, Stavropol krai, and Nizhegorodskaya oblast had meaning in understanding their model. They wrote: "United Russia and the presidential apparatus were able to use rewards and incentives as a means of making inroads into political machines at the regional level during Putin's presidency once the removal of elections made regional executives accountable to and increasingly dependent on the Kremlin for political survival."[47]

Such studies parallel the part of this book which focus on the peoples' access to the political process and I oftentimes remembered their work as I was writing this publication.

Another publication which has had much bearing on some of the issues studied in this book is Joanna Szostek's work(s) concerning Russia's "strategic narrative." Her studies are fascinating in consideration, quite correctly, of how messages meant for domestic audiences have opposing effects for domestic audiences. While this book does not dwell on foreign audience receptions so much, it has been a pleasure to consider her quite valid arguments when writing this book.[48] Her work on "popular geopolitics" has been widely inspirational as well.[49] Referencing Russia's military doctrine, Szostek says it best: "It is the domestic audience that, however, matters the most to the Kremlin. Russia's latest military doctrine identifies "information influence on the population" amongst the "main internal military dangers" threatening the country."[50]

For the Center for Eastern Studies, Maria Domanska wrote a report published in November 2017 titled, "Conflict Dependent Russia: The Domestic Determinants of the Kremlin's Anti-Western Policy."[51] In Domanska's study, she covers some of the same bases that I do here in this book and does a wonderful job of analysis therein. However, I do disagree with any depictions of the Russian people as "allies" of the Putin regime in promoting an aggressive foreign policy or the suggestion, as discussed before, that the "Soviet man" (or Homo Sovieticus) is still a typology or characteristic of some great percentage of the Russian populace.

The Russian people, I argue, are not to blame for many of their ills in the post-Soviet world. I do argue, very strongly in fact, that the Russian populace today is fully capable of exceeding the "inferiority complex" or dependency on the state that is referred to, if (again) given access to the "tools" necessary to make an informed political choice, including a better civil society and media atmosphere.

Lastly, Vladimir Shlapentokh's and Anna Arutunyan's 2013 book on *Freedom, Repression, and Private Property in Russia*[52] is probably one the best books that focuses on parallel topics to this book. I have nothing but respect for Shlapentokh's and Arutunyan's contributions to this field and I will relate back to their work, both as individuals and together, a host of times over the course of this book.

This point forward, I shall move on and talk about our first aspect and relevant analysis; that is the "Idea of Russia" in Russian society.

NOTES

1. Galeotti, Mark, *The Vory*, Yale University Press, New Haven, CT, 2018.
2. As I will mention more than once over the course of this book, and as much as some analysts (that will not be named here) would like to put Russia in the context of some strong moral terminologies, I as an author and analyst of Russia for more than fifteen years do not see how hostile associations of segments (or all) of Russian politics with historical monstrosities can square with the notion, which I support, of at least trying to view the Russian state and the Russian people in the mindset of their own points-of-view in this era. Hence, differing from some of my colleagues, Putin is not a "Hitler," he is not even close to conceptually being Hitler; Putin is Putin, and he has his own plans and ways, especially rooted in the Russian outlook and tradition. People love absolutes, especially journalists, because they enhance airtime, or sell newspapers or whatnot, but I dislike absolutes absolutely, and I will stick to this view as such.
3. Although ideology does have a significant influence.
4. Translation of the specific into the general and back again is nothing new; this has relevance in all political cultures in all countries and has been the subject of much political analysis throughout history. However, I believe it is the case that in Russia, and as I will seek to explain, Russian people approach this uniquely, especially in view of their perceived internal and external "enemies," and how, both in the past and present, Russian political culture has had a uniquely antagonistic approach on both sides of this transitory "coin," but, again, I will cover more on this here.
5. As of the writing of this book, see Perlroth, Nicole, Michael Wines, and Matthew Rosenburg, "Russian Election Hacking Efforts, Wider Than Previously Known, Draw Little Scrutiny," *The New York Times*, 1 September 2017, https://www.nytimes.com/2017/09/01/us/politics/russia-election-hacking.html?hpw&rref=technology&action=click&pgtype=Homepage&module=well-region&region=bottom-well&WT.nav=bottom-well.
6. Hale, Henry E., "The Myth of Mass Authoritarianism in Russia: Public Opinion Foundations of a Hybrid Regime," The National Council for Eurasian and East European Research, University of Washington and George Washington University, Seattle WA, 2009, pp. 19–20.

7. A Russian once told me near one of those protests/events in the center of Moscow that the speakers on the platform, some of which were Navalny's people, were "talking to the cats." I kind of liked that metaphor, and I made sure to remember it for publication one day, but never found the chance to work it in anywhere.

8. See my first book: Vaughn, Jason C., *A Socio-Political Model of Lies in Russia: Putin Against the Personal*, University Press of America, Lanham MD, 2016.

9. Though, due to the Eurasian region's potential, its vast resources, and bourgeoning post-war economic might, I would argue that Russia and its empire under any constitution was due for some recognition in the post-Second World War-era. If anything, Communism could be argued to have held back Russia from even greater achievements, but this argument is for others to pursue.

10. To understand the Holomodor, one of the first books I ever read on the subject and still the best is: Conquest, Robert, *The Harvest of Sorrow: Soviet Collectivization and the Terror-Famine*, Oxford University Press, Oxford UK, 1987.

11. Главное управление лагерей, Glavnoye Upravleniye LAGerej, or GULAG, translated: Main Administration Camps were a central facet of the Soviet regime where many political prisoners, indeed many who spoke out against the Soviet regime, were kept, plus a fair number of non-political criminals as well. Some of the Soviet Union's brightest artists and writers spent time in the vast GULAG system, including perhaps most prominently Alexander Solzhenitsyn. There are many histories and varying counts of the residents and forced laborers of the GULAG system, including one written by Solzhenitsyn himself. One of the relatively more recent books studying the Soviet Union's camp system is by Anne Applebaum, which won the 2004 Pulitzer Prize. See Applebaum, Anne, *Gulag: A History*, Anchor Books, New York NY, 2004.

12. "Racism and Xenophobia in March 2017," SOVA, 3 April 2017, Retrieved 16 April 2017, http://www.sova-center.ru/en/xenophobia/news-releases/2017/04/d36730/.

13. As it always has been, the ideas of ethnic and civil Russian identity, of russkie and rossiiskii, continue to be central to debate even to the current day. Is being "Russian" a matter of birth and ancestry or a matter of getting a certain "passport?" Denoting the worthy subject, many academics and analysts have explored these concepts in great detail. In this publication, outside of certain sections, these ideas will be discussed in the context of other arguments presented while generally avoiding an extensive exploration solely on this point. One can get caught up completely in such arguments and that is not the basis for this book. As such, for purposes here, these questions must for the most part be left to others who have specifically explored that debate in other publications. For one more recent article that can provide an opening to the subject for new readers, see (in English): Tishkov, Valery, "The Russian People and National Identity," *Russia in Global Affairs*, No. 3, 2008.

14. Here I am referencing the work of my former academic supervisor, Dr. Peter J. S. Duncan, who is a continuing source of inspiration for my work. See his book, which is very good: Duncan, Peter J.S., *Russian Messianism: Third Rome, Revolution, Communism, and After*, Routledge, London UK, 2000.

15. The number of academic publications that have referred to pre-modern literature within the context of explaining modern Russian sociopolitical standards is notably large. I do not argue that this is an incorrect way of analysis on some types of Russia public opinion, it is fascinating indeed, I only argue that my work mostly exists pragmatically parallel, and not descendant, to these studies.

16. The Admiral Kuznetsov's ship classification as a "heavy aircraft-carrying cruiser" largely for purposes of traversing the Turkish straits, notwithstanding. Whatever the case may be, Kuznetsov will never be mistaken for an American Nimitz-class or (new) Gerald R. Ford-class large-scale so-called "super" aircraft carrier, which are much more capable of a larger collection of mission sets by a factor of perhaps four or more.

17. Not that Russia can even remotely afford a blue-water navy in 2017, as the Russian defense minister Sergey Shoigu has suggested. See: Rezchikov, Andrey,

"Россия больше не может позволить себе океанский флот," (In English): "Russia can no longer afford itself a blue-water (oceanic) fleet," *Vzglyad*, 21 April 2017, Retrieved 24 April 2017, https://www.vz.ru/politics/2017/4/21/324418.html.

18. One of the best summaries of why Putin supports Hafez and Bashar al-Assad (the regime) in Syria actually comes from a September 2015 posting on the blog of the Economist. See: "Why Russia is an Ally of Assad," *The Economist*, https://www.economist.com/blogs/economist-explains/2015/09/economist-explains-22.

19. Stewart, Phil, Idrees Ali, and Lin Noueihed, "Exclusive: Russia appears to deploy forces in Egypt, eyes on Libya role—sources," *Reuters*, 13 March 2017, Retrieved 22 December 2017, https://www.reuters.com/article/us-usa-russia-libya-exclusive/exclusive-russia-appears-to-deploy-forces-in-egypt-eyes-on-libya-role-sources-idUSKBN16K2RY.

20. Khasov-Cassia, Sergei and Robert Coalson, "Russian Mercenaries: Vagner Commanders Describe Life Inside The 'Meat Grinder,'" *Radio Free Europe/Radio Liberty*, 14 March 2018, Retrieved 15 March 2018, https://www.rferl.org/a/russian-mercenaries-vagner-commanders-syria/29100402.html.

21. "Vladimir Putin," Levada Centre, *Press-Vypuski*, 20 November 2017, Retrieved 21 November 2017, https://www.levada.ru/2017/11/20/vladimir-putin-5/.

22. Skillen, Daphne, *Freedom of Speech in Russia: Politics and Media from Gorbachev to Putin*, Routledge, New York and London, 2017, p. 18.

23. As I debated in my first book, and which I will not here go over again, I prefer the "electoral regime" characterization as defined by Richard Rose and Neil Munro back in 2002, but at this point I digress. For the original academic argument as referenced in my first book, see: Rose, Richard and Neil Munro, *Elections Without Order*, Cambridge University Press, Cambridge, 2002, p. 60.

24. "Populism" is a term I dislike, as the meaning has only been implied and never entirely clear, yet it is still common among analysts and academics and I will use it in limited situations.

25. The best explanation for this is from my once-academic advisor at University College London, now-Professor Alena Ledenova, and her two primary books in which she explains "sistema," that is, the shared constitution of corruption and internal self-attachment to ones' fellow corrupt actors in Putin's Russia. See: Ledenova, Alena, *Can Russia Modernise? Sistema, Power Networks and Informal Governance*, Cambridge University Press, Cambridge UK, 2013 [and] Ledenova, Alena, *How Russia Really Works*, Cornell University Press, Cornell NY, 2006.

26. Referring of course to the head of the mafia family in the movie series, The Godfather. Andrey Piontkovsky famously referred to Putin as Al Capone: See: Piontkovsky, Andrey, "Андрей Пионтковский: Кремлевский Аль Капоне," (In English: "Andrey Piontkovsky: The Kremlin Al Capone,") *Radio Svoboda*, 27 November 2017, Retrieved 29 January 2018, https://www.svoboda.org/a/28876197.html.

27. Skillen, Daphne, *Freedom of Speech in Russia: Politics and Media from Gorbachev to Putin*, Routledge, London and New York, 2017, p. 69.

28. Zygar, Mikhail, "Putin Likes to Pretend 1917 Never Happened," *The Atlantic*, 1 April 2017, Retrieved 17 April 2017, https://www.theatlantic.com/international/archive/2017/04/russia-putin-revolution-lenin-nicholas-1917/521571/.

29. As of the time of this writing, the anti-corruption marches of 26 March 2017 following the publication of Navalny's video detailing Prime Minister Dmitry Medvedev's many homes have been duly impressive, with substantive numbers of Russians coming out on the streets in a large number of major cities. Yet, we'll see if there will be a valid and long-lasting ability of Navalny's people to follow-up these protests and accomplish something of major value. I don't doubt that it is possible, and I am hopeful, but again, we'll see. For a media article about these protests, see: Higgins, Andrew, "Aleksei Navalny, Top Putin Critic, Arrested as Protest Flare in Russia," *The New York Times*, 26 March 2017, Retrieved 09 April 2017, https://www.nytimes.com/2017/03/26/world/europe/moscow-protests-aleksei-navalny.html?_r=0.

30. I am not a big fan of fifty-page-long literature reviews such as I had to generate for my graduate degree works. I am far more interested in focusing my time on what I have found and the results of my own study. Nevertheless, in the interests of being complete, I will try to give all due mention to those books and chapters of importance, not only here, but as a running commentary on my results.

31. Carnaghan, Ellen, *Out of Order: Russian Political Values in an Imperfect World*, Pennsylvania State University, Pennsylvania State University Press, University Park PA, 2007, p. 30.

32. Ibid, p. 266.

33. Dawisha, Karen, *Putin's Kleptocracy: Who Owns Russia?*, Simon and Schuster, New York NY, 2015.

34. Gessen, Masha, *The Future is History*, Riverhead Books, New York NY, 2017.

35. Gessen, Masha, *A Man Without a Face*, Riverhead Books/Penguin, New York NY, 2013.

36. Shevtsova, Lilia, *Putin's Russia*, Carnegie Endowment for International Peace, Washington DC, 2005.

37. Harding, Luke, *Mafia State: Spies, Surveillance and Russia's Secret Wars*, Guardian, London UK, 2012.

38. Skillen, Daphne, *Freedom of Speech in Russia: Politics and Media from Gorbachev to Putin*, Routledge, New York and London, 2017.

39. Ostrovsky, Arkady, *The Invention of Russia: The Journey from Gorbachev's Freedom to Putin's War*, Atlantic Books, London UK, 2015.

40. Whether I accomplish this is of course up to the reader to decide.

41. Petrov, Nikolay, Maria Lipman & Henry E. Hale, "Three Dilemmas of Hybrid Regime Governance: Russia from Putin to Putin," *Post-Soviet Affairs*, Volume 30, Issue 1, 2014, p. 3 (pp. 1–26).

42. Hale, Henry E., "The Myth of Mass Authoritarianism in Russia: Public Opinion Foundations of a Hybrid Regime," The National Council for Eurasian and East European Research, University of Washington and George Washington University, Seattle WA, 2009.

43. Clunan, Anne L., *The Social Construction of Russia's Resurgence: Aspirations, Identity, and Security Interests*, The Johns Hopkins University Press, 2009.

44. Christensen, Paul T., "Russia as Semi-periphery: Political Economy, the State, and Society in the Contemporary World System," *The Political Economy of Russia*, ed. Neil Robinson, Rowman & Littlefield, Lanham MD, 2013, pp. 169–90.

45. DeBardeleben, Joan and Mikhail Zherebstsova, "'Managerial Patronage' and the 'Power Vertical,'" *The Politics of Sub-National Authoritarianism in Russia*, ed. Vladimir Gel'man and Cameron Ross, Ashgate Publishing, Surrey UK, 2010, pp. 85–106.

46. Belokurova, Elena, "NGOs and Politics," *The Politics of Sub-National Authoritarianism in Russia*, ed. Vladimir Gel'man and Cameron Ross, Ashgate Publishing, Surrey UK, 2010, pp. 107–22.

47. DeBardeleben, Joan and Mikhail Zherebstsova, "'Managerial Patronage' and the 'Power Vertical,'" *The Politics of Sub-National Authoritarianism in Russia*, ed. Vladimir Gel'man and Cameron Ross, Ashgate Publishing, Surrey UK, 2010, pp. 88.

48. Szostek, Joanna, "Defence and Promotion of Desired State Identity in Russia's Strategic Narrative," *Geopolitics*, Routledge, August 2016, pp. 1–23.

49. Szostek, Joanna, "Popular Geopolitics in Russia and Post-Soviet Eastern Europe," *Europe-Asia Studies*, Volume 69, Issue 2, 2017, pp. 195–201.

50. Szostek, Joanna, "News Consumption and Anti-Western Narratives in Russia: A Case Study of University Students," *Europe-Asia Studies*, Volume 69, Issue 2, 2017, p. 285, (pp. 284–302).

51. Domanska, Maria, "Conflict Dependent Russia: The Domestic Determinants of the Kremlin's Anti-Western Policy," *Point of View Series*, Centre for Eastern Studies, Number 67, Warsaw Poland, November 2017, (pp. 1–56).

52. Shlapentokh, Vladimir and Anna Arutunyan, *Freedom, Repression, and Private Property in Russia*, Cambridge University Press, Cambridge UK, September 2013.

TWO

The Idea of Russia

INTRODUCTION

Asking the question: "What is, actually, the "Idea of Russia?" probably is the first "port of call" here. Extending from the Idea of Russia as a nationalist concept held by a "people," the collective imagination of a large aggregation of individuals from what we know now, and in the past, as Rossiya, general theory usually implies that the Idea of Russia is inevitably connected in some way to, either in opposition to or as beholden to, the "European Other."[1] [2]

Over the course of this chapter (and, to a degree, this book) I will speak on that nationalist concept (or, more accurately, understandings of or variations on that). As to be examined in-depth, other theoretical analysts focus on imperial characteristics[3] of post-Soviet Russian politics (and that will factor in my analysis as well), but I want to focus centrally on the Russian people as we know now and what the Idea of Russia means for them.

In summary, as many aspects will be discussed herein, I will assert that the Idea of Russia is the (1) collected meaning that the Russian people (at least in aggregate) exalt it to be and what they as a people (2) symbolically and, to some extent, (3) morally hold their country to be. The Idea of Russia will be seen here to encompass all three of the aspects of Russia by Russians, that is, the concepts of Eternal Russia, Independent Russia, and Unique Russia.

Having studied Russia for some seventeen-plus years now, this is a fascinating question, and one which I find to be highly worthwhile in asking. Much can be learned about the Russian narod through an analysis of their understanding of the fundamental basis (the "Idea") of their own country from their own point-of-view. Furthermore, a deepening extant of my research has focused on this aspect of their "house," as I began to put into focus this examination in the preparation for undertaking the research contained herein.

It must be mentioned also that I asked questions concerning the Idea of Russia parallel to my previous studies on Russian public opinion, the wars in Chechnya, and then the examination of the culture of lies in Russia which was, respectfully, the subject(s) of my academic research thesis and then my first book on these and related topics.[4]

Further of note: in the building, maintenance, and renovation (if so possible), of their "house," the Idea of Russia for Russians has ebbed and flowed over time, and it should not be forgotten.

As an archetype for overtly nationalist Russians, the Idea of Russia (and the idea of never-forgotten past situations, both good and ill) remains in many ways an attractive one. All the horrors of the past are of course overlooked in their concept.

It serves to mention again of course that for non-ethnic Russians and for those who live in Russia but would, to put it lightly, rarely would even to consider calling themselves Russian, this view on the Idea of Russia is profoundly negative. Here we reference again the ethnic vs. civil concept, officially the so-called "Rossianiye" or civic Russian identity (as opposed to the ethnic identity or "russkii"[5]), much like many other such peoples, they are the Russian but non-Russian. They live in Russia, maybe they use their Russian passports when they travel to other countries, but it is point not easily reconciled for the peoples in question. In observation of the Putin regime's naturally-continuing tendency to focus the acceptance of itself as the only way to make Russia governable, Putin is perhaps not a nationalist on this question, as I agree with academician Marlene Laruelle,[6] but there are many groups on Russia that slide towards the nationalist angle and their influence must not be dismissed.

Extreme nationalism in Russia has had a substantial role to play over time in post-Soviet period Russia amid allegations that some groups, such as the former ruling United Russia party-affiliated and Kremlin-affiliated youth movement Nashi and the pro-Kremlin group SERB (South East Radical Block) movement, have had significant positions in Russian society. The SERB movement is alleged by media sources to be responsible for attacks on the opposition figures; such attacks will be discussed again later in this book.[7]

Such aspects however should not be over-stressed; I do not believe that, in general, Russians as a people are in the least more isolationist now despite the implications of policies followed by the regime of President Vladimir Vladimirovich Putin. The post-Soviet era in general has perhaps not been as conducive to fostering openness to new ideas both foreign and domestic for ordinary Russians as could have been possible. This is partly because of their choice of leader(s). Why this is the case will be an on-going subject of this chapter, and of course it is reflected in part by the difficult and competing past(s) which the country has had to accept in a new era devoid of both a clear pre-Soviet and/or a Soviet-defined status quo to fall back on.

Indeed, from this standpoint beginning with the history of the subject, this chapter seeks to explore the different facets of what constitutes the Idea of Russia in the popular and latent Russian mindset.

THE HISTORY AND PERCEPTIONS OF THE RUSSIAN IDEA

The idea of Rus' and Russia is a spring from which a whole people grew but which has been somewhat alternatively difficult to define almost for its entire existence. As few nations are an "island," especially one that would develop in the middle of a major land mass, the idea of proto-Russia first sprang, as it were, from influence from other peoples, not least of which the Mongol Empire of the thirteenth century, and sometimes from strong opposition and great amounts of suffering (and of course these three parameters are sometimes greatly mythologized in the Russian national "imagination").

The "original" state of Russia was of course Kievan Rus' based from Kiev, which was the first real unification of what was before then a bunch of East Slav tribes. From the ninth to the thirteenth century, Kievan Rus' dealt with managing the area's trade routes and gleaning what money it could from commercial relations with what would later be called Byzantium. Establishing a Christian substance for this new state, according to religious chronicle, a disciple of Jesus, the Apostle Andrew, came to the river banks of Kiev and built a church there, thereby becoming the "Apostle of Rus'."[8] Thus began the eventual primacy of Christianity as the predominant religion in Kievan Rus' and eventually across Russia, and would become one of, if not the most, defining attributes of the "Idea of Russia."

Western sources invariably talked about harsh rule, authoritarianism, and dictatorial admonition in Russia and the stereotype that Russia is "dependent" on the harshest rule. My own experience, growing up in America, and using as examples when my teachers spoke of Russian rule, they always spoke of the terrible threat and bogeyman of Communism, suggesting that Russia only wanted to conquer all freedom-loving peoples.

For history as known in Russia, however, oftentimes the periods of chaos are held up to be the most difficult and arduous for the Russian people, including those time periods when usurpers reigned, and/or the monarch was not clearly represented or not in control. Russians, or at least the ones I've talked to, surveyed, and related to, thought of those previously-mentioned authoritarians as almost a symptom of circumstances/or and the passage of time. Given the right atmosphere, as they say, the Russian people are as freedom-loving as anyone else. The threat from the very beginning, except for some rare circumstances, has been external for Russia; Russians, they say, are loyal, self-reliant, and dedicated to the family and so on, but they have much to fight against.

Beyond looking at "threats," through Russia's expansion in all directions of antiquity, but particularly west, it brought the nation into conflict with other powers. Russia's insertion of authority in relation to the powers of Europe and against the Ottoman Empire of the Russian south-west had its own ups-and-downs on numerous occasions since that point. Not insignificant for the world today, as of May 2017, France's newly-elected President, Emmanuel Macron, made a point of confronting Putin regarding past positive Russian policies such as Peter the Great's Europeanism when Putin visited a Peter the Great exhibition in Paris.[9]

Even though the Soviet Union fell over twenty years ago, its shadow still haunts Russia as if it fell yesterday. Arguably the Russian pre-Soviet empire continues until today, although some emphasis on the Soviet past is still predominant. Almost every decision in everyday life can be called into reference to the Soviet past and before. Denoting the strong influence of Communism and Imperialism from their respective heydays, much of the social, political, financial, and economic spheres in Russia have a strong heritage and tradition from elements of each.

In general, Levada Centre data shows that pride in Russia trends high among Russians through the Yeltsin and Putin eras, as seen from Figure 2.1.[10]

At face value, one could consider that the Idea of Russia, proposed by the Putin regime, rings true for at least a generalized proportion of the Russia population.

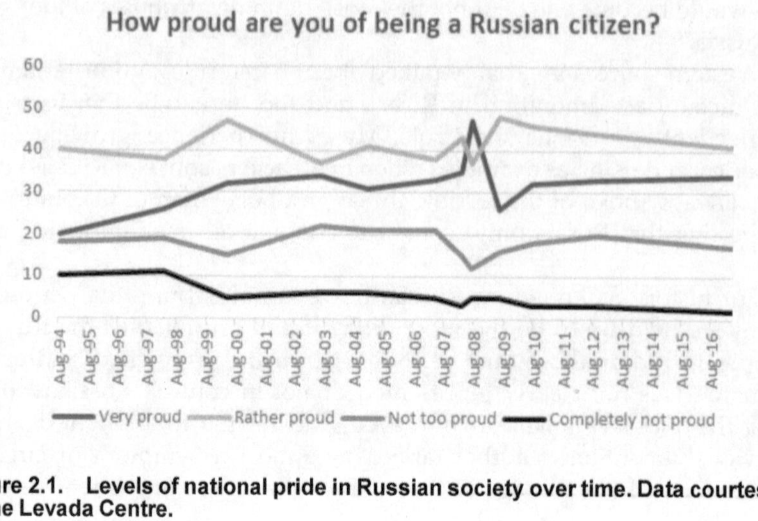

Figure 2.1. Levels of national pride in Russian society over time. Data courtesy of the Levada Centre.

In my own experience, having taught a fair number of them, this is the case with Russia's youth as well. My findings generally show that the children of the post-Soviet era are proud of Russia and are indeed, in some ways, conservative in thinking, however quite flexible in outlook, but perhaps not in the way that some progressive Russian opposition leaders and critics wish them to be. Notably when discussing Russian "democracy" in the older generations and sometimes in the newer, any movement towards democracy is also complicated by frequent misunderstandings in Russian public opinion of what "democracy" in fact is, and that is a point on which the Putin regime has taken advantage of as well.[11]

Over the course of this book, we will continue to examine these points as we focus more on the present and future beyond the ups-and-downs of the past. Nevertheless, as is well-known, and as I mentioned in the introductory sections to this book, the domestic idea of Russia is caught up to varying extents in the modality of the past.

SYMBOLOGY

As with many modern states, and especially former or current empires, symbols of modern Russia dominate much of the Idea of Russia in Russian society.[12] This is internationally recognized, specifically regarding Russia. For instance, when the International Olympic Committee chose to discipline Russia at the 2018 Olympic Games, some of the first things that the IOC decided to take away were Russia's abilities to present itself through its flag and hymn at the Olympics in PyeongChang, South Korea; a decision that was widely reviled in Russia and which reflected my own research.[13]

Assertively, elements of all three of the concurrent themes discussed within this book are embodied in varying perspectives regarding the symbology herein. Not surprisingly, Russia is at times repeatedly "Eternal," "Independent" and "Unique," in that most, if not all, of the symbols here have recalcitrant value in the promotion of nationalism in Russia, and this cannot be forgotten in context.

Russia therefore had to define itself relative to and, to some extent, apart from Soviet strictures, but also redefine elements of past Russian features and characteristics from pre-Soviet periods, if the country was not to wholly reinvent itself in some a-historical completely new context; this being ever so unlikely, as that would almost never happen for any peoples on Earth.

The Pre-Soviet era is also befitting modern Russia, as the government led by the Putin regime is revolutionary (particularly in terms of international relations in a historical context) without any real ideology, in some ways like the Tsarist governments before the Soviet era.

In this respect on a social level, and although this is also the case with other former monarchical and/or imperial powers, at least in the modern post-Soviet era, many of the ideas supporting symbols of modern Russian society still have more of a uniquely nationalist ethnocentric and thereby implicitly racialist appeal combined with them. In a nationalist discussion, the inability of Russia to escape the age of empires in the post-Soviet era, and President Vladimir Putin's regime's use of those same concepts to maintain his power, is a recurring arc within this book.

In practice, Russia's attempts at normalizing Russian culture and nationalism in such places as Tatarstan has led to deepening expansive ways to locally broaden ethnic national cultures ("ethnic minority nationalism") even in an illiberal state.[14] Russia cannot crack down on such displays and opportunistic minority national displays for fear of the backlash, which would be swift and would endanger the Russia's thin hold on regional control, especially when Kremlin-appointed local and regional officials are duly failing to appeal on those same levels. Additionally, one need only further look at the North Caucasus to verify this, but I will touch on this theme (i.e., another example of the ethnic vs. civil argument) periodically in later sections.

The St. Georges Ribbon is a much seen symbological example in today's Russia. The black and gold ribbon and colors represented aspects of the highest military decoration of the Russian past, including its scheme being seen on Great Patriotic War medals although it had limited impact on Soviet ideology. Today, in modern Russia, it is a representation of Russian nationalism, and has been considered as such by the peoples of Russia's neighbors.[15] It is a relatively-new phenomenon, also; when I first came to Russia in 2001, I rarely saw the "black and gold" anywhere. Now, the colors and ribbons are everywhere, most typically, they can be seen tied to many a rear-view mirror in cars on the roads and streets. I've asked many Russians about what it means to them. They have told me that it represents Russia's past and pride, or some variation of that combination. Although I will not venture to guess an exact date or time period when these ribbons started showing up (I remember them just kind of coming out "of the woodwork" very quickly, if you will), Putin's mouthpieces in the Russian media, RT (Russia Today) for one,[16] have been eager to point out this new symbol in popular society in the last ten or so years.

Just to comment, this is one example of how the Putin regime is seeking symbols to separate Russia from Western ideals, and the Russian people seem to like this symbology and so it has become more prominent in society. Hence, it was a good choice of symbol from the Putinist point-of-view, and a great contribution to the Idea of Russia insofar as promoting Russia's place in the world for domestic audiences.

The constitution is an equally facile subject for the Putin regime. While, as President, Putin is supposed to be the guarantor of the Constitution of Russia, when ordinary Russians are asked if the government (not Putin, you might notice) indeed guarantees the Constitution, there is a notable lack of belief in the government's reliance to do so. In surveys conducted by Levada Centre in November 2016, only 9 percent said that the government "fully" observed the constitution, 35 percent said "basically" (whatever that means), 37 percent said "only in part," and 12 percent said absolutely not at all.[17]

The Hymn of the Russian Federation, the national anthem, is perhaps the longest-running and most prominent controversy internationally in Russian symbology, based as it is on the Soviet national anthem. Since Putin re-instituted it in 2000, the anthem has often been focused on by Western analysts, particularly those who believe that exultation of the Soviet Union and its murder of its own citizens and those of its empire, as something that should be de-legitimized in popular cultural settings.[18] Giving the chance as it does to have that proud Soviet anthem played in front of the peoples of the former Soviet empire and republics, it does still rile some observers even many years later.

Symbology in Russia cannot of course be limited to the officially designated representations; there are symbols of the past that still carry much meaning today, if only because they linger. This goes beyond the red stars and other overt symbols of the Soviet Union; this extends to such things as the architecture and the statues which remain in Russia from past eras. While there is architecture today that is thoroughly modern; in certain districts of Russia, there are skyscrapers as new, shiny, and mirrored as anything built in London over the past two decades. Indeed, as of 2017 Europe, that Moscow has possessed that marker much mentioned nowadays dealing with cities, of having the tallest building in some region, is a prominent indication. Once vaulted huge buildings like Stalin's seven sisters (although they were never called that in Russia itself) still dot the skyline of today's Moscow.

More broadly however are the statues of Lenin, Stalin, their political comrades, and the numerous dedicatory monuments and statues to Russia's military past. Indeed, Andrew Foxall of the School of Geography at the University of Oxford points out how General Alexei Ermolov, he of Russian colonial fame in the North Caucasus, still has his statues at myriad places, including one which Foxall focuses on in Stavropol (Stavopol Krai), which of course is part of the broader North Caucasus region which Russia long fought to subdue.[19]

The question always stands; can a Russian country exist when large numbers of its citizens are kept, symbologically-speaking, in the shadow of an Ermalov statue dedicated to the conquer of their ancestors?

There are slightly more living symbols of past empire and the Soviet Union as well; Leader of the Communist revolution Vladimir Ilyich Lenin still lies pickled in his mausoleum in front of the Kremlin. Various stories which I don't feel the need to recount all talk about the level of preservation of Comrade Lenin and fortunately, even according to state-backed VTsIOM polling data, a majority favors burying the carcass at some point in the future.[20]

Yet, even Putin the "realist," who compares Lenin's body to "holy relics" knows that there is some value still left in Lenin's preservation. In Putin's own words: "Вот смотрите, Ленина положили в мавзолей. Чем это отличается от мощей святых для православных, да просто для христиан? Когда мне говорят, что нет, в христианстве нет такой традиции, ну как же нет, в Афон поезжайте, посмотрите там, мощи святые есть, да и у нас вот здесь тоже святые мощи." Or: "Look, Lenin was put in a mausoleum. How is this different from the relics of saints for the Orthodox, and simply for Christians? When they tell me that they do not, in Christianity there is no such tradition, well, how not, go to Afon, look there, there are relics of the saints, and we have here also holy relics."[21]

Russia, as concerning the Idea of Russia, goes however far beyond many of the tangible symbols discussed here. Russia is having a dacha, a country house, even though it might only be a garage in the forest. Russia is on having a shashlik (meat on metal sticks over an open flame) party with your friends, along with a few bottles of vodka. Russia is solyanka, preferably with well-cooked meat. Russia is bolscht, always with well-cooked meat. Russia is that happiness from being alive. These are all symbols of Russia; I cannot, and will not, lessen these wonderful things about the Idea of Russia.

Yet, again, I will not harp on the symbological nature of Russia "half-heartedly" escaping the Soviet Union. The Russian idea has never had any clean public break from Soviet and pre-Soviet times. Many notable Russians, of the many I have talked to and discussed their country with, also always have one eye dead-set on the past (Eternal Russia here considered), on a history that once was and which could (somehow) return some day, a Russia different from other global anachronisms (Independent and Unique Russia), and one that must be "prepared," as a good Russian friend of mine once histrionically stressed.

THE RUSSIAN LANGUAGE

On the question of socio-political dominance, Russian language can be considered a significant part of the Idea of Russia. Even though modern Russian language is relatively new, originating mostly with reforms in the eighteenth century from Peter the Great's time, it became the dominant language of the administration of the Russian Tsars and achieved domination within the Soviet Union. In that regard, and as a side note, in comparison as far as languages go, Ukrainian is older, originating from old Ruthenian and Kievan Rus', though Ukrainian ironically became the repressed language of the two.

It must be mentioned also that while the linguistic basis for the Idea of Russia is Russian language, other traditional languages continue to exist and are of great interest. In the non-Russian ethnic regions/oblasts/and so on of Russia (such as Tatarstan among others), the bilateral teaching of the non-Russian language to all children (including Russian children) as well as Russian language continues to be a divisive topic. In those respective regions, of course some of them are also co-official with Russian language in their respective territories. Alongside Russian language, Tjeerd de Graaf of the Mercator Centre has documented many of these languages and the results of his study are available on-line for interested parties.[22]

On a broader international level, as is well-known, Russian language, and the notable[23] Cyrillic script which underpins it, cannot be overlooked, as it is one of the most prominent in the world, competing with (various forms of) Arabic, English, French, Chinese, and other languages on the global list of most speakers. Yet, even in the Putin administration's desired "sphere of influence," aspects of language, namely the vaunted Cyrillic script, are questioned, such as in Kazakhstan where recent decisions have promoted a move of Kazakh towards the Latin alphabet.[24]

Externally, however, the biggest issue of this is the concern surrounding potentially large percentages of primarily Russian speakers in the former Soviet republics, and the degree to which those Russian speakers might be more loyal to the Idea of Russia, and thereby (possibly) the Russian state, rather than to the state of their citizenry (if not Russia) and/or their residing republic. Those former Soviet republics, particularly the Baltic States, sometimes see their Russian speakers and any lingering Russian culture as a threat, not to mention the seeming efforts of foreign Russian-language media supported by Putin's Kremlin in attempting to somehow affect those populations.

For many people in Russia originating from the post-Soviet sphere, knowledge and fluency in Russian language can be considered a gauge in assessing their right to commerce and be socially accepted in the Russian sphere.

Indeed, knowing Russian language in Russia to the level necessary to daily work is a regular barrier for any immigrant in Russia, especially when combined with those other realms of knowledge which come more naturally from Russia's educational system; these include the knowledge of Pushkin and Tolstoy at a level where those (and other) writers and poets produced unique phraseologies, sayings, and, hence, memorized passages that can add whole new meanings to many a conversation.

This I usually refer to as the "language rule of peculiarity." By this, I mean to say that Russian language becomes part of the Idea of Russia by using peculiar cultural facets and archetypes that many gather only by growing up in Russian culture. While this is not wholly unique to Russia, I am aware that every culture has its in-jokes and sayings, Russia has a well-endowed list of them coming from everything afield, such as from literature, from old Soviet jokes, and from cartoons. I've met Russians who can speak from memory entire children's books, while (though I read much) I can only remember maybe ten lines of Dr. Seuss from my own memory. This literary memory ingrains the Idea of Russia into ordinary Russians in some ways which are impossible to overlook.

All in all, the Russian language is a potential wellspring for the Russian people and for the Idea of Russia, but only while also accepting Russia's traditional non-Russian language speaking regions and the concerned views within them. From the language, Russians can establish culture and meaning, refer to their childhoods, and teach their children the same. This same wellspring, however, in the post-Crimea truth, has been used aggressively by the Putin regime, and thereby can equally be threatening for those of the former Russia/Soviet Empire where the influence of Moscow is less welcome or not welcome at all.

THE CHURCH

The Idea of Russia usually runs parallel also to the principal traditional religion of Russia, that of Orthodox Christianity. With surveys regularly saying that something around 60 to 70 percent of the population[25] express their religious identification as Orthodox Christian, the Russkaya Pravoslavnaya Tserkov, i.e., the Russian Orthodox Church (ROC), presupposes itself to speak for its adherents and is headed by the Patriarch in Moscow, currently Kirill. In theory, the Church represents one of the guiding forces for adherents to the faith, and over time, to a debated extent, it has had an alternating working or confrontational relationship with the government of Russia.

Whatever the case, in public opinion, and politically-speaking in the post-Soviet era, as far as the head of the church, Patriarch Kirill, goes, in trust ratings of the last few years he hovers in the low single digits, as seen in Figure 2.2:[26]

In turn regarding the state's policies toward the church, Alexander Skorobogatov of the Higher School of Economics (HSE) writes, referencing his own work and that of Paul Froese:

> Over roughly the past century, religious policy in Russia has come full circle—from strong support under the Tsarist regime to brutal violence under Lenin, Stalin, and partly Khrushchev, to chiefly moral oppression of the late Soviet years, to more liberal treatment during perestroika, to moderate benevolence in the 1990s, and back to the strong support evident today.[27]

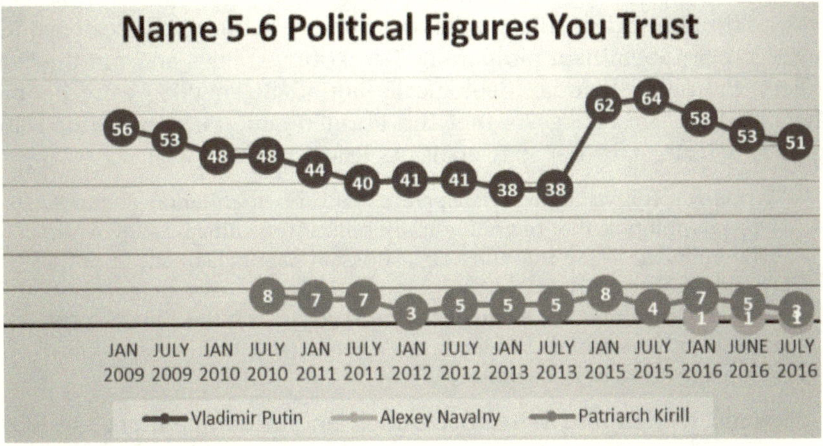

Figure 2.2. On-going trust surveys of Russian public figures. Data courtesy of the Levada Centre.

While the Church has managed to re-gain and gain adherents in the post-Soviet era, the ROC has also managed success in significantly broadening church doctrine and establishing its policies both on an interpersonal level and towards a process of official state adoption, applying religious principles to some parts of the general education system and the military.[28] Senior officials of the Moscow Patriarchate, including Archpriest Dmitry Smirnov, are known for making extreme statements on occasion to gain attention and possibly strike fear in the general Orthodox population, such as in early May 2017 when Smirnov on Soyuz television said that Europe will no longer be Christian in thirty years and Russia will no longer be Christian in fifty.[29]

As in Soviet times, with some justification, there is always the allegation of interference, or "control," of the Church by the Russian security services, amid corresponding legislation that (arguably) is meant to "support" a public information interest, but which can be construed as being doctrines specifically supporting the government's monitoring and informal leadership of the institution.[30] Nevertheless, focused studies have found that there is no quid pro quo on most, if not all, of these points, and in fact the relationship between church and state is at present profoundly muddled, albeit nationalistic in normative cooperation.[31]

However, there is evidence that, in actual practice, ROC rhetoric could be decisive in the Putin regime's processes. In a 2018 opinion piece for The New York Times, academician and professor at Loyola University Chicago, Michael Khodarkovsky attributes potentially nationalist anti-Semitism to November 2017 remarks by Bishop Tikhon Shevkunov (a top aide to Patriarch Kirill and noted spiritual adviser to President Putin) in which Skevkunov suggests that the 1918 killing of last Tsar Nicholas II was a "ritual murder," using a loaded phrase that implied (corresponding to the anti-Semitism rampant in Tsarist times) Jews and not the true killers, the non-religious, ideologically-bound Bolsheviks, were behind the murders. This suggests that the Putin regime is using Church-inspired rhetoric to further state goals. As Khodarkovsky writes:

> In today's Russia, where transparency is rare, speculation abounds. One possibility is that reigniting traditional anti-Semitism is a Kremlin ploy intended to tap into ultra-right Russian nationalism ahead of the presidential elections in March. [. . .]
>
> The fact is that the Kremlin has been relying on the church more than ever, unleashing fundamentalist forces and turning a political campaign into a moral crusade.[32]

Beyond church and state cooperation and/or competition, the ROC however places few strictures upon its adherents, and it cannot be overlooked as also a stabilizing force in Russian society: "For an institution like the ROC, this means that what at the center looks like an inert religious monopoly with minimal sacramental participation appears much livelier along its edges, where the ambient presence of Orthodox aesthetics stabilizes a frayed social fabric."[33]

Owing to a level of competition with other faiths, namely the Muslim faith, which has been gaining adherents faster than the ROC relative to the decreasing ethnic Russian overall population, higher birth-rate of the Muslim populations of Russia, and to increased indoctrination in majority-Muslim regions of Russia,[34] the Church is struggling to maintain its predominance in the evolving social, political and economic spheres. As Russia's hold on its regions becomes unclear so does the relative localized hold of the ROC.

Nevertheless, in my own experience, looking strictly at Russian believers and adherents to the ROC where they can affect polity, they are very faithful to their church and are very quick to recognize its position in society.

On the other hand, some adherents to other faiths debate why the Church should have any special function in either day-to-day society or in government. Assuming a secular government, it's an interesting dilemma.

The ROC does not always completely welcome diversity as well. Indeed, anti-gay laws effectively supported by the Church which criminalize rallies and various forms of Lesbian, Gay, Bisexual, and Transgender (LGBT) expression were passed in 2013, leading to at least state passivity to acts of violence against the LGBT population. Consequently, a significant study by Harvard University found that violence is common and suicides among the Russian LGBT community are strikingly high. Researchers at Harvard found that: "The Putin-led Parliament and the Russian Orthodox Church are united against Western liberalism and permissiveness that they argue "corrupts" Russian youth." [35]

Back in 2012, Peter Pomerantsev, in an article on Church opposition, quoted one Archpriest Alexei Uminsky when Uminsky said: "The tragedy of the church is that it has always grown too close to the state, and then it pays for it. Now the church is trying to prove to the Kremlin it is a serious and useful player." [36]

The Putin regime can of course backhandedly attempt to imply, probably off-the-record of course, that restrictions on the LGBT community are popular, using Kremlin-inspired Public Opinion Foundation (FOM) data.[37] As such, it is a question as to whether the ROC will turn against nationalism and find a more pacifist position in Russian society when presented with any possible "other," indeed peacefully coexisting alongside the growing Muslim populations.

Concerning the future, in trying to be optimistic, it is at least possible that Russia's overall religious climate may indeed liberalize, the Church's predominance relative to government notwithstanding. It is possible that the ROC can be repositioned as equal to other religions in Russia, though the general conservatism dominating the post-Soviet ethnic Russian population quite likely will be inclined against this. The ROC's political influence includes the concurrent prospect that the Church itself may oppose aspects of Putin's policies in future political subject matters (this is all assuming of course that the Church in fact has some modality of independence in this regard). Therefore, more of a clear separation between church and state and a normalization of the Church's role relative to the government could come to pass.

The negative outlook, however, seems more likely in any case; that the government, the ROC, and the traditional ethnic Russian segment continue to dance parallel to one another in the same way as they have for at least the last hundred years (and much longer); that of a balance of love, of hate, sometimes distaste, and the periodic proscription of the ROC outright, while other faiths continue to grow in regional adherence when possible.

Indeed, this bodes ill for the Idea of Russia as promoted by nationalist elements, especially concerning Russia's continued empire (such as it is), not least because, as stated previously, Russia's other substantial religious segments, notably its Muslim populations, will not relegate themselves to live constantly in the shadow of Moscow's Orthodox church spires forever. Allowing Tatarstan's autonomy to end in 2017 and the spreading of patriotic history in local centers (including in the Tatar capital Kazan) with the support of state gas giant Gazprom has not helped matters as well.[38]

Even for President Putin, perhaps recognizing a possible future himself, he himself gave a relative fig leaf to non-ROC populations: he opened a grand new mosque in Moscow (reflecting the city with the largest Muslim population in Europe with some estimated 2 million adherents) in 2015 called the Moscow Cathedral Mosque which is quite expansive and can accommodate 10,000 people.[39]

The big question is whether these grand gestures, and possibly others, might be enough to address concerns of "civic" Russian Muslims and non-ROC populations when such displays are paralleled by periodic nationalist rhetoric by Church officials advising Putin, by ROC-inspired anti-diversity lawmaking, and general conservatism prevalent in Russian society.

ROMANTICISM

One lasting element of the Idea of Russia, one which has been expressed to me personally more times than I can even begin to remember, is the romantic and idealistic memory of the Great Russia. This element is often figurative and mythological (sometimes involving movies and cartoons and such) yet I think it at least bears mentioning. Old ladies and young guys have told me of the great "bear" that cannot be beaten; the older populations remember the Soviet Union with almost a tear in their eye. In no other country I've been to, and I've been to a few, has there been such a mourning for the past. President Vladimir Putin himself expressed this idea in his famous quote about the fall of the Soviet Union being the greatest disaster of the twentieth century. Other analysts refer to this in other ways more academic, but I will stand on my own impressions on this aspect of Russian thought.

Even many in the global sphere love certain aspects of the idea of Russia. I admit that, in some ways growing up back in America, I recognized this romanticism. It is the idea of "simpler times," of the fundamental opposition: of the Cold War; of Capitalism versus Communism; of Western versus Russian ideas.

Whatever the case, many such considerations in view of the idea of Russia are often romanticisms on some level. The negative and the positive; Russia has been brutal, and Russia has been seductive.

Be what it may, any Soviet romanticism should be noted as contrary to some who lived through and viewed the regime at its birthing decades as well, hating every remotely-positive conceived "positive" aspect. As Dmitri Shlapentokh found in relation to Alexandr Solzhnitsyn who could find even no hint of good Russia when he was writing his novel, The Red Wheel:

> But the data presented quite a different story. In 1914–1917 Russia underwent a societal meltdown and the Bolshevik regime—with other alternatives—was the response to anarchical push of society. This, however, required at least partial legitimization of the regime, which became in a way an organic outcome of the country's history.[40]

Russia as the foundation of the Soviet Union killed unknown numbers of people in the Gulag yet sent the first person into outer space. Russia had many problems with efficiency and even basic production yet built modern cities, railways, and electronics.[41] Russia has beautiful cities like St. Petersburg, Moscow, Nizhni Novgorod, Krasnodar and Vladivostok. Indeed, Moscow is one of the largest cities in Europe, yet proceed not far from Moscow and Petersburg, including in some big cities, and you find life that has changed not so much in the last 100 years. This is good some ways; the tastiest jam and homemade preserves on Earth can be found in the regions of Russia, yet in terms of such things as modernization and infrastructure, this has led to a minority of rich in the biggest cities and many in poverty outside.

Politically, this has translated into a rich elite who supports the Putin regime running parallel to a weak elite in opposition and relates to a majority of Russians in the middle-to-low population cities and countryside who buy into Eternal, Independent, and Unique Russia (again those themes), who only receive pro-Putin media, and who also generally support the Putin regime.

With regret, Putin's sky-high approval ratings (60 percent +, while not genuinely that high, is believable in some contexts) do not come out of thin air, it comes out of some genuine support for him and his rule from the countryside.

To use that old trope, American President Richard Nixon's "silent majority" supported him because much of the American people silently but strongly supported him. Putin has a silent majority; they are rarely vocal, yet they would vote for him with admiration given any opportunity. My own research inside and outside or the major cities has found the Idea of Russia is rarely so strong as among Putin's often-unnoticed supporters in the mid-level towns and broad countryside of modern-day Russia.

One way that Putin's support could be undermined, in fact, is on this point. It is my own opinion that a "parallel Great Russia" must be presented to the Russian people. The opposition must find a way to access the Russian people, and that "majority" must be shown how much better life could be without corruption, with better and less opaque leadership, without Putin, and with the West as a friend of Russia and not as the constant antagonist. The Russian opposition, with or without Alexei Navalny or Mikhail Khodorkovsky or their colleagues, must present an alternate better Russia to the Russian people through all means possible. Parallel to that, only the Russian people can change the political trajectory of Russia, and the Russian opposition, in whatever form it takes, must be responsible for guiding this.

In this endeavor, and not for the first time, I say good luck.

Back to the immediate subject at hand, while young people come to the major cities to go to university, to learn to speak, to think about politics, to sing protest songs and to dream about travel to the farthest edges of Europe and beyond, their parents and relatives continue their works and machinations in the mid-to-low population cities and countryside. By extension, when young people come to the major cities and learn about the world, according to their own words, few of them want to return to their home towns and the countryside to continue life there (except to visit), to make preserves, and figure out or think about how to change the views of their usually older relatives.

Once they see the comparative riches of Moscow or Petersburg, in my experience, it is sometimes a hard sell to get Russians to return to even the larger cities of Siberia, the small towns and farms of Russia's eastern center. Hence, even Russia's youth become to some extent the "other."

The same can be true with Russia's military as well, in its ongoing rocky transition from being a primarily draftee to a voluntary (contracted) one. While Russia's military has been hastily trying to modernize to compete with other (Western) militaries, Russia's army continues to lag in many areas. As each successive call-up is initiated, Russia's poorest youth, i.e., those who cannot get into university or whose families are unable to subsidize their avoidance of the draft, end up coming into what is still a broken institution despite any reforms, with significant numbers of unnecessary deaths associated with the armed forces and fear rampant of being sent on Russia's military adventures in Ukraine, Syria, and elsewhere.[42] Adding to that are the recent attempts to tighten standards and close loopholes for those who can avoid the draft, as Putin signed a new law in New Year 2018 eliminating some medical exemptions for those who failed their medical exam the first time around.[43]

Back on the cultural idea, in my own studies (and others[44]), I've found that there is subtle pressure for draftees to return not to Moscow but to their hometowns and regions when their service ends, which usually is only one year in length nowadays (by law, two years if you agree to be a professional soldier).

Therefore, in a broader view of the Idea of Russia, what do ordinary Russians want? How long can any romanticism for a "Great Russia," to what extent it decreasingly exists, sustain them as their social contract net declines (a point which I will discuss more on in a later chapter)? Most (if not all) Russians are proud of the "Idea" of Russia: of their culture, their music, their science, their films, their cartoons, their poetry, all of which are world-renown. I've been told a million times of the greatness of Russian culture and of the Russian idea. Russians are entirely proud, and rightly so, of their victory in World War II.

Events like Victory Day on May 9, signifying Russia's (successor to the Soviet Union's) conquest of Germany in 1945, further represent this. That day is one of the proudest non-religious dates of the Russian calendar, with correspondingly high public opinion responses.[45] In my own experience, having stood out in the cold and asked Russians in several cities, albeit unscientifically, what they thought about Victory Day, their answers were often blasé and promoting the opportunity to drink (as with all major holidays, I must say). Whatever the case, this victory and signifying holiday inhabits the Idea of Russia to such an extent that it is inculcated in some ways into the Russian psyche, if you will. Particularly in the major cities, Russians watch a local military parade, or of course the major parade on Red Square, where indeed so many Cold War Kremlinologists tried to predict the future by watching who stood where at the ceremony.

Without a doubt, Russians want to continue this tradition, to honor the Idea of Russia, and to continue the romanticisms inherent to that Idea of Russia. Indeed, this public love of the Russian idea (or ideal) has to some extent been manipulated by every leader and administration of Russia, both local and national. Again, those symbols discussed in a previous section of the Russian idea, the St. George's orange and black ribbon, the Russian flag, they are publicly supported and all over the place in Russia for a reason. In city and town, on every flag pole, on memorabilia, on key chains and T-shirt, they contribute to the Idea of Russia but perhaps oftentimes more than that, a view of romanticizing Russia and what it can do in the future "if they unify," as they say, in supporting a United Russia (as with the Russian political party), and that furthermore means only one thing usually:

The Putin regime, although this must be changed.

Currently, the Russian people not surprisingly have little idea as to what a "Great Russia" might look like without Putin, except perhaps the chaos of Yeltsin. To aid a new "romanticism" in Russia, the opposition needs to do what it can to show and create this alternative.

Get to it.

PUTIN CONSTITUTING THE IDEA OF RUSSIA

As suggested in the previous section but to focus on it a bit more, the regime of Vladimir Putin, with his domination of the Russian media, has sought to conflate his own "wonderful" visage and his depictions with the symbols and expressions of cultural and social Russia. When I've asked Russians why they support Putin and his regime, seen commonly (though not always) at the 60 percent + popularity mark in my own studies (much more according the other sources[46]), they often answer me with some variation of Putin's embodiment of the Russian ideal, his ability to establish some form of "law and order" to a potentially unruly country but also that he commands respect both internationally and domestically. They like his image of strength and how he represents the strength of the Russian people and government. When he takes his shirt off in public,[47] practices judo for the cameras,[48] shoots tigers,[49] and flies with the birds,[50] it is very much seen by ordinary Russians to be representative of Russia's greatness and abilities, naturally with "a grain of salt" though, for in my experience Russians are not (normally) all that gullible, mind you.

As discussed elsewhere in this book, coinciding with this is the passage of laws meant to control the media and consolidate internet and communications in line with the purposes of the regime.[51] My own research as well as the research of others[52] further confirmed and documented Putin's applied public personage. Also, in my previous work, I documented some aspects of this phenomena and public opinion survey results which supported Putin's symbolist usage.

Further, symbols of Russia, the flag and various military pieces of hardware/units of Russia, are often co-mingled with the face of Putin in a variety in commercial respects in the 2010s era. Virtually every trade center in major cities has in fact at least one store or kiosk dedicated to the sale of merchandise sporting various depictions of Putin in every conceivable fashion.

You want a coffee cup with a picture of our dear President in front of the newest iteration of Russia's brand-new Armada tank line? Well, you've come to the right place! Here you go.

This commonality of depiction, what I argued in my last book as something of a "cult of personality" around the Putin idea certainly has a great deal of social and political ramifications. Yet beyond the "cult of personality" that so many often talk about in respect to Stalin and other past leaders, this commonality of depiction is usually an entirely voluntary one; few if anyone is forcing anyone to wear a Putin t-shirt. In fact, reflecting Putin's not-insignificant popularity[53] (not entirely depicted with all necessary nuance in associated opinion polls) many Russians want and indeed love to associate themselves with the leader with an open heart.

While peoples opposed to Russia, Ukrainians for one, wonder how it is possible that such a "dxxkhead" (one of many curses in external popular media I've heard to depict Putin by peoples opposed to the Putin regime) can be voluntarily depicted everywhere, the abrogation of Putin's negative politics and adulation of his positive qualities bears much relation to how Russians perceive the Idea of Russia in the 2010s.

As an English teacher in Russia in 2015 and 2016, I often had students in my classes with crass Putin t-shirts on. I found this intriguing and when possible, I did ask them: what do you (and your parents) think about their leader? Most of their responses centered on how Putin was defending Russia from outside influences, and that, in some respects, he was embodying the ideal of the strong Russia. Other research for this book in the regions oftentimes confirmed this abstract. Putin embodied to some extent both the fortress mentality and the fears of ordinary Russians.

What happens though when this idea, this co-mingling, of Russia with Putin is shaken? There will be difficulties in the future for Russia, perhaps even sooner than some analysts imagine, especially as Russia's economy is hamstrung by Western sanctions and the new protests of corruption in 2017. That is perhaps the most intriguing question for the future. It is useful to not however overlook that Putin's wiliness, willingness to fight, and the fact that he now possibly has a "friend" (Donald Trump) in the American White House (albeit one seriously hobbled by on-going investigations and rejection on this issue by the American Congress) do seem to promote his staying power far beyond his projected reelection on 2018 (at least as of 2017).

Nevertheless, of course even Putin cannot live forever and will inevitably have a successor in one form or another in the future. I can vouch for the fact that his linking his image with Russia is only temporary and will disappear along with him. However, although in comparison with Western democracies where leaders come and go, Putin can afford to look at the long game, as he no doubt does, even he has a "shelf life" or a "half-life," if you consider him a toxic radioactive element like another Ukrainian in Kiev once told me.

THE RUSSIAN OPPOSITION AND THE IDEA OF RUSSIA: EMBODIMENT OR ANTIPATHY?

It is far from correct to say that there is no real opposition to the regime in Russia, indeed far from it. Instead, it is to say that the opposition is functionally fragile. As such, it is instead more accurate to say that the opposition is confined to elites, capable observers, and critics, albeit some of them that can spark real peoples' initiative, but not necessarily to any real authoritative or qualitative leadership. Ineffectively, the opposition still confines its rallies to one-off exercises as well, unlike the multi-day, long-term protests which have dislodged regimes in places like Ukraine.

Further in relation to this publication, the opposition has so far had little traction in embodying the Idea of Russia as popularly supported by most of the Russian people, on which Putin has been able to take so much advantage of over the course of his rule.

Shown oftentimes by its ineffectiveness and the divisiveness of their attempts to challenge the rule of Putin, the opposition trips all over itself as to how to pragmatically address events and policies which could, at least theoretically, be used as some type of foundation to ultimately challenge the Putin regime. The closest that they have come in recent history is Alexei Navalny's March 2017 anti-corruption protests, which got young people moving in cities across Russia, but they have yet far to go to have a multi-pronged assault on the regime.

Navalny, as mentioned in chapter 1, is a powerful force in some ways in modern Russia, perhaps the most powerful non-Kremlin force, in relation to general politics and each election that comes and goes. As a lawyer and activist, he founded his Anti-Corruption Foundation, "Фонда борьбы с коррупцией," or FBK,[54] in 2011, he ran for mayor of Moscow in September 2013 (coming in second to the Kremlin's choice, Sergei Sobyanin), and he has been instrumental in maintaining some level of consistent support for Russia's opposition since then. He is (in theory) rivaled in the opposition lineup, at differing times and occasions, by a billionaire (and Civic Platform party leader) Mikhail Prokhorov, a former State farm manager (and Communist party guy), Pavel Grudinin,[55] a traditional liberal economist and politician (and long-time head of the Yabloko party), Grigory Yavlinsky,[56] and the young TV presenter and socialite, Ksenia Sobchak, amongst a few others.

Today's opposition is in some ways overshadowed by those who have died opposing the Putin regime, or while simply trying to uphold human rights in Russia. Most notable of those who have died is probably former (Yeltsin-era) Deputy Prime Minister of Russia Boris Yefimovich Nemtsov, who was assassinated on a bridge in central Moscow within sight of the Kremlin on 27 February 2015. His roles as a longtime opposition figure, critic of Putin's rampant corruption, as co-chair of the Russian opposition party RPR-PARNAS, and as a leader within and of several regions of Russia made him a prime candidate to one day possibly lead Russia as President. His stature is much missed in what constitutes the opposition in Russia of today, although his daughter, Zhanna, still carries the Nemtsov "torch," and both the elder and younger Nemtsov will be mentioned multiple times over the course of this book.

Another similar assassination, also highly professional and in the Kremlin area, was the January 2009 killing of Stanislav Markelov, who sought to bring charges against members of the Russian security forces accused of violating human rights in Chechnya, and the murder of Novaya Gazeta reporter Anastasia Baburina, who was walking with Markelov when he was shot and killed.

Remarking on the "silence of the Russian authorities," when they said nothing for quite some time, regarding the Markelov and Baburina assassinations, as Dmitry Sidorov wrote for Forbes magazine:

> The Kremlin's efforts to block information about how rights and freedoms are violated in Russia, and to prevent the free discussion of this issue in society and the press is a fine example of so-called "sovereign democracy" in action. Hiding behind this clever phrase, the Kremlin has convinced itself that is has carte blanche, both within its borders and beyond. In so doing, Russia is a "truly" democratic nation.[57]

As of this writing, the 2018 presidential election is the next artifice through which Putin will most likely find dominance in terms of his expected reelection. Not surprisingly, since he is the central opposition figure, Navalny was banned by the regime from participating in the election because of the prior criminal charges against him. As the obviously[58] semi-"official" opposition, Ksenia Sobchak (who, among other things, says she is "against all"[59] others in the election) is all over the news in Russia, yet Navalny does have a "pre-election" program of his own, containing a myriad promises which are surprisingly concrete in some ways.[60] The Communist party candidate Grudinin and the usual presidential candidate (and Kremlin loyalist, and not even funny anymore, the "Liberal Democratic Party of Russia" candidate, still the ultimate contradiction in terms) Vladimir Zhirinovsky, will be running in that election as well.

All this makes one question if it is really an "election" at all, yet it's a moot point as Putin has the votes to win regardless. Partly by the Putin regime's design, in view of the Russian people I've conversed with, many in the true Putin opposition are ineffective in overcoming the Putin regime's media control. Most of the false opposition likely will play by the "rules" of the election, like Grudinin and Zhirinovsky, as the Communists and LDPR people always do. Navalny's talks of a boycott likely will get him nowhere as well.[61]

Worthy of mentioning as well is that I've talked to at least one Russian who believes that even Navalny is not really an opposition figure but is merely another cog in the governing machine that is the Putin regime. Could it be that all modern Russian politics is a concerted set-up of some sort? It is certainly possible (in studying Russia, absolutely nothing is impossible, of that I have no doubt), however, as to defining that here, it represents a certain difficulty in trying even to define the "beast" that is the Putin regime in that case. Nevertheless, it is one that I keep in mind but which I usually put to the side during my research.

Back on the issues, in one approach relevant here: how can the Idea of Russia be greater than the Idea of Putin? (It's a rhetorical question, but I can never resist.)

The Idea of Russia is a beautiful thing, as I've been told by numerous, sometimes-inebriated, Russians. The enduring nature of Russia is something, again I've been told, that must be upheld. The opposition in Russia is also dependent on showing that the Idea of Russia can be great, but without Putin as the leader. If the Putin regime is ever to be defeated, Putin himself or his successors (whomever that may be), in favor of a more democratic and rule of law-based form of governance, then the opposition cannot allow itself to preach in obscurity, and it must focus on what a great Russia would look like without Putin; what Russia could, should, and must be.

To summarize here most importantly, Navalny and his people, or whoever is the opposition now or in future, must answer the question: "Why?" Simple question, eh? I must elaborate. Navalny talks constantly about corruption, which is a very big problem and is literally strangling Russia's progress. Yet, in my experience, corruption has little traction as a critical issue regarding the Putin regime outside the major cities. They all do it, you know . . . or so I've been told with a wink and a shrug and anyway, Navalny is no better, etc. etc.

I've heard the rejoinders more than once:

"Ok, so Medvedev and Putin are stealing the entire treasury, so what?"

Or, as I was asked rhetorically by an elderly chap near Belgorod: "what's the difference between Putin owning everything and the state owning everything?"

To those who vote for Putin because they like him, because some of them aspire to "be" Putin, to those who wear clothing with his visage on them, or because they like his strength in judo and his abilities to fly with the birds, etc.: why is corruption so important?

In my experience, the opposition has yet find a quick and snappy response to such questions. They need to.

These questions are not unique to corruption as well; in today's Russia, to overcome the Putin-philia explained here, any opposition candidate needs to explain the reasoning behind whatever issue they choose to stress in their campaigns. Otherwise, it is just background noise while Putin seeks to find some way to ensure turnout.

Just to take on another issue, as with amongst many elites in Russia, the Crimean question has been one of paramount importance for the Russian opposition. As I will be talk about in more depth over the general course of this book overall, should and, in Russian general and elite public opinion, "must" Crimea be part of Russia?

Watching the Russian opposition tie itself in knots over this question has been something of mild interest, at least for this analyst, over the years that I have researched this book. Navalny has been unclear on the subject;[62] Ksenia Sobchak has said that Crimea belongs to Ukraine, for which the excitable LDPR party head and usual presidential candidate, Vladimir Zhirinovsky, called for her imprisonment.[63]

The first true prominent opposition figure to the Ukraine invasion was Boris Nemtsov before he was assassinated; a conflict on which he sought to clarify as truly Putin's war and push against the regime's propaganda.[64] Commentators on the opposition from freer Russian outlets like TV Rain also further debate the return of Crimea vociferously.[65] Each opposition member must ask him or herself, should I back the annexation of Crimea or not?

Naturally, if the answer is yes, if Crimea should be kept, then they risk walking into a trap laid by the Putin regime; they are somewhat obviously losing any moral high ground which, in the next step, constitutes a "rug" which can be pulled out from under them in their argument against Putin's supporters and the media which is ever so firmly on the regime's side. While appealing to the Russian nationalist argument; that Crimea was, is, and always will be firmly a part of Russia; little support can be alternatively gained. From that point, those opposition figures who support the annexation have nowhere to go but down.

If the answer is no, Crimea should be allowed to return to Ukraine, then the opposition is faced with the full fury of the nationalists who will put them in check through the media, in saying that the opposition leader in question is failing to uphold the Idea of Russia. So what direction is there to go in, one must rhetorically ask?

Overall, the central question is on how the opposition deals with the Idea of Russia. Navalny's prominence and position, by trying to side-step potential hot-button issues like Crimea (sometimes it pays to be unclear), does offer hope to many who want Russia to be a freer society and country, and that should not be undervalued or overlooked.

As another abstract for the Russian idea relative to political opposition, there remains in Russia the idea of the externally-based "exile." There is right now a substantial amount of young Russian democrats leaving Russia for sunnier shores; some like BBC characterize it as a "generation."[66] As mentioned in that article, political exile status is embodied by several notable figures; one of the most famous is Mikhail Khodorkovsky.

Khodorkovsky was once a triumphant oligarch, and a friend of the top elite. He, however, decided to take a political stand early in Putin's presidency, he became another thorn in the Putin regime's side, and so he lost his oil empire, Yukos, and was arrested in 2003. Over the course of the next ten years, until 2013 when he was released, Khodorkovsky argued with some legitimacy that his arrest and eventual guilty sentence was politically motivated. From 2014 on, he left Russia for the mountains of Switzerland, amongst other places, and started the civil initiative, Open Russia, which continues to call for civil reforms in Russia to this day.

As such, from European exile, Khodorkovsky spends his days as a critic of the Putin regime. His status as a politically-influential figure secure, when considering that past exiles, like say, Vladimir Lenin, were exiles at one point, his position is not unprecedented in representing a point of opposition to the Putin regime. Yet due in large part to the regime's media controls, he, like Navalny, has only the most strenuous ties to that great percentage of unheard Russians around Russia, particularly outside Moscow and Petersburg.

Garry Kasparov, the former chess player, also has some status as a major liberal opposition figure, although he isn't spoken about on the streets all that much, at least according to my own experience.[67]

As mentioned before, the daughter of Putin's former boss (Anatoly Sobchak, when Anatoly was mayor and Putin was but a young newly-political sprout in St. Petersburg in the 1990s), Ksenia Sobchak, is also a potent opposition figure in Russia, if only due to her prominence as a television presenter. Her decision to run as Putin's opponent in the 2018 Presidential election has limited viability and has (and will) split the opposition at least a bit.

In aggregate, these opposition figures and others do have some hope of motivating the Russian populace to perhaps choose an alternative to Putin's rule one day. Yet, as I mentioned before, as of mid-2017, while the March 2017 protests were significant, there must be more unity, they must last longer, and must evince a certain constant drumbeat for change in Russia, and that drumbeat unfortunately has not fully manifested itself and must be supported with initiative.

AN OPPOSITIONIST IDEA OF RUSSIA: NEO-EURASIANISM AND WHAT IT IS

Since the times of Peter the Great, when the idea of Russia's mated dance with the Western countries of Europe was more (or less) established alongside the construction of the new sometimes capital that is known as St. Petersburg today, the Idea of Russia has been attached to a Europeanized mindset, or however one wishes to call it. Russia always had great status as a source of agriculture for Europe in Russian Imperial times.[68] Simply put as explored herein before, Russia is a part of Europe and possibly even a great European power as seen through the Napoleonic era and the Cold War.

As such, many Russians, both the general classes and the ruling classes, have often thought of themselves as European. However, in a Russia under Putin which has had its share of great turmoil in its relationship with those same Western powers, up to and including sanctions, there has been some move towards redefining the Idea of Russia by a number of Russian thinkers and figures, some of them suggesting that Russia should realign itself as a truly unique force of some nature, as a Eurasian power divested from both European influence and from any China-inflected association as an Asian power.

This movement, if one should call it that, generally follows a separate course of the Unique and Eternal Russia, based on the Church as an anchor, and follows the paradigm that Russia can exist wholly as a Eurasian power in the world. This is a far-flung theory, but one which is repeated on occasion: "There are marginal theories like neo-Eurasianism, which, however, are incapable of representing at least one example of a functional social institution."[69]

Acknowledging at the same time that Russia might have to adjust itself to speak and trade with other countries and foreign powers, the movement seeks to generally create a holistic and absolutist centrality to a Russia impregnable and isolationist in its own affairs at an axis between the European and Asian, except to the extent that the umbrella can be expanded to cover ethnic and political Russians further outside her current borders. For the Eurasian Russia, Crimea was a no-brainer, if you will. It simply had to be taken from Ukraine and, if possible, more bits of Russia taken illegally from it over the centuries can and must be reacquired.

In public opinion, Eurasianism has a certain percentage of adherents; such adherents are usually eager to oppose the West and strongly supportive of the Putin regime whatever it may do.[70] Further, this percentage often naturally supports the more nationalist elements of society including the nascent fascist and neo-Nazi movements in Russia and is predictably rejectionist when it comes to the large percentage of non-ethnic Russians and immigrants in modern Russian society.

On leadership, such names as Alexander Dugin often come up in mainstream press, and his noted role in the official Russian government included being seen on occasion with Putin himself.[71] Other prominent names come up in connection with this concept periodically in the press; names like, for example, the so-called "Cardinal of the Kremlin" (officially a one-time Deputy Prime Minister) Vladislav Surkov, although Surkov's concept of "sovereign democracy" only shares certain aspects with Eurasianism.[72]

For the Idea of Russia, it is a mistake to assume that Eurasianism is in any way new.[73] Although not prominent in the singular apparition which was the Soviet Union, Eurasianism has existed in Russia since time immortal, although I believe it grows from the pre-state emptiness which persisted from the founding of Kievan Rus' and then the evolution into the pro forma Russian era itself.

Throughout its time from the ancient era, Russia has been a tough place, Siberia and the steppes surrounding it bred a tough people who managed what little farming was possible and a great many fast-moving populations on horseback who took their dear sweet time in roaming and pillaging the settlements, including modern-day Moscow, which slowly sprang up. This openness is especially the case when compared to ancient empires and population centers in lower Europe and in China.

From this open land came a certain desperation, and when some means of long-term establishment became available, as with the now-major cities of Russia, thus came a remarkably different outlook on life which was far different from the city-states of Europe. This was what one might call predominant Eurasianism. When various Tsars brought Russia together, Petersburg was built, French became the fashionable language, and various wars started being fought, including when Napoleon came to visit Moscow itself, predominant Eurasianism never disappeared, in fact it built an undercurrent of reliability that ideologies of the twentieth century didn't like but could not eliminate.

In substance, the idea of Eurasianism is a nationalist facade which might can bring a certain element to the polls, might bring support for the regime, and might even bully immigrants, but cannot hold a candle to the power of Russia's inevitable dalliance and unification again (one day) with the European idea.

The social and political figures that support Eurasianism are inevitably, much to their own displeasure, going to be left out in the cold. Hopefully, sanctions and the antagonism between Russia and the West will not last forever, probably involving a Russia without Crimea, and Russia will again seek to add its name to the list of legitimate European powers. Whatever one might say on the topic, barring some catastrophe of global proportions (God forbid Russia should ever fight the West and we should see a Third World War), one day Russia will be back in all those European processes and making trouble in all those European capitals as an equal, and not as something of an exile as is increasingly the case today.

CONCLUSIONS

Russia is doomed to be Russia, for all the good and ills that that portends.

Through public opinion research, through all the interviews that I have conducted of Russian public opinion throughout all the cities, locales, and country sides that I have visited, that theory has remained the same.

This chapter finds that the Idea of Russia is relatively strong, but guarantees the continuing risk of being politically manipulated, and it will likely stay that way for the conceivable future. How is this different (one might ask) from other national ideas? The combination of history, the Church, the military, the Putin regime, and the response given by neighboring and coexisting nationalities leads to the argument that the Idea of Russia is far from attractive to those who might have the option of joining it now or in the future.

In this first way, the Russian idea is part of the framework of that theoretical "house" posited in the introduction. It is a strong framework, mind you, but one which is only being replenished by its own limited regeneration without the positive addition of new building materials, "boarding," or "nails." The basic structure of the Russian idea is falling apart slowly in view of Russia's population decline as well, but also steadily by the failure of reform of laws and by the existence of an aggressive foreign policy, as to be talked about in more detail later, that makes the Russian idea unattractive to many of those who would otherwise be happy or in that case beneficial to be joined with it. For those wish to see a strong Russia in the future, the framework not in total but in part must be stripped of its anti-inclusive elements.

For a comparative idea, although not continuous (particularly as of late), a central part of the American and British national ideas was that immigration was good, and it could bring skills to those strong empires/countries if controlled in a properly functioning process. No such process exists in the Russian idea; in fact, certain facets of the Russian idea are reliant on terminal processes which do not regenerate.

The Russian language continues to exist uncomfortably alongside non-Russian languages even within Russia itself, and there are rumors of laws that could change Russia's dangerous balance of languages in non-Russian regions of Russia (Bashkortostan, Tatarstan, etc.). The Church, while seeking expansion, also seeks to be a political force and sometimes it can be exclusive. To some extent, such processes must change into a more regenerative model if the Russian idea is to survive confrontational ideas both within its boundaries and in the context of the higher birth-rates of non-Russian and non-Russian Orthodox nations living within its operational territory.

Given all this background on cultural "Russian Idea" presupposition, looking at the domestic front, again especially with the help of Putin's media, when Russians see the post-Cold War North Atlantic Treaty Organization (NATO) spreading from country to country coming ever closer to Russia, and saddling up closer to Russia's heart as Lithuania, Estonia and Latvia do, many Russians don't see a neutral collective actor or some fellowship of friends that could one day invite themselves to the party. Instead, no matter how much NATO stresses that it is a defense, non-culturally-dominating, organization (as it is), Russians see a threat to their culture: a military organization, state-of-the-art "war-making" technology, ready to take judgment on those which NATO, collectively and through its elite construct, sees as a threat. As long throughout Russian history, the Putin regime points to this threat as one to be opposed, and hence, here we are.

With this Russian Idea explored, I progress to the Respect of Russia, for which the regime of Putin is wholly obsessed, at least far beyond Russia simply being one in the family of European nations.

NOTES

1. Neumann, Iver B., *Russia and the Idea of Europe*, 2nd ed. Routledge, New York, NY, 2017.

2. Maria Engstrom connects current Russian globalism to Russia's counter-culture of the late 1980s and early 1990s insofar as the rises and falls of the "imaginary West" image (something Russia wants to join) and the "imaginary anti-West" (something Russia wants to fight against). Engstrom argues that the "anti-West" variant is gaining strength now, and it is a worthy argument. See: Engstrom, Maria, "Late Soviet Counterculture and New Russian Globalism," *Riddle*, 20 April 2018, Retrieved 28 April 2018, http://www.ridl.io/en/late-soviet-counterculture-and-new-russian-globalism/.

3. This is a worthy but elite-level involved argument on which to study Russian politics. Nevertheless, for those interested in this question, read the works of such esteemed scholars as Emil Pain, Dominic Lieven, and Alexander Motyl. For two, see: Pain, Emil, "The Imperial Syndrome and its Influence on Russian Nationalism," *The New Russian Nationalism*, chapter 2, Edinburgh University Press, Edinburgh UK, 2016. [and] Lieven, Dominic, "Empire, History and the Contemporary Global Order," *Proceedings of the British Academy*, Volume 131, 2004 Lectures, Oxford University Press, Oxford UK, 2005, 127–56.

4. See again: Vaughn, Jason, *A Socio-Political Model of Lies in Russia: Putin against the Personal*, University Press of America, Lanham MD, 2016.

5. As first touched upon in the introduction, the difference between the two is large but not absolute. In this book, we will refer back to the two abstracts, the civic and the ethnic, as necessary in view of the argument made. For more information and discussion, most recently see: Laruelle, Marlene, "Misinterpreting Nationalism: Why Russkii is Not a Sign of Ethnonationalism," *PONARS Eurasia Policy Memo No. 416*, PONARS Eurasia, George Washington University, January 2016.

6. Laruelle, Marlene, "Russia as an Anti-Liberal Civilization," *The New Russian Nationalism*, chapter 10, Edinburgh University Press, Edinburgh UK, 2016.

7. "When far-right 'activists' from the SERB movement commit attacks in Russia, what's the police response? (Spoiler: there isn't really one)," *Meduza*, 12 September 2017, Retrieved 26 March 2018, https://meduza.io/en/short/2017/09/12/when-far-right-activists-from-the-serb-movement-commit-attacks-in-russia-what-s-the-police-response.

8. *The Chronicle*, known as Povest' vremennikh let, has several viable manuscripts; this one (http://hudce7.harvard.edu/~ostrowski/pvl/, Retrieved 10 April 2017) from Harvard University placed by Donald Ostrowski (https://daviscenter.fas.harvard.edu/about-us/people/donald-ostrowskihttps://daviscenter.fas.harvard.edu/about-us/people/donald-ostrowski, Retrieved 10 April 2017) who is renowned for his work on such materials.

9. R ubin, Alyssa J. and Aurelien Breeden, "Emmanuel Macron Challenges Putin on Syria and Gay Rights," *The New York Times*, 29 May 2017, Retrieved 2 June 2017, https://www.nytimes.com/2017/05/29/world/europe/emmanuel-macron-putin-france-russia.html?_r=0.

10. On-going survey of 1600 respondents, eighteen or older, in 137 population points of 48 regions of the country. "Национальная гордость," (In English): "National Pride," *Levada Centre*, 4 May 2017, Retrieved 31 May 2017, http://www.levada.ru/2017/05/04/natsionalnaya-gordost-2/.

11. Hale, Henry E., "The Myth of Mass Authoritarianism in Russia: Public Opinion Foundations of a Hybrid Regime," The National Council for Eurasian and East European Research, University of Washington and George Washington University, Seattle WA, 2009.

12. It is important to mention that I will address here general Russian symbology indicative of the Idea of Russia, but there are symbols abound across Russia for territories and for formally pre-Russia dominant dominions and/or empires such as, for just one example, Kazan's descendent symbols of Turkic origin. If anything, many of said symbols act against the Idea of Russia and could be the basis for independent states should the Russian Federation at some point in the future fail and break apart itself, yet that is the basis for a separate book and will not be discussed in-depth here.

13. Schreck, Carl, "'Spitting in Our Face: Russia Olympic Ban Stirs Anger, Conspiracy Theories, Support for Athletes," *Radio Free Europe/Radio Liberty*, 6 December 2017, Retrieved 7 December 2017, https://www.rferl.org/a/russia-olympics-ban-reactions-anger-conspiracies-support/28900475.html.

14. Yusupova, Guzel, "Cultural Nationalism and Everyday Resistance in an Illiberal Nationalizing State: ethnic minority nationalism in Russia," *Nations and Nationalism*, ASEN, John Wiley & Sons Ltd., 2017, pp. 1–24.

15. Karney, Ihar and Daisy Sindelar, "For Victory Day, Post-Soviets Show Their Colors—Just Not Orange and Black," *RFE/RL*, 7 May 2015, Retrieved 10 April 2017, http://www.rferl.org/a/victory-day-st-george-ribbon-orange-and-black/26999911.html.

16. "St. Georges Ribbon recalls Russian heroism," *Russia Today*, 7 May 2009, Retrieved 10 April 2017, https://www.rt.com/news/st-george-ribbon-recalls-russian-heroism/.

17. S urvey of 1600 respondents, eighteen or older, in 137 population points of 48 regions of the country. "день конституции," (In English): "Constitution Day," *Levada Centre*, 8 December 2016, Retrieved 8 December 2017, https://www.levada.ru/2016/12/08/den-konstitutsii/.

18. Warren, Marcus, "Putin revives Soviet national anthem," *The Telegraph*, 9 December 2000, Retrieved 11 April 2017, http://www.telegraph.co.uk/news/worldnews/europe/russia/1377685/Putin-revives-Soviet-national-anthem.html.

19. Foxall, Andrew, "A Contested Landscape: Monuments, Public Memory, and Post-Soviet Identity in Stavropol', Russia," *Communist and Post-Communist Studies*, Volume 46, 2013, pp. 167–78.

20. "Press-vypusk No. 3359," VTsIOM, 21 April 2017, Retrieved 21 April 2017, https://wciom.ru/index.php?id=236&uid=116172.

21. "Путин сравнил тело Ленина в мавзолее с мощами святых," (In English: "Putin equates the body of Lenin in the mausoleum with holy relics,") T V Rain, 14 January 2018, Retrieved 15 January 2018, https://tvrain.ru/news/putin_sravnil_telo_lenina_v_mavzolee_s_moschami_svjatyh-455043/.

22. De Graaf, Tjeerd, "Description of Minority Languages in Russia on the Basis of Census Data, Sound Archives and Fieldwork," Mercator Centre, Budapest, 28 April 2015, http://www.nytud.hu/archiv/eloadasok/degraaf2015.pdf.

23. After all, who can miss the difference when coming from any other country using, say, Latin, Arabic, Chinese, or Japanese script?

24. Trafimovich, Anton, (in Belarusian): "Гэта выхад з «рускага міру». Чаму былыя савецкія рэспублікі адмаўляюцца ад кірыліцы?" (In English): "It is out of the Russian world. Why are Soviet republic refusing Cyrillic?," *RFE/RL*, 21 April 2017, Retrieved 24 April 2017, http://www.dvnovosti.ru/eao/2017/04/21/65346/.

25. Differing polls give markedly different numbers. Pew Center polls put the number as high 72 percent. See: "Russians Return to Religion, But Not to Church," *Pew Research Center*, 10 February 2014, Retrieved 15 January 2018, http://www.pewforum.org/2014/02/10/russians-return-to-religion-but-not-to-church/.

26. Levada Centre, On-going trust surveys, Retrieved 1 May 2017, www.levada.ru.

27. Skorobogatov, Alexander S., "A provocative event, media, and religious choice in post-Soviet Russia," *Post-Soviet Affairs*, Volume 32, Issue 6, 2016, pp. 513–14 (pp. 512–41). Skorobogatov references: Froese, Paul. "After Atheism: An Analysis of Religious Monopolies in the Post-Communist World." *Sociology of Religion*, 65, Vol. 1, pp. 57–75, 2004.—AND—Froese, Paul. "Forced Secularization in Soviet Russia: Why an Atheistic Monopoly Failed?" *Journal for the Scientific Study of Religion 43*, Issue 1, pp. 35–50, 2004.

28. Blitt, Robert C., "Whither Secular Bear: The Russian Orthodox Church's Strengthening Influence on Russia's Domestic and Foreign Policy," *Fides Et Libertas: The Journal of the International Religious Liberty Association*, p. 89, 2011; University of Tennessee Legal Studies Research Paper No. 173. 2011. Available at SSRN: https://ssrn.com/abstract=2008331 or http://dx.doi.org/10.2139/ssrn.2008331

29. "В РПЦ предрекли конец христианской цивилизации через 30 лет: Европа станет мусульманской, а христиане "будут жить в полуподполье," (In English): "The ROC foretold the end of Christian civilization in 30 years: Europe will become Muslim, and Christians "will live in a semi-underground," *Newsru.com*, 5 May 2017, Retrieved 8 May 2017, http://www.newsru.com/religy/05may2017/eu_islam.html.

30. Lunkin, Roman, "Doktriny Bezopasnosti ot Religii," *NG Religii*, 21 December 2016, retrieved 23 December 2016, http://www.ng.ru/ng_religii/2016-12-21/5_412_doctrina.html.

31. See: Richters, Katja, *The Post-Soviet Russian Orthodox Church: Politics, Culture and Greater Russia*, 1st ed., Routledge, New York NY, 2013.

32. Khodarkovsky, Michael, "Reviving Old Lies to Unite a New Russia," *The New York Times*, 11 January 2018, Retrieved 11 January 2018, https://www.nytimes.com/2018/01/11/opinion/russia-jew-bishop-lies.html?hpw&rref=opinion&action=click&pgtype=Homepage&module=well-region&region=bottom-well&WT.nav=bottom-well.

33. K ormina, Jeanne, and Sonja Luehrmann, "The Social Nature of Prayer in a Church of the Unchurched: Russian Orthodox Christianity from Its Edges," *Journal of the American Academy of Religion*, Oxford University Press, 2017, p. 23. (pp. 1–31)

34. U sing Russian State Statistics Service and Pew Foundation studies, Stratfor charts that's Muslims made up 11.7 percent of the population in 2010 and will rise to 13.3 percent by 2020 and 15.6 percent by 2030. See: "Russia's Growing Muslim Population," *Stratfor*, 8 August 2013, Retrieved 12 April 2017, https://www.stratfor.com/image/russias-growing-muslim-population.

35. Kucheyavenko, Oleg, Kirill Guskov, and Michael Walker, "Cost of indulgence: Rise in violence and suicides among LGBT youth in Russia," *Health and Human Rights Journal*, Harvard University, 18 December 2013, Retrieved 30 April 2017, https://www.hhrjournal.org/2013/12/cost-of-indulgence-rise-in-violence-and-suicides-among-lgbt-youth-in-russia/. See also: Manson, Jamie, "The Orthodox Church's Role in Anti-Gay Law," *National Catholic Reporter*, 14 August 2013, retrieved 2 March 2017, https://www.ncronline.org/blogs/grace-margins/orthodox-church-s-role-russia-s-anti-gay-laws.

36. P omerantsev, Peter, "Putin's God Squad: The Orthodox Church and Russian Politics," *Newsweek*, 10 September 2012, Retrieved 30 April 2017, http://www.newsweek.com/putins-god-squad-orthodox-church-and-russian-politics-64649.

37. "Об отношении к сексуальным меньшинствам и их правах," (In English): "On relations with Sexual minorities and their rights," Public Opinion Foundation (FOM), 12 April 2012, Retrieved 30 April 2017, http://fom.ru/obshchestvo/10404.

38. Khodarkovsky, Michael, "Reviving Old Lies to Unite a New Russia," *The New York Times*, 11 January 2018, Retrieved 11 January 2018, https://www.nytimes.com/2018/01/11/opinion/russia-jew-bishop-lies.html?hpw&rref=opinion&action=click&pgtype=Homepage&module=well-region&region=bottom-well&WT.nav=bottom-well.

39. MacFarquhar, Neil, "Putin Opens New Mosque in Moscow Amidst Lingering Intolerance," *The New York Times*, 23 September 2015, Retrieved 12 April 2017, https://www.nytimes.com/2015/09/24/world/europe/putin-opens-moscows-most-elaborate-mosque.html.

40. Shlapentokh, Dmitri, "Historical narrative and emotional paradigms: The case of Solzhenitsyn's The Red Wheel and his other works," *Communist and Post-Communist Studies*, Vol. 26, 2016, p. 199.

41. Fischer, Stanley, "Russia and the Soviet Union Then and Now," *The Transition in Eastern Europe*, Vol. 1, ed. Olivier Jean Blanchard, Kenneth A. Froot, and Jeffrey D. Sachs, University of Chicago Press, Chicago IL, January 1994.

42. Dzhorzhevich, Alexandra and Anastasia Kyrilova, "По всей срочности закона," (In English: "The urgency of the law for all,"), *Kommersant Daily*, 1 April 2017, Retrieved 3 January 2018, https://www.kommersant.ru/doc/3255326.

43. "Путин подписал закон, разрешающий ограниченно годным к службе проходить новый осмотр," (In English: "Putin signed law allowing for citizens to undergo reevaluation," *TASS*, 29 December 2017, Retrieved 3 January 2018, http://tass.ru/armiya-i-opk/4852580.

44. For one recent, see: Braw, Elizabeth, "Russia's Conscription Conundrum," *Foreign Affairs*, 25 August 2015, Retrieved 12 April 2017, https://www.foreignaffairs.com/articles/russia-fsu/2015-08-25/russias-conscription-conundrum.

45. Survey of 800 Russians, 22–25 April 2016, 4.1 percent margin of error; "РОССИЯНЕ О ПРАЗДНОВАНИИ ДНЯ ПОБЕДЫ," Levada Centre, 5 May 2016, http://www.levada.ru/2016/05/05/rossiyane-o-prazdnovanii-dnya-pobedy-3/.

46. See "Approval of Putin's Activities," Levada Center, 12 April 2017, Retrieved 12 April 2017, www.levada.ru.

47. "Vladimir Putin Bares All for the Latest On-Camera Stunt," *The Guardian*, 26 August 2011, Retrieved 12 April 2017, http://www.telegraph.co.uk/news/worldnews/europe/russia/8725106/Vladimir-Putin-bares-all-for-the-latest-on-camera-stunt.html.

48. "Putin Puts Judo Skills to the Test in Sochi (VIDEO)," RT, 9 January 2016, Retrieved 12 April 2017, https://www.rt.com/sport/328376-judo-putin-sochi-gamba/.

49. G lendinning, Lee, "Putin Shoots a Tiger as Europe Grapples with Russian Aggression," *The Guardian*, 1 September 2008, Retrieved 12 April 2017, https://www.theguardian.com/news/blog/2008/sep/01/russia.

50. Kr amer, Andrew E., "Putin Pulls Off Latest Feat: Flying With the Birds," *The New York Times*, 5 September 2015, Retrieved 12 April 2017, http://www.nytimes.com/2012/09/06/world/europe/putin-pulls-off-his-latest-feat-flying-with-migratory-birds.html.

51. Of note, one such proscription for parliamentary passage is the so-called "Yarovaya Law." See RFL/RL's coverage: "Russia's 'Yarovaya Law' Imposes Harsh New Restrictions On Religious Groups," *RFE/RL*, 11 July 2016, Retrieved 18 October 2017, https://www.rferl.org/a/russia-yarovaya-law-religious-freedom-restrictions/27852531.html.

52. Sperling, Valerie, "Putin's Macho Personality Cult," *Communist and Post-Communist Studies*, 2015, http://dx.doi.org/10.1016/j.postcomstud.2015.12.001.

53. As always, you can check Putin's running approval rating. I've sure especially his lackeys do. See: "Odobreniye Deyatel'nosti V. Putina," (in English) [Do you] approve of V. Putin's activities?" *Levada polling front page*, 12 April 2017, Retrieved 12 April 2017, http://www.levada.ru/.

54. See the foundation's website, Retrieved 17 December 2017, https://fbk.info/.

55. Grudinin is the successor to the long-time Communist presidential candidate (since the Yeltsin-era) and normalized politician, Gennadi Zyuganov. See: "Съезд КПРФ утвердил кандидатуру Грудинина на выборах президента РФ," (In English: "Congress of the KPRF confirms candidate Grudinin on the RF presidential election,") *Ren TV*, 23 December 2017, Retrieved 27 December 2017, https://ren.tv/novosti/2017-12-23/sezd-kprf-utverdil-kandidaturu-grudinina-na-vyborah-prezidenta-rf.

56. Yavlinsky has in many ways carried the flag of the social-liberal opposition in Russia since having a role in the transition of the USSR to the Russian Federation, most prominently through authoring the "500 Days Program" in 1990 to aid in Russia's passage into a market economy. He has been a candidate in every presidential election of the post-Soviet Russia era. For a contemporary view of his political position (in Russian), see his website: Yavlinsky web site, Retrieved 9 January 2018, http://www.yavlinsky.ru.

57. Sidorov, Dmitry, "Stanislav Markelov," *Forbes*, 24 January 2009, Retrieved 20 January 2018, https://www.forbes.com/2009/01/24/markelov-murder-budanov-oped-cx_ds_0124sidorov.html#199ec31fb7ef.

58. As has been the standard operating procedure in the past, the Putin regime has to give the Russian people another choice in the presidential election other than himself. In the last election, it was the aforementioned Prokhorov who served as the designated alternative, this time, it's the daughter of Putin's old Petersburg boss, Anatoly Sobchak.

59. "В Кремле отвергли причастность к решению Собчак участвовать в выборах," (In English: The Kremlin denies participation in the decision of Sobchak to participate in the election,") TV Rain, 19 October 2017, Retrieved 19 December 2017, https://tvrain.ru/news/peskov-448033/.

60. Dmitriev, Denis, Yevgeni Berg, and Alexandr Polivanov, "Алексей Навальный опубликовал подробную предвыборную программу. К ней есть вопросы," (In

English: "Alexei Navalny published details of his pre-election program. It has questions.) *Meduza*, 13 December 2017, Retrieved 17 December 2017, https://meduza.io/slides/aleksey-navalnyy-opublikoval-podrobnuyu-predvybornuyu-programmu-k-ney-est-voprosy.

61. "Navalny Calls For Election Boycott As Commission Blocks His Presidential Bid," *RFE/RL*, 25 December 2017, Retrieved 27 December 2017, https://www.rferl.org/a/russia-navalny-presidential-candidacy-rejected/28937989.html.

62. Some of this infighting among Russia's opposition over the Crimea question has been publicized both in Russian media and in Western sources. Alexei Navalny hedged on the Crimea question in an interview with Echo Moskvy, resulting in a multitude of Twitter responses by other opposition figures, and that was in turn further picked up by the New York Times, for example, here: Mackey, Robert, "Navalny's Comments on Crimea Ignite Russian Twittersphere," *The New York Times*, 16 October 2014, Retrieved 9 March 2017, https://www.nytimes.com/2014/10/17/world/europe/navalnys-comments-on-crimea-ignite-russian-twittersphere.html?_r=0.

63. "Sobchak Stirs Controversy In Russia By Saying Crimea Is Part Of Ukraine," *RFE/RL*, 25 October 2017, Retrieved 9 January 2018, https://www.rferl.org/a/sobchak-stirs-controversy-russia-saying-crimea-is-part-ukraine/28815695.html.

64. "Boris Nemtsov's Parting Shot," *The Economist*, 13 May 2015, Retrieved 30 January 2018, www.economist.com/news/europe/21651130-posthumously-completed-report-details-russias-involvement-war-ukraine-boris-nemtsovs.

65. "«Крым будет либо частично потерян, либо полностью»: спор Чичваркина и Милова о проблеме полуострова," (In English: "Crimea will be lost in part, or entirely: Debate of Chichvarkin and Milov about peninsula problem."), *TV Rain*, 27 December 2017, Retrieved 28 December 2017, https://tvrain.ru/teleshow/debaty/krym_budet_libo_chastichno_poterjan-453919/.

66. "Goodbye Russia: A generation packs its bags," BBC, 23 December 2017, Retrieved 24 December 2017, http://www.bbc.com/news/stories-42431009.

67. Kasparov, Garry, Web site, Retrieved 11 May 2017, http://www.kasparov.com/winter-is-coming/.

68. "Trading Profile: Russia Guards Against its Vulnerabilities," *Assessment Series*, Stratfor, 9 January 2018, Retrieved 11 January 2018, https://worldview.stratfor.com/article/trade-profile-russia-guards-against-its-vulnerabilities.

69. Original Russian: "Существуют маргинальные теории вроде неоевразийства, которые, однако, не способны представить хотя бы один пример действующего социального института.," "Россия и Европа: единство на почве национализма," (In English: "Russia and Europe: Unity on the Basis of Nationalism"), Levada Center, 16 August 2016, Retrieved 12 April 2017, http://www.levada.ru/2016/08/16/rossiya-i-evropa-edinstvo-na-pochve-natsionalizma/.

70. "Россия – Запад: восприятие друг друга в представлениях россиян," (In English, "Russia–Europe: The Perception of Each Other in View of the West,"), Levada Center, 26 June 2015, Retrieved 12 April 2017, http://www.levada.ru/2015/06/26/rossiya-zapad-vospriyatie-drug-druga-v-predstavleniyah-rossiyan/.

71. Shekhovtsov, Anton, "Aleksandr Dugin's Neo-Eurasianism: The New Right *à la Russe*," *Religion Compass*, Volume 3, No. 4, 2009, pp. 697–716.

72. Laruelle, Marlene, "In Search of Putin's Philosopher," *Intersection*, 3 March 2017, Retrieved 16 April 2018, http://intersectionproject.eu/article/politics/search-putins-philosopher.

73. B assin, Mark, "Classical Eurasianism and the Geopolitics of Russian Identity," *Ab Imperio*, February 2003, pp. 257–66.

THREE

The Respect and Spectacle of Russia

INTRODUCTION

Russia, and further amplified by how Putin's policies, personal activities, and comments have depicted the country, demands Respect. Putting the regime's possible spin on this concept of respect, President Vladimir Putin makes direct references to the same[1] and mirrors unsurprising rhetoric (albeit reflecting the intentions, but not always the effects of his policies). As of the late 2010s, Putin's policies have had mixed results in projecting Russia's image abroad as an influential world power, as shown by on-going Pew Research Center polls.[2]

However, what do the Russian people think? How do the Russian people, of which I've spent a significant amount of time studying, consider this application of respect?

Following from the Idea of Russia, the "ordinary" historical Russian point-of-view, that is to say, that which is understood to be the case (though far from necessarily true in and of all circumstances) by the every-man and every-woman image of Russia as a salient power, religious sanctum, and cultural whole, further holds the position that, as with every other people on Earth, Russia is demanding of "Respect."

Relevant to this chapter, it must be stressed, this could be called the—special big "R" respect—of Russia, perhaps as a chosen people with messianic properties, perhaps as a country and nation deserving of special acknowledgment in the world based on historical reasoning, perhaps as a powerful empire (and if you/they agree with that sentiment), perhaps as a "mover and shaker" in the world (as influential people might colloquially say), and, not least of which, possibly including even the most simplistic brute-force applications of the notion (respect me, because I command respect).

All people seek respect and all countries, particularly those with histories and imperial pasts such as Russia, seek respect writ large. To focus on this for a bit however, what is "Respect" for Russia and for Russians?

Once being an acknowledged global superpower, as the pre-Russian Federation Soviet Union was, for one idea, at its most basic level a sign of respect vies-a-vie the international community. The question stands: what is a superpower, or a great power, or what you make of it anyway, except for a word or series of words that sound inspirational, positive, and/or worthy of glorification when it refers to your own country?

Firstly, a superpower as the term is applied by many a thinker is that of a country that could successfully press its morals, or its economic/financial goals, or its military goals globally. Scholarly and analyst-driven thought on the matter is indeterminate. Some prominent individuals like for example former American President Jimmy Carter emphasize the moral side of being a superpower.[3] Others link relative economic power to possession of some technological edge to determine a superpower.[4] Whatever the case may be, Russia (or at least President Putin and his regime) strives for it, and I will bypass the open question. By extrapolation on the next level, a great power, or regional power, is presumably a bit less within those definitions in each category, focusing in each case on its own neighborhood, as it were.

All these thoughts have been debated in depth by other analysts; is modern India or China a superpower? To be a superpower, does a country need the will to be a superpower? Put another way, does a country "need" to think like a superpower to be a superpower, or does it just flow from economic, financial, or military strength? These questions will and must only be discussed here to the extent that it is important in the Russian case, yet this should not lessen the significance of the questions.

The post-Soviet period has not been kind to Russia and to Russians by any stretch of the imagination, as Russia has both lost obvious superpower status as well as has had to deal with a changing role in the world. Concerning even Russians' own view of their country, Vladimir Shlapentokh wrote that: "Openness has had a major impact on Russian society by diminishing the loyalty and respect Russians have toward their country."[5]

This best sums up the fact that, once the (relatively-) closed fish tank of the Soviet era was lifted, which was reinforced by that regime's grand efforts at propaganda and population control, and given that their world (or sphere of influence, or whatever you wish to call it) "shrunk" considerably, ordinary Russians did not necessarily like, to put it kindly, what they saw when comparing their economic and financial positions to Western powers, especially after economic reforms in the 1990s generally failed. Yet, there are indications that Russians' view on the matter are unchanged since Soviet times. As considered by Hanna Smith at the University of Finland: "However, it also seemed that from the Russian point of view, the status that had fallen down was that of the Soviet Union not of Russia. In the Western world's eyes Russia's status had changed, in the Russian view it had not."[6]

Over the course of this chapter, I will examine how Russians' view their world in consideration of their own respect for their country, as well as within the attitudes of those foreign to Russia, and how this has changed over the course of the post-Soviet era, and I will then examine what we can learn on these points which is of relevance to our world today, as extending from the 2010s decade more than twenty years after the fall of the Soviet Union.

Firstly, though, I will discuss a short history of superpower-ism or great power-ism, or whatever you choose to call it, and what it means for Russia.

RUSSIA AND A HISTORY OF RESPECT AND EMPIRE

Russia, by its current standard of big-R Respect, exists completely within the evolutionary purview of European (and, in furtherance, global) history; Russia, given its past and high levels of education, resources, and technology, found due a certain rise to global prominence in the twentieth century and now in the twenty-first century. Russia's turns in affecting the history of Europe were heightened and at times decisive.

Putting aside that reasoning, according to Russians themselves, at least from polling data shown in Figure 3.1,[7] there are a myriad of reasons for Russians, indeed, people in general, to have respect for Russia:

Comparisons here for Russia as a "power" are, of course, relevant both to the modern era, as with the current widely-acknowledged superpower, the United States, but also with pre-modern and ancient times, referring to the Roman empire, and so on.

The rhetoric by some that Russia is a kind of "Third Rome" must be mentioned as well, although I myself prefer to avoid the implication of "destiny" of any country.[8] Having some relevance to concepts of Eternal, Independent, and Unique Russia of which I will examine, as history defines respect for Russia to an extent, and this is one of the central analyses of this book, I am not as interested in the predestination for greatness aspect. The "Third Rome" idea is just one (potential) facet of the Russian public's view of its collective history, but not more.

Whatever those observations, historical Russia alongside other empires demanded respect, and those who were ruled by them were forced, in a myriad number of ways, to acknowledge, such as it was, the recognition of the overlord, or if only the need to overthrow it in various cases. Over the course of more than a few centuries, Britain, France, Turkey, China, Spain, Belgium, Japan and, yes, Russia all had turns engaging in "grand" imperialistic endeavors, sometimes against each other.

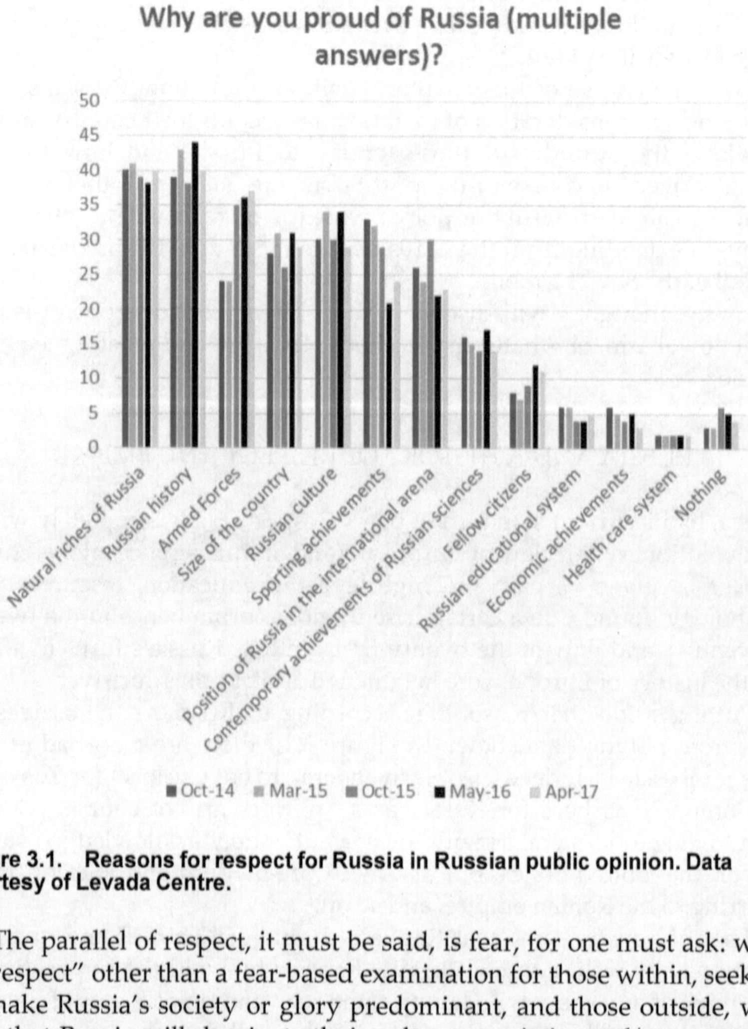

Figure 3.1. Reasons for respect for Russia in Russian public opinion. Data courtesy of Levada Centre.

The parallel of respect, it must be said, is fear, for one must ask: what is "respect" other than a fear-based examination for those within, seeking to make Russia's society or glory predominant, and those outside, who fear that Russia will dominate their cultures, societies and/or countries? In Russia's dealings with its nearest neighbors and with its rivals for global power, respect can be most tied to defense and the fear of Russia's offense, particularly concerning Russian President Vladimir Putin's aggressive foreign policies in the so-called near-abroad, the former Soviet states once under Moscow's domination. Russia's post-Cold War history is well-known, its Warsaw Pact allies ran to join the North Atlantic Treaty Organization (NATO), backstopped by the United States, when the USSR fell (though that changing reliance on U.S. support has been controversial for some of those same countries in its own way).

While many analysts, myself among them, stress that the NATO alliance is strictly a defensive alliance meant for common goals and to engender the general cooperation of its members, I at least acknowledge (though definitely not support) Moscow's opposing view on the matter of the last twenty to thirty years; that NATO is taking new members amazingly close to Russia in (possibly) an imagined attempt to box it in. While this involves a fundamental misconception of NATO's mission, it is at least a relevant position to take, even if not true. Geographically-speaking, it's hard to ignore that, post-Cold War, NATO came closer and not further from Russia.

By extension, Russia says that it is being "disrespected" as such, and NATO took advantage of Russia's 1990s weakness to aggressively move NATO's borders to Russia's doorstep. It is an attractive premise; it is not true, but it is an attractive premise, especially for elites in Moscow within the Putin regime who can use such antagonism to maintain power.

Fear and respect of Russia's potential has also sparked Ukraine and Georgia to seek NATO membership for some of the same reasons, considering Russia's aggression in those two countries. On the other hand, respect for at least the perceived "positives" of Russia's status to some extent has brought countries like Belarus and Armenia to seek a closer pro-Russian political framework, although that has been weakening as of the 2010s decade[9] and there are many opposed at the grassroots level in those countries.

To the east, countries like China, Kazakhstan and the other Central Asian states oftentimes seek to balance the positives of Russia's geopolitical position with the positives of pro-Western policies. Russia could always make trouble for China, and Russian friendship is always wanted, yet China's strong and rising economy benefits a pro-Western trade and economic policy that Russia cannot even dream of matching.

Perhaps Peter Rutland addressed some of these issues best when he wrote of Russia concerning a difficult to define future and the evolving nature of respect: "Russia is facing a double challenge: learning to live in a post-Soviet and post-modern world. [. . .] Simplistic notions of Russia as a recidivist empire, or a nascent market democracy, do not match this complex reality."[10]

Another aspect of respect in this context is the respect for law; a notable facet that has been noticeably lacking in the Russian case, though most countries which suffered through Communism shared this outcome. As written by Ase B. Grodeland recently about other formerly-Communist countries when comparing them to Western respect for law, but by extension easily applied to Russia: "The supremacy of the law, that is, the rule of law is a key feature of Western democracy and also an important part of Western legal culture. In Eastern Europe, which was under Communist rule for more than fifty years, such rights were until fairly recently non-existent."[11]

Indeed, the lack of respect for the rule of law, and Russian society's laxity in expectations for it, provide a key advantage for Putin and his regime's rule of the last fifteen years.

One major ongoing international problem for those who truly respect the rule of law has been the Putin regime's attempted export of Russia's failed civil society and observance of the rule of law. The Putin regime's desire to externalize Russia's problems, and Russia has many, separate from sequentially taking Crimea, supporting eastern Ukrainian separatists, and deploying troops to Syria, is a key facet of understanding the respect that these foreign policies attempt to earn. As to be covered further in chapter 4, all this while conveniently overlooking the fact that outside Russia's major cities there is poor infrastructure and valuable parts of Russia inaccessible to natural resource collection (as such, technological failure) except to the most dedicated of adventurers.

To be argued next, these sometimes counter-intuitive relationships of internal and external respect for Russia and the Russian state, parallel to the Putin regime's externalization of Russia's problems, and the lack of respect for ordinary Russians by the Putin regime make the question of "Respect" in Russia an extremely complicated paradigm to analyze.

RESPECT FROM THE "ORDINARY" RUSSIAN

As well they should, ordinary Russians have and demand a great respect for their country and for its achievements. Given Russia's past as a former superpower, this tendency is amplified in absolute terms in a myriad of directions. Russia is well-known internally and externally for its efforts in space exploration, manufacturing, industry, arts and literature. Socially, albeit overblown in some popular contexts, Russians have and are known for their enjoyment of a good party but also of a certain respect for traditional aims and authority.

It is on that basis, focusing on a traditionalist paradigm (thereby the theme of Eternal Russia), which is the deepest source of political support for Russian President Vladimir Vladimirovich Putin and his regime. Foreign analysts, diplomats, civil, private actors, and military officers have all asked me how and why the people of Russia support Putin's regime despite obvious moves towards authoritarianism and aggression towards countries and peoples that might once have had at least friendly relations with Russia (albeit with serious caveats befitting deals with a former colonial empire). Depending on how much time I had to answer that question, it went something like this:

As I covered in much detail in my first book, Putin uses and manipulates a culture of lies in Russia that both pits ordinary people against the government but also against their fellow neighbors and compatriots, thereby creating a closed circle where all information is gamed to benefit those in the know, and to disadvantage those who by time, place, or circumstances are not in a position to have their hand in the "well," such as that is. Putin takes advantage of Russians' respect for others, for society, and for authority and turns it inward, and, further, in many ways no less so than the case with previous more overtly authoritarian governments of Russia, namely that of the "big names" like Stalin and so on that we read about in the history books.

At this point, it is useful to stress a side issue, something which is a popular oversimplification: according to the arguments of some analysts and commentators, Russia and Russians are·overly acclimated to be a "superpower," and are willing to go along with Putin and their government in general to regain that same position in the world. Many point to President Putin's well-publicized quote (and I will paraphrase) that the fall of the Soviet Union was a major geopolitical disaster.[12] Although I'm sure Putin enjoys the thought, I do not agree with the adherence or overreliance on this quotation to assume that it should necessarily be taken at face value, nor do I believe that it is the policy of even Putin himself to attempt purely to regain superpower status.

Up to and including even the hardest "SERB-ite" nationalist in Russia, ordinary Russians in general are foremost cognizant of the fact that Russia cannot re-do that past, to expand and extend itself on some grand ideological bender; they have no desire to reenter other peoples' wars, or fund faraway ventures that have little meaning for the Russian people.

"Russia's adventure" in Syria is more accurately called "Putin's adventure," as in my experience, ordinary Russians care little about it. The Syrian case is a special point on which I will discuss later in this book. Instead, as I relate, Russia, Russians, and Putin in specific, are dedicated to national interests and domestic defense of the status quo (but for differing reasons), with the current regime in control at all costs, and absent some notable examples, Putin's quote should be taken in that context, rather than as a suggestion of re-attaining indiscriminately-broad foreign policy attractions.

As Andrei Tsygankov has covered before in both his books and his articles: "What Russia wants from the world is recognition of its right to rebuild a system of a strong state, to preserve the status of a great power, and to advance its national interests in Eurasia and adjacent regions."[13]

As for my own opinion, Putin is quite aware, I think, of many of the concerns present with Russia's status. As I have noted previously in this book, Putin is not a stupid individual. I posit that he is not the smartest person either, that is, probably not as smart as he thinks he is, but not stupid. Although I will flash back to this idea multiple times in future, he is in fact in the best position to know that life particularly outside of Moscow—the infrastructure, the quality of life, the technology—does not lend itself to gaining respect to those who regularly examine and analyze Russia. Nevertheless, it is frank to assume that he knows that he can gain respect in expansive ways, in those ways that he can gain the largest amount of respect for his regime.

One of the most important things for his regime backers (not surprisingly, very far and different from the people of Russia, mind you) is to engender respect, and thereby force opportunities to improve the all-important regime's financial situation making use of current Russian political thought.

Again, as discussed in the last chapter, this touches on the image of Putin as commanding respect. Such an image was not however built without some major flaws and mistakes made in the past. Many of these overt past mistakes are being swallowed up by history, however. Relatively early in his presidency, the 2001 sinking of Russia's flagship submarine, Kursk, and Putin's lazy reaction to the tragedy denoted a serious learning curve to the concept of attaining respect for his regime. With the deaths of all aboard the Kursk and the failed technology of the Russian navy involved in attempting to save the Kursk sailors, there was a black mark upon the respect of Russia and the regime's conscious and competence which could have been long-lasting had Putin not immediately recognized the danger to his regime and made all efforts to get perceptions of him back on an even and stable foundation.

Furthermore, dealing with the financial crisis of 2008–2009 and 2014 to the present-day (as of this writing, 2017–2018), Putin was and is faced with a potentially dangerous threat to the economy which could dent the Russian people's respect for his regime. Putin in part countered this crisis to a limited extent with additional military spending, but this has limitations as well.[14]

Of course, Putin has the usual help of a strongly pliant media machine that he himself had a distinct hand in building;[15] there is "spin" implying or directly suggesting a Western cause or causes for the crisis and so the financial disaster can be directed at the foreign "menace."[16] Hence, it is not yet clear whether there will be any lasting effect of the steady "dripping" failure of the economy on the Putin regime in the near-term. This in fact brings us to our next point.

Putin is vulnerable to losing the respect of Russians; a fact that he himself almost certainly knows quite well. As has been persuasively proven by Mikhail A. Alexeev and Henry Hale using public opinion surveys surrounding 2013 and 2014, any rise in Russian nationalism amongst the people surrounding Russia's embarkation on the Crimean invasion is by no means solid or sustaining.

> As regards many kinds of nationalist thinking, the increase was actually rather slight; and some aspects of Russian nationalism, including support for further territorial expansion, actually declined after Crimea was annexed. Moreover, we also discern strong indications that the "rally-around the leader" effect may not be long-lived. Members of the public have remained deeply concerned about economic problems that

have only grown worse since the crisis, as well as about other problems that the wave of patriotism has not actually resolved.[17]

Putin's image is therefore sometimes connected directly to the general respect for Russia, both celebrated and reluctantly defended in sometimes nearly-equal dynamics. The personalization of his image as leader has brought some analysts to consider that his words and deeds mean something in exacting detail. Therein, this has also led to a reemergence of what was called during the Cold War, Kremlinology, when the minutest arrangements of every public appearance were and is examined for hints of what is happening "behind the scenes" in Kremlin politics.

Indeed, observers today watch for every change in President Putin's schedule, every arrangement of pencils on his desk, every meeting with foreign officials both abroad and domestic and even the cleanliness (or lack thereof) of Putin's clothing.[18] Some even speculate that Putin has had (possibly botched) plastic surgery, although little direct evidence has ever been forthcoming (not that it necessarily ever would be).[19] Having observed Putin for some seventeen years now as of the late 2010s, I've never gotten the impression that he was so concerned about his appearance, albeit he's happy to show off his bod, but anyway, I digress. All of this lends to the perception that Putin as a personage demands "respect."

As a figure of "respect," Putin himself has that rare bi-polar image where his policies can be seen by older generations as being indicative of restraint and, and in no small part due to his aggressive foreign policies, also possibly be rebellious, thereby appealing to the younger generations. This is quite a good dualistic image for someone who is, at root, a rather realpolitik and doctrinaire decision maker. In this context he has several avenues in which to portray his desired policies, without endangering his own respected position or respect for Russia from insiders and outsiders.

As such, many of his policies can further be portrayed in Russian culture as being restraining and rebellious at the same time; the Crimean annexation has been portrayed in this context and will be discussed in more detail as this book goes on. It can be regarded as axiomatic in that the taking of Crimea from Ukraine and making it whole with Russia can be seen on one hand as "restraint," in that Putin is conservatively defending Russia and Russians by bringing home a piece of Russia left behind by "stupid" (i.e., Soviet) people in the past (presenting a problem to Putin's demonstrable periodic Soviet-philia). On the other hand, taking back Crimea can also be "rebellious" in that Putin is upending the Western political norms and past agreements where Russia was forced, supposedly against its will, to honor that Crimea was a part of Ukraine when in fact, according to Putin's rhetoric, it never was.

In other countries, the number of politicians who can attain this level of unbridled "respect," of parallel restraint and rebellion, can probably be counted on one hand. Most politicians have to choose in some way, shape, or form to either be more restraining, or closer to the restrictions of adhering to political normalcy, or to be more rebellious, in order to supposedly bring change and rebuke the status quo.[20] Many politicians try to attain this duality, or change with more subtlety between the two poles over the course of their political careers, or perhaps try for a softer abstract "magnanimous" practical (and logical) duality far softer than the aggressive tendencies of Putin (again, there is no escaping here of the taking of Crimea, Europe's first major change in borders since the Second World War), but few attempt to do the hard form of this all at the same time.

This is however not to imply that this duality grants Putin invulnerability to opposition, far from it in fact. The manipulative use of his image in this fashion is indicative of the fact that even Putin knows that there is some danger to his regime as Russia faces a depressed economy in relation to Western sanctions. While as generally judged by Russian public opinion over time based on Levada Centre polling data (as seen from the following Figure 3.2[21]), Western sanctions are survivable, the featured impact on "respect" over the long-term is yet up in the air and dependent on Putin maintaining his hold on the predominant cultural "initiative" in Russian society. Hence, simply put, for Putin, no one can be allowed to get ahead of the regime in positioning the cultural narrative.

Further indicative of Putin's weakness, during my research, rarely did anyone wearing a Putin T-shirt answer me that, even though I asked, Putin's image meant hope for the future; it almost always meant instead some variation of a rapacious defense of Russia's past glories. There is always the possibility that this respect for Putin and his regime could

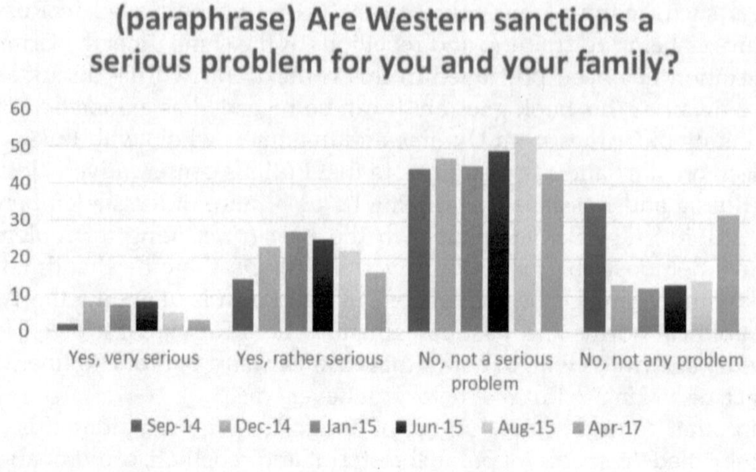

Figure 3.2. Reasons for respect for Russia in Russian public opinion. Data courtesy of Levada Centre.

come to an end, although as of the middle of the 2010s decades given Putin's current hold on power and given an assumed reelection in the 2018 presidential election, I still maintain that the last shoe has yet to drop on the current regime.

For Putin himself to be extracted from power, or to endanger Putin's own peacefully managed transition (no doubt to a contemporary), some external event would have to bring this about or a significant downturn in the economy would have to be forthcoming. Maybe Navalny, or a billionaire like Mikhail Prokhorov (but not him) or a television personality like Ksenia Sobchak (but not her), will yet surprise me, but I remain skeptical.

Nevertheless, people do (slowly) get tired of the status quo; eventually it is at least possible, and indeed conceivable, that Putin's duality might become stale (hard to imagine in Russia's contemporary culture, I know) and fail to turn the hearts of even the harshest supporter of the current regime's ideal of "respect." Maybe the regime's close elite supporters might suddenly decide that they want to one day visit those avenues of Italy or slopes of Switzerland again, regardless of what point Putin is trying to make in foreign policy. Having researched, lived, and worked in Russia for a considerable amount of time, I just don't see an "endgame" yet, but surprises do happen.

It must also be recognized that respect for Moscow in the outer regions of Russia, that is, outside the major cities, has been highly questionable as of late. For one thematic protest in March to April 2017, striking truck drivers across Russia have put Putin's rule into some small doubt.[22] These protests have been growing significantly and have met with some response from Moscow, although that response, basically with silence and rhetoric, has been duly cognizant of the protesters' capacity to create problems.[23] The government restraint therein provides some hope that the strikes and so on might one day come to affect Moscow and the Kremlin's calculations for the future. As of 2017, it is however unlikely that there will be some larger type of "March on Moscow" in the near-future, and Putin's remaining control over regional governors and, in turn, the governors' control over their regions, while showing signs of weakening, have not shown any indication of truly dangerous trouble for Putin, or at least not yet.

Whatever the case may be, any Moscow opposition that promotes a parallel for Russia's respect and "greatness" has not been forthcoming. Russia's opposition has been all but sidelined except in Navalny's corruption investigations and Putin, his regime and his party, United Russia, are aware of this. In the run-up to Russia's September 2016 parliamentary election, one notable poster for Putin's United Russia promoted three reasons why Russia's electorate should vote for United Russia. The third and final major reason was basically asking the rhetorical question:

"If not United Russia, then who else?" This is a notable and valid question given the opposition at hand.

As Putin's regime has already gutted much of the opposition, except for Navalny who's rarely attracted major support,[24] and driven certain members, including former Yukos driver Mikhail Khodorkovsky, into exile outside of Russia, there is a notable lack of further possibilities. In oblique reference to Navalny's attempt at some type of election boycott, Yekaterinburg's Mayor, Yevgeny Ruizman, who somewhat-uniquely ran against corruption, spoke out on the dearth of functional opposition: "These are not elections. I have known the result for a long time and so has everyone else. The only unknown is the turnout. If there is a low turnout, the victory will feel incomplete."[25]

These deterrents do not however stop some analysts from constantly predicting that this or that development, or this or that year (in this article's case, 2016), is the beginning of Putin's downfall or Putin's loss of control and so on.[26] I completely understand such pronouncements, as I completely respect much of this work, and (for my own part) I hope that they have some degree of accuracy, however I do not think that the end of Putin's reign will necessarily be apparent at the time it happens or even be systematically predictable, given all the "balls in play," if such a thing happens at all (Putin could leave voluntarily with a chosen successor at the end of his practically-imminent re-elected term in 2024, which is always a definite possibility in my mind).

All things being equal, for the regime, the defense and domination of Putin's image has therefore had the desired effect. As of the late 2010s, internal "respect for Russia" and "respect for Putin" is difficult (but not impossible) to separate. From most appearances, and in line with much of my research and interviews in Russia, the peoples' respect for Russia remains, at least in the short term, currently bound to its leader, and its leader is bound to indirect self-promotion in the process of supporting the ordinary Russians' respect for the state. Bearing on the future, this has given Putin a continuing platform on which to base a newly-aggressive foreign policy backed by the military which he would not have had otherwise.

Nevertheless, as a small bit of good news, there is at least some evidence that the Russian people are losing patience with Putin, although such reports are admittedly sporadic.[27]

As to be examined in the next section, the opposite of respect for Putin is not necessarily the case, and this must be explored in detail here.

RESPECT FOR THE "ORDINARY" RUSSIAN

The respect that the ordinary Russian has for Russia and the Putin regime is rivaled with the lack of respect that the Putin regime has for the people of Russia.[28] One might think that respect for Putin as discussed in the previous section would engender some amount of responding gratitude for the Russian popular trust in him. To put it more bluntly, one would think that, Putin's touches of empathy on television notwithstanding, the Putin regime would have the common courtesy to have a high regard for the people who have allowed it such riches and broad support through multiple elections and some very difficult times. In this regard, one would however be most mistaken.

Furthermore, and contrary to any fear of possibly losing that trust, Putin and his regime have no problem in putting the Russian people in their "place," if you will; while paying lip service to their needs, and countering with self-serving economically debilitating policies which can only leave Russian home shelves bare.

Putin's lack of respect for ordinary Russians can be seen by his efforts to control public opinion through the media. The Putin regime's control of the media and electoral landscape overall, especially through state media, is legendary.[29] As to be addressed shortly, the Putin regime takes over media companies and places few restrictions on its efforts to directly control it, co-opting (and, in some cases, killing) journalists who dare to write anti-regime features, manipulating elections, and in general subverting even the possibility of a free and open civil society developing in Russia.

This includes the 2017 branding of Voice of America and Radio Free Europe/Radio Liberty (RFE/RL) as "foreign agents"[30] (which is a notably more dangerous label in Russia[31] than in freer countries such as the United States), and attacks and convictions leveled on journalists for the two organizations, like for example RFE/RL's Mykola Semena in Russian-controlled Crimea.[32]

Not unlike other semi-authoritarian regimes, these policies all (it shouldn't need to be said but I will say it anyway) represent an automatic lack of trust by the Putin regime in the people.

As a relevant side-note, as seen from the Putin regime's aggressive influence campaigns against the United States during the 2016 Presidential election there, and possibly against certain European votes including the British exit vote ("Brexit") in the United Kingdom, the Putin regime has been working on internationalizing its domestic psychological operations on the world stage. (Not to mention Russia's covert direct actions as, for example, the assassination of Alexander Litvinenko and the attempted-assassination of former UK spy, Sergei Skripal and his daughter, both in London and both from exotic substances that almost certainly came from Russia.[33]) These facets will, I argue, surely wake up foreign governments as to the true dangers of the Putin regime; dangers that, it must be mentioned, have been expressed by Russia specialists for years.

Russia's culture, if respect for Russia's people is honest, must be of heightened concern. Apart from the internet, which does not yet reach as much of Russia as the opposition hopes it would (as it is limited as discussed in the next section), many Russians outside the major cities rely on the state media, and the Putin regime, not surprisingly, is reluctant to grant any favors here to independent storylines.

All these aspects coincide with the Putin regime ideal of holding power (with and without Putin, when one day he relinquishes power either voluntarily or involuntarily) and, not coincidentally, this is all consistent with the expression of Putin's "law and order" establishment which has developed well into its second decade.

Again, as is well-known, the list is quite long of journalists and journalistic entities persecuted by the Kremlin for taking a non-regime line. Amongst the lengthening list of correspondents who died on duty, perhaps the best-known journalists are such luminaries as Anna Politkovskaya, a famous Chechen war correspondent who died in 2006 in the elevator of her own apartment block from four bullet wounds, and Natalya Estemirova, also a famous Chechen conflict reporter who was kidnapped and killed in the North Caucasus in 2009.[34]

As for organizations and journalistic entities which have suffered in the Kremlin's quest for silencing those who could damage its image of respect for Russia, the list is also long. Excellent human-rights organizations like "Memorial," long examining both the past and present and investigating the criminal elements that was Stalinism, have been reduced to barely operational status. The list of specifically media sources and journalistic entities is longer still. Media sources like Television Rain (TV Dozhd), Novaya Gazeta, for which the aforementioned Politkovskaya and Estemirova worked, and pretty much every other media organization which dared to maintain its independence has been brought to ruin or taken over by state entities such as the state-controlled Vserossiyskaya Gosudarstvennaya Televizionnaya i Radioveshchatelnaya Kompaniya (VTGRK, All-Russia State Television and Radio Company) and rich state-backed or state-owned oil conglomerates like Gasprom, etc.[35]

For the Putin regime and its supporters, the necessities of breaking journalists and journalistic entities are portrayed as being a prerequisite for upholding the respect of Russia. Theses traitors must be silenced, as has been argued by every authoritarian regime in history, up to and including the one under discussion here. Nevertheless, respect for Russians by the regime is further reduced.

Ordinary Russians are presented with the necessity of abiding by the regime's rules or being compartmentalized and exiled to outer regions or to foreign countries, although yet the methodology through which the regime does this has not quite amounted to the overt strong-arming of the Soviet period. The Putin regime of the mid-2010s uses its unofficial supporters more than through direct policy; with a wink and a push, the Putin regime's supporters put pressure on any who might seek to change the system, such as when Alexey Navalny was doused with green paint by unknown assailants while opening a campaign office in March 2017.[36]

Not insignificantly, the judiciary also supports these policies; people like Mikhail Khodorkovsky lost much of their wealth to flee the regime and mount an opposition from foreign shores. This is not a new concept to Russia, it must be mentioned; Lenin himself spent his time fomenting "revolution" from the quiet mountain cities of Switzerland, nevertheless, it is a fundamental facet that this has not changed in the many years of Russia's history. Still, even these policies do not fully explain the compartmentalization of the Russian people amid their forced abeyance to the Putin regime.

Again, as I discussed in my first book,[37] the Putin regime induces and contributes to a "normalcy" of lies in Russian society, a normalcy which in many ways is a continuation of Soviet society, wherein the Putin regime lies to the people and, quite rightly in turn, most (if not all) Russian people vies-a-vie Russian civil life lie both to the Putin regime and to each other, although this systemic existence has many disadvantages for the regime as well. In a society where there is no trust and many (if not all) are lying, how can the regime gauge and collect its own support?

Therein, no one knows really if any information is true, it contributes to Russian social and cultural stagnation, and Russians doubt whether the opposition across Russia is real (although, as of March 2017, Navalny's anti-corruption marches got information out better than previously); and for the regime no one knows if the taxes collected are the taxes owed.

At the highest levels, avoiding state attention to one's taxes and liability is truly an art form that develops alongside influence in modern Russia. While this is but one part of the so-called post-truth paradigm globally, especially with America President Donald Trump's frequently untruthful pronouncements, in Russia it is unique because it has so much more historical precedence. Russia also has few of the constitutional or legal guards against abuse that America has, and so the first principal of becoming influential in Russia, or even in running your own business or, really, doing anything in Russia, is to avoid unwanted and/or unnecessary attention from the Putin regime.

The limitations of civil freedoms are paralleled further by economic, financial, and foreign policies that the Putin regime intends to engender respect for Russia among Russians, but in fact only serves to make for a lot of bare shelves and hungry Russian people. Indeed, even the basic foreign policies of the Putin regime are not meant so much for a foreign audience as they are meant for the domestic audience.

Beyond that however, as policies with Ukraine and regarding Western-based sanctions can and will be discussed elsewhere in this book, including in the next section, few ways has the Putin regime tried to create respect for Russia among its citizens more than fighting the "war" of sanctions versus counter-sanctions. Putin's counter-sanctions have only made certain imported goods more difficult to get, i.e., more expensive, for the Russian people, without in any way damaging the foreign producers of said items, although, it must be said, as studied by the Centre for European Policy Studies, the "sanctions and counter-sanctions have a relative low direct impact on the trade flows of targeted products."[38]

Further, Putin has instituted policies to ban foreign goods that could, some only theoretically, be reproduced in Russia by Russian producers (import substitution). These policies have failed to successfully promote Russia's economic sovereignty, as much of Russia's "manufacturing output is not competitive on global markets and is consumed domestically,"[39] thereby they are products of quintessentially lower quality. Nevertheless, as seen from the following Levada centre polling data in Figure 3.3,[40] bowing to Putin's unsurprising media portrayal of them as necessary, the counter-sanctions have been generally popular among the Russian people:

Plus, as to be discussed more in chapter 4 regarding such areas as oil exploration, given that many sources in the deep Arctic of Siberia can only be approached and exploited by people using advanced Western

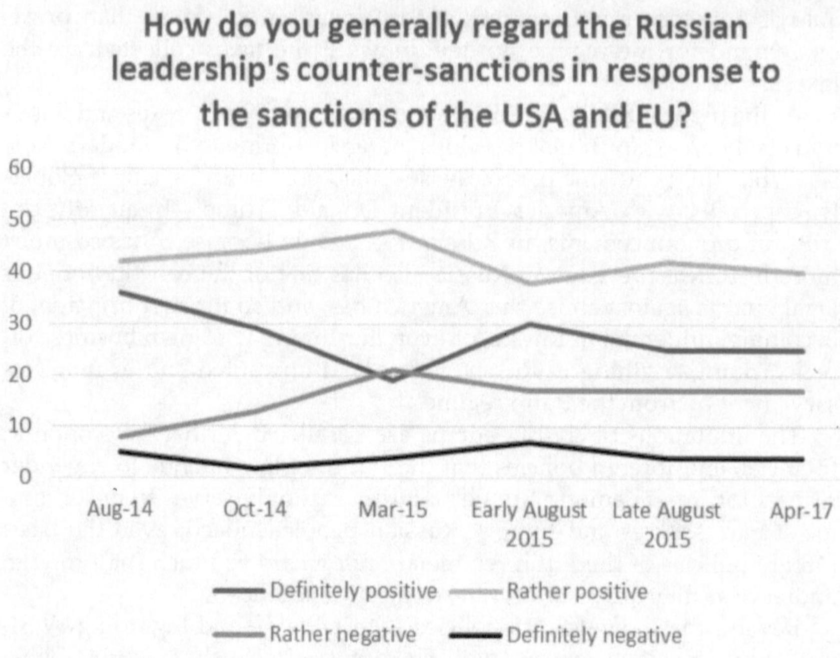

Figure 3.3. Support for counter-sanctions in Russian society. Data courtesy of Levada Centre.

technologies, Russia has had to forgo for the conceivable future ever reaching these promising areas. Putin's counter-sanctions argument that such technologies can be produced domestically rings decidedly hollow. In an economy that could use all the help that it could get even without sanctions, Putin's Russia is quite simply hobbled by the necessity of serving its own media portrayal for domestic consumption; that of a strong power, if not really a superpower as remarked upon earlier.

The Putin regime's dogged support for stability and the status quo even when corruption is rampant is another significant marker for the lack of respect for the people by the Putin regime. Putin knows that the people will not rise against him if stability (phantom stability it may be) is supposedly endangered (suggesting a return to the more chaotic Yeltsin era before him). Recent investigatory findings by opposition leaders like Alexei Navalny have had little impact on regime support in part for this reason. As I will discuss more, given that Putin is "respected" by the people of Russia, while the regime respects the people less on this unequal paradigm, where no one is surprised by really anything, then there is little chance of breaking the status quo in any meaningful way.

Finally, the regime has also allowed the social safety net, part of the Russian social contract, to degrade, due to lack of investment and funding. The Russian people's access to medical care is steadily getting worse, and pension funds,[41] are being drained to bankroll the economy under sanctions and, effectively but indirectly, to fund the regime's foreign policy adventures. These developments are slowly but surely making life more difficult for those most vulnerable in Russia. They also show the lack of respect for the Russian people by the regime and demonstrates Putin's general lack of concern.

Through his pragmatic policies, neglecting necessary domestic investment while antagonizing foreign "enemies," Putin and his regime show little to no respect for the Russian people, serving the regime and the heightened sense of itself. Figuratively speaking, as much as the Russian people respect the Putin regime, the Putin regime has shown little to no respect, or even basic acknowledgment, for the plights of the citizenry.

If one day, Putin is to lose his vaulted position in Russian society, given some sequence of events or some new occurrence which is almost impossible to predict beforehand, the root cause of his loss will be exactly here where he could be construed to be weakest.

The Russian people for now have little end in their respect for him (and by default his regime); this could however change, and it could change more quickly than perhaps he, myself, or some other observer could seek to imagine. Putin is vulnerable, but not from his "front," if you will. To venture somewhat poetic just for a moment, Putin's rear quadrant, as oftentimes with many leaders domestic, international, military, and so on throughout history, is almost certainly the most vulnerable segment of his furtive projected being. When he loses, assuming he does not retire quietly at some unrevealed point, he will lose here.

"THE CRIMEAN QUESTION," INVASIONS, AND RESPECT

Russia's military interventions in the near-abroad, with the invasion and forced annexation of Crimea as a cornerstone, are at their core about respect. Indeed, as posited by Mikhail Suslov at the very beginning of an early 2017 article:

> The annexation of Crimea in March 2014 and the War in Donbas have made a strong impression on the popular imagination and substantially changed perceptions of Russia's place, role, and mission in the world amongst the Russian population. Mass media and social networks have hyped up these events as Russia's return from historical obscurity and transformation from geopolitical periphery into international pivot.[42]

These interventions I will talk about outside of Russia's desire to be a superpower again if such a desire exists (which I do not necessarily agree with). Secondarily, I will also most often focus on Crimea because that is the focal point on which the ideas of respect have most virulence as to be explained shortly.

To some extent, "respect" is at the heart of the Crimean question in part because of a general failure to satisfy a small minority of Russians with the results of the fall of the Soviet Union. That minority responded to Putin's manipulation of the issue for his own desire for respect and made Crimea into an issue that could collect a majority of Russian public opinion. There are numerous reasons why that minority was unhappy in the beginning: failures of treaties and organizations like the Commonwealth of Independent States (CIS) to sustain goodwill in the post-Soviet space, bad-neighbor decisions by Russia and (to a lesser extent) former Soviet countries, and failures at all levels to regulate disagreements in the post-Soviet era have not helped matters any.[43]

On this precise point, my own research (and the research of some others from the period[44]), talking to hundreds if not thousands of ordinary older Russians, has most often seen an expansion of the idea that Russia had lost "something." It became a codification of the idea that for Russia, when the Soviet Union fell, except for perhaps the Baltic republics, life in Soviet times as a friendship and somewhat cooperating groups of diverse peoples was expected to continue. Of course, the other nation-states of the Soviet Union did not see it that way. The Baltic republics of course disappeared very quickly, but then so followed the other republics with many seeking broad ties with Western countries, and (as said in the beginning) some even attempting with varying degrees of success to join the Western military alliance, NATO,[45] which for years had been set in making entirely-responsible plans to deal with the Soviet empire.

Expanding from that early minority of Russians and continuing until today, Russians were, and are, (supposedly) appalled by this state of events. In a patriotic tizzy, while paradoxically backing off from any need for superpower status, I've had more than one Russian citizen suggest to me that they would never have "allowed" the Soviet Union to fall apart if they had known that Western countries would seek to "take advantage" of Russia in the post-Soviet aftermath.[46] Many Russians saw NATO's expansion to be a lack of "respect" for Russia, and they thought, and think, that Russia's strong president Putin should do something about it, like what he is doing now in bolstering (more or less) Russia's military position, though most are yet against military adventurism.

On a broader scale now in the 2010s, with all that has happened, ordinary Russians have questioned many things about their Soviet past, and the perception has lingered that the other fourteen republics benefited more upon independence from the Soviet Union than Russia did. On a more personal, albeit informal, basis, from the point-of-view of some of my closest Russian friends, they have told me that the other fourteen former Soviet republics, in declaring independence and nationalizing assets on each respective territory, have pretty much stolen something from Russia. Soviet decisions, like the transfer of Crimea to Ukraine way back when, are now questioned and seen as giveaways at a time when Russia could not oppose them, given that all the countries gave an effective fait accompli through separation and even, shockingly in their view, joining Western military alliances.

As a point of contention, I say this regarding particularly Crimea, but many Russians don't see the issue of an unequal breakup of the Soviet Union only about that issue. Many of the factories that were Soviet, but became Ukrainian, because they were in Ukraine at the time of the Soviet fall; some Russians wonder where their "compensation" was for those factories. All the material in the post-Soviet republics that Russian resources, to some extent, went towards building those factories and industrial facilities, where is that money now?

This is again in conflict with the view that many considered the breakup of the Soviet Union in the years shortly afterwards. Many experts of the 1990s gave much heed to the fact that the major central states of the Soviet Union (Ukraine, Belarus, Russia and Kazakhstan) had a relatively "orderly" breakup. However, the fact that the breadth of the Soviet Union did not immediately break out into mass civil war should not suggest the lack of reasons to do so; it was only representative of the fact that a fundamental tiredness overwhelmed many of these states as they each considered their own problems and what to do next.

Now that we are twenty-five years on, in the 2010s decade and onwards, what do these grievances mean insofar as the "Respect" of Russia? Well, time, financial, and natural resources have a lot to say about old issues.

Money, and the ever-evolving quest for more money in Russia for the oligarchs, belie the systemic creation of "respect" in and for Russia as a concept, even more so than in other countries, democratic and authoritarian, where respect is interlocked with the financial gains of the elite.

One can never forget the issue of natural resources, oil and related further development, when talking about Russia. Putin's ability to fund a newly-risen Russian military and his limited (now-decreasing) ability to support the Russian social welfare has existed much on the backs of high oil prices, as many analysts[47] have agreed over the 2000s and 2010s decades. Even given the sanctions of the 2010s decade, now that Western countries have sought to punish Russia for taking Crimea and its more-forward foreign policies, there is an economic backbone behind this airing of post-Soviet grievance, which was and is the seed for the annexation of Crimea by Russia.

By extension, the general citizenry, as their dependency on the social net (pensions, etc.) has been financially-monopolized and taken advantage of by the regime and its elite segment, are duly headed by a Putin regime which is more than happy to try to regain prestige on issues like Crimea. This is nominally to "regain" the respect of Russia, but effectively used to maintain support and the regime's own financial gains while the economy is something of a serious problem, if not an imminent catastrophe.

As such, while members of the Putin regime often call for upholding sovereignty at all costs, this understanding is only for when it benefits the Putin regime and its dependent oligarchs. This further implies that the Putin regime wants respect with added benefits beyond past understandings of international relations; a subject that I regard as Russia's aggregate international prestige, i.e., a kind of respect that exceeds any normal understanding of a country.

RESPECT+

Based on the annexation of Crimea and the historical invasions of many of its neighbors, I understand that the Putin regime wants to have what I call: "Respect+." What is this new concept of "Respect+," you might ask?

Respect+ is not-quite-empire but exceeds the boundaries of international law concerning what one power can do in respect to smaller or less imperial-inclined countries near and far. Respect+ uses the concept of sovereignty when the concept benefits the state that desires it. Other analysts suggest that "Russia" wants added influence on former imperial possessions to unduly influence them. This indeed is half of Respect+. Respect+ is more than that though. Respect+ is about influence, yes, but it is also about having not-quite empire, using military forces with abandon, without any negative consequences. Respect+ is a self-serving perspective on international law, and little else.

Respect+ is good for the Putin regime both from the ordinary and elite Russian point-of-view; it can lead a neo-superpower (but dismissing superpower status for socio-political reasons and partially from lack of fortitude) while still feigning non-interference in foreign countries. Respect+ is bad from the Western point-of-view, as it involves the daily flaunting of international law in almost all its forms.

Barring someone, or something, seriously hindering the Putin regime's quest for Respect+, there will never being an "ordinary" country when Russia is concerned.

In view of the election of the notably pro-Putin Donald Trump administration in the United States, the Putin regime will continue to seek Respect+, and there is no indication at present as of the mid-2010s that Russia will not receive it.

THE "SPECTACLE" OF RUSSIA

Parallel in many ways to the Respect of Russia, is the fact that in some ways, albeit not as a superpower and existing secondarily to the regime's domestic needs, I think Putin wants to put on a "show" for the external world as well; this is the "Spectacle" of Russia, which is the second and lesser concept of the title of this chapter. This is different from Respect in that a portrayal (a "Spectacle") for international audiences honoring Russia's abilities and technology by potential opponents versus accurately determining the perception of Russia both domestically and on the world stage (the "Respect") is indeed significant. One cannot avoid the examination of Russia's position in the past, present, and future without delving into this aspect of investigation.

Further by the "Spectacle" of Russia, I mean to imply that the depiction of Russia both internally for Russian social and cultural consumption, and externally by those deterministic factors for external people; they all love a spectacle. This is part of the romanticism of chapter 2; the people love the depiction of Russia as being beautiful, of being strong, of being cultural progressive but conservative on some issues.

"They," those Russia sympathizers inside and outside the country, love the depiction of Russia as a kind bear that stands up to those who would make a mockery of such a "power," whether you agree with the concept of Russia as a great power or whatnot in the 2010s decade in the first place.

Of course, while perhaps not central to the Russian daily view, for most of course are more concerned with putting food on the table not so different from the peoples of other countries, Russia and Russians still have a long and detailed conceptual view of Russia descending as it were from the Soviet era and which still has dominance in the Russian world view of the 2010s decade and most likely beyond.

Ultimately, the Spectacle of Russia, I posit, is a further extension of Respect+.

It is the feeling by the Putin regime that Russia is above the law and can do anything it wants. It is a fundamentally negative concept, and I venture that Russia must be pulled away from it in future, at the risk of a frightening future confrontation with other powers that may be cataclysmic in scale.

This short section runs parallel to the earlier section; it is written to explore and examine these aspects of the "spectacle" of Russia and will be conceptually seen through a single ideal. It is that of the "proud Russia." This view should be depicted as a dependent part of the Russian cultural worldview which President Vladimir Putin himself has tried to both benefit from and hold in check, as this ideal can and does have both advantages and disadvantages, as to be explored herein. In the context of this book, this ideal is important to mention in understanding how Russians have both looked outwards to understand their new post-Soviet role in the world as well as understood their own specific and peculiar circumstances relative to the "house" of Russia.

The idea of a proud Russia is a predominant categorical ramification of Russia's past, present and what hoped-for future. The nationalistic idea of pride is of course not exclusive to Russia and is not universally negative. Unfortunately, much as in the past, Russia's idea of a proud Russia for most Russians has co-mingled with the idea of a strong central power held by a perceived strong central leader. As has been well documented by a host of literature, authoritarianism and Russia's step back from the democratic ideals in the post-Soviet era are well-known and has been written about in detail by many experts, academics, analysts and the like. This aspect of spectacle of Russia is unavoidable, I would argue, in the post-Soviet era and cannot be completely condemned, given the difficulties faced by the Russian people since 1991. Neither however can excessive pride be overlooked and should not be tolerated if Russia is to become a strong world power again.

One popular (and overblown) manifestation of the spectacle of Russia is and has always been Russia's military, the Red Square still rumbles to the sound of tanks every Victory Day (as I have discussed and will discuss more in coming sections), but also means Russia's sports output. Stretching back to the Soviet era, Russians saw their Olympic medal collection in each successive Olympics to be an expression of Russian personal, governmental and physical prowess. Much like in other countries, Russians had high expectations in their international sports accomplishments.

Examining the Russia of today, the abstract spectacle of Russia has been damaged in many eyes, both internationally and domestic, with the allegation of state-sponsored doping within (and by) Russia's sports community. This has led to the likelihood that Russia's athletes might be banned from future athletic competitions; in 2017 the focus was on participation in the 2018 Summer Olympics in Rio. The Putin administration has countered that any such allegation is false and politically-motivated. In turn, ordinary Russians I've talked to tend to agree with these counter-allegations of the Putin administration on this issue.

Teaching English in Russia, I met many young students, many of which were very interested in sport, who said that it was all political, and that any international sports sanctions on the Russian team(s) were political motivated. Sergey* [*not his real name] from a seminar I gave in Moscow, for examine, vociferously denied any such systematic doping policy; instead, he told me many times the old trope of "whataboutism?," ("Americans do dope too, Jason . . . What of them?") in order to imply that all athletes from all countries have a doping edge, despite being informed that other countries have well-known and well-trodden anti-doping testing and procedures that Russia might or might not adhere to.

By extension, the spectacle of Russia has been damaged significantly by other events, such as Russia's mentality in the Syrian Civil War, by supporting the Assad regime despite chemical weapons use in the operational theater in April 2017. Extending from that (as well as the Ukrainian situation), and so forth, as Russia becomes more isolated, so does its ability to display its worth on the world stage in many potentials avenues and outlets.

The Spectacle of Russia, while worth mentioning, is rapidly diminishing in the eyes of the international community, and that is perhaps how it should be as long as the Putin regime is in power.

CONCLUSIONS

A conclusion can be simple in this segment, and I for one am always looking to simplify things as much as possible.

Russia seeks respect as does ever country on Earth, yet the Putin regime seeks the concept of Respect+ which is the normalized surpassing of international law in almost all respects.

While the Russian people have great respect for President Vladimir Putin personally, and his regime by default, he and his regime have little respect for the Russia people. The regime is willing to drive the people into poverty to forward its goals of regime-friendly elite defense at home, mostly through domestic financial consumption of resources, and added prestige abroad through aggressive foreign policy, not unlike many other authoritarian regimes since time immortal.

Given this adherence to respect within and outside of Russia, Russia has little opportunity and advantage to ever becoming more than an aggressive power, and a rudimentary civil-social construct within. For those who hope for peace, the most that ordinary Russians can hope for is a future protest that could endanger the regime, or perhaps the accession of Putin's successor who, through whatever means that that will happen, will be more open to peace with potentially broad Western trading opportunities and less reliant on confrontation.

More importantly, one should hope that a future leader will be less reliant on Respect+, which I posit is a fundamentally negative concept and one that, if Russia is to progress, must be relegated to something far less than it is now.

NOTES

1. "We will never enter the path of self-isolation, xenophobia, suspicion and the search for enemies. All this is evidence of weakness, while we are strong and confident.," Russian President Vladimir Putin, "Presidential Address to the Federal Assembly," Kremlin website (Kremlin's translation), 4 December 2014, Retrieved 4 May 2017, http://en.kremlin.ru/events/president/news/47173.

2. Vice, Margaret, "Publics Worldwide Unfavorable Toward Putin, Russia," Pew Research Center, 16 August 2017, Retrieved 21 December 2017, http://www.pewglobal.org/2017/08/16/publics-worldwide-unfavorable-toward-putin-russia/.

3. Carter, Jimmy, "What is a Superpower?" *Tikkun Magazine*, Volume 26, Number 1, Duke University Press, Winter 2011, p. 35.

4. Brooks, Stephen G. "The Once and Future Superpower," *Foreign Affairs*, May-June 2016.

5. Shlapentokh, Vladimir, "Russia's Openness to the World: The Unpredicted Consequences of the Country's Liberalization," *Communist and Post-Communist Studies*, Vol. 45, 2012, p. 358.

6. Smith, Hanna, "Russia as a Great Power: Status Inconsistency and the Two Chechen Wars," *Communist and Post-Communist Studies*, Volume 47, 2014, p. 362, (pp. 355–63).

7. On-going survey of 1600 respondents, eighteen or older, in 137 population points of 48 regions of the country. "Национальная гордость," (In English): "National Pride," *Levada Centre*, 4 May 2017, Retrieved 31 May 2017, http://www.levada.ru/2017/05/04/natsionalnaya-gordost-2/.

8. See again: Duncan, Peter J.S., *Russian Messianism: Third Rome, Revolution, Communism, and After*, Routledge, London UK, 2000.

9. There are signs that Belarusian President Alexandr Lukachenka's rule has been weakening as of late (circa 2017) due to unpopular laws targeting the jobless in that country, which has in turn caused much distress for Moscow and the Putin regime as of late. The possibility of losing such a key ally is no doubt distressing in the Kremlin. See: "Thousands Protest in Against Law Targeting Jobless," *Associated Press*, 26 February 2017, Retrieved 11 March 2017, http://hosted.ap.org/dynamic/stories/E/EU_BELARUS_PROTESTS?SITE=KYB66&SECTION=HOME&TEMPLATE=DEFAULT.

10. Rutland, Peter, "Still Out in the Cold?: Russia's Place in a Globalizing World," *Communist and Post-Communist Studies*, Vol. 45, 2016, p. 353.

11. Grodeland, Ase B., "Perceptions of Civil Rights, Security and the "War on Terror": East and West Compared," *Communist and Post-Communist Studies*, Vol. 48, 2015, p. 327, (pp. 317–35).

12. Including famously by John Bolton, former American Ambassador to the United Nations. See: Sanders, Katie, "Did Vladimir Putin call the breakup of the USSR 'the greatest geopolitical tragedy of the 20th century?'" *PunditFact*, 6 March 2014, Retrieved

12 April 2017, http://www.politifact.com/punditfact/statements/2014/mar/06/john-bolton/did-vladimir-putin-call-breakup-ussr-greatest-geop/.

13. Tsygankov, Andrei, "Russia has an inferiority complex, America has a superiority complex," *Russia in Global Affairs*, 6 August 2014, Retrieved 7 June 2017, http://eng.globalaffairs.ru/book/Russia-has-an-inferiority-complex-America-has-a-superiority-complex-16859.

14. T anas, Olga and Andrey Biryukov, "Putin's Stealth Economic Weapon Loses Its Punch," *Bloomberg*, 3 April 2018, Retrieved 4 April 2018, https://www.bloomberg.com/news/articles/2018-04-03/putin-s-stealth-economic-weapon-loses-punch-as-recovery-falters.

15. Most recently, Daphne Skillen discussed this best in her book: Skillen, Daphne, *Freedom of Speech in Russia: Politics and Media from Gorbachev to Putin*, Routledge, New York and London, 2017.

16. Gregory, Paul Roderick, "A Russian Crisis With No End in Sight, Thanks to Low Oil Prices and Sanctions, *Forbes*, 14 May 2015, Retrieved 14 March 2017, https://www.forbes.com/sites/paulroderickgregory/2015/05/14/a-russian-crisis-with-no-end-in-sight-thanks-to-low-oil-prices-and-sanctions/#18ee916c11a5.

17. Alexeev, Mikhail A. and Henry E. Hale, "Rallying 'Round the Leader More than the Flag: Changes in Russian Nationalist Public Opinion 2013–14," *The New Russian Nationalism*, chapter 7, Edinburgh University Press, Edinburgh UK, 2016, pp 193.

18. There are many examples, but for one, see: Taylor, James, "Japanese Reporter Thinks There is Something Strange Afoot with Putin's Schedule," *The Washington Post*, 2 September 2016, https://www.washingtonpost.com/news/worldviews/wp/2016/09/02/a-japanese-reporter-uncovered-something-strange-about-vladimir-putins-schedule/?tid=pm_pop_b.

19. Elder, Miriam, "Has Putin Had Plastic Surgery?" *The Guardian*, 26 September 2011, Retrieved 13 April 2017, https://www.theguardian.com/world/2011/sep/26/putin-plastic-surgery.

20. This duality in Putin is also shown most starkly when he preaches sovereignty while at the same time violating Georgia's sovereignty in North Ossetia and Abkhazia.

21. Surveys of 1600 respondents between 21 and 24 April 2017 of people eighteen or older from 137 population points of 48 regions. Margin of error regressive as normal from 3.4 percent. See: "Санкции и контрсанкции," (In English): "Sanctions and Counter-Sanctions," *Levada Centre*, 15 May 2017, Retrieved 28 May 2017, http://www.levada.ru/2017/05/15/sanktsii-i-kontrsanktsii-3/.

22. "Truck Drivers in Russia Continue Strike Against Road Tax," *RFE/RL*, 30 March 2017, Retrieved 12 April 2017, http://www.rferl.org/a/russia-truck-drivers-protest-road-tax/28399194.html.

23. Filipov, David, "The latest protest Moscow is trying to ignore: Thousands of angry truckers," *The Washington Post*, 21 April 2017, Retrieved 4 May 2017, https://www.washingtonpost.com/world/europe/the-latest-protest-moscow-is-trying-to-ignore-thousands-of-angry-truckers/2017/04/21/13f87080-1a2d-11e7-8598-9a99da559f9e_story.html?utm_term=.c65d48468ec9.

24. Again, as mentioned in the first chapters, Navalny's 2013 Moscow mayoral campaign can be some kind of indicator of the possibility of greater things. Navalny's campaigns, including his rallies and his call for direct elections for heads of federal subjects, have had influence. Yet, many Russians of whom I've interviewed still dismiss him and give him little attention, although his impact has been greater as of the 2017–2018 time period.

25. "Yekaterinburg Mayor Yevgeny Roizman on Why Russians Should Boycott the Elections," *The Moscow Times*, 29 January 2018, Retrieved 30 January 2018, https://themoscowtimes.com/articles/-not-voting-is-a-matter-of-principle-60319.

26. Whitmore, Brian, "The Daily Vertical: Putin's War at Home," *Radio Free Europe/Radio Liberty*, 29 December 2016, Retrieved 29 December 2016, http://www.rferl.org/a/daily-vertical-transcript-putins-war-at-home/28203389.html.

27. "Народ утратил доверие государства," (In English): "People losing trust in the state," *Rosbalt*, 5 May 2017, Retrieved 9 May 2017, http://www.rosbalt.ru/blogs/2017/05/05/1613449.html.

28. On rare occasions, a Putin regime lackey will say this out loud. Igor Yurgens, presidential advisor, said at a press conference in 2010 that the "indifference of the population to innovations, as well as the low civilian activity of the population" was in part to blame for Russia's difficulties in modernization. See: Sergeev, Mikhail, "В провалах модернизации виноват народ," (in English: In the failures of modernization, the people are to blame), *Nezivisimaya gazeta*, 16 September 2010, Retrieved 13 April 2017, http://www.ng.ru/economics/2010-09-16/1_modernize.html. For commentary in English, see: Kara-Murza, Vladimir, "Russia's 'Backward' People," *World Affairs*, 21 September 2010, Retrieved 13 April 2017, http://www.worldaffairsjournal.org/blog/vladimir-kara-murza/russia%E2%80%99s-%E2%80%98backward%E2%80%99-people.

29. See: Khvostunova, Olga, "A Complete Guide to Who Controls the Russian News Media," *Index on Censorship*, 09 December 2013, Retrieved 12 April 2017, https://www.indexoncensorship.org/2013/12/brief-history-russian-media/. See also: Reporters Without Borders, 2016 World Press Freedom Index, On-going, Retrieved 12 April 2017, https://rsf.org/en/ranking.

30. "Russian Duma Bars RFE/RL, VOA As 'Foreign Agents,'" *Journalists in Trouble, RFE/RL*, 7 December 2017, Retrieved 19 December 2017, https://pressroom.rferl.org/a/russia-duma-bars-rferl-voa-foreign-agents/28903371.html.

31. This is the case given the labels' strongly-negative association in Russia with Cold War espionage and subjecting the organization(s) to increased audits, difficulties with registration, and even possible jail-time for employees under certain circumstances. Multiple NGOs and even Levada Centre has been subject to the "Foreign Agent" label as well, making their jobs all the more difficult and even curtailing their activities in some cases.

32. "Russia-Imposed Court In Crimea Upholds Journalist Semena's Verdict," *Journalists in Trouble, RFE/RL*, 18 December 2017, Retrieved 19 December 2017, https://pressroom.rferl.org/a/crimea-semena-appeal-russia-journalist/28925107.html.

33. G reenfield, Patrick and Marc Bennetts, "Who is Sergei Skripal, the ex-spy exposed to 'unknown substance'?," *The Guardian*, 5 March 2018, Retrieved 28 March 2018, https://www.theguardian.com/uk-news/2018/mar/05/who-is-sergei-skripal-ex-spy-exposed-substance-salisbury-hospital.

34. The Committee to Protect Journalists does a respectable job of listing and documenting the circumstances of journalists who died in the line of duty globally. See their website: www.cpj.org.

35. See Freedom House's Freedom in the World overview for Russia 2016: Retrieved 12 April 2017, https://freedomhouse.org/report/freedom-world/2016/russia.

36. "Russia's Navalny Goes Green After Antiseptic Attack," *RFE/RL*, 20 March 2017, Retrieved 12 April 2017, http://www.rferl.org/a/russia-navalny-campaigns-after-green-antiseptic-attack/28380741.html.

37. Vaughn, Jason, *A Socio-Political Model of Lies in Russia: Putin against the Personal*, University Press of America, Lanham MD, 2016.

38. Gros, Daniel and Federica Mustilli, "The Effects of Sanctions and Counter-Sanctions on EU-Russia Trade Flows," *CEPS Commentary Series*, 5 July 2016, Retrieved 28 May 2017, https://www.ceps.eu/publications/effects-sanctions-and-counter-sanctions-eu-russian-trade-flows.

39. Connally, Richard and Philip Hanson, "Import Substitution and Economic Sovereignty in Russia," *Russia and Eurasia Programme Research Paper*, Chatham House, June 2016, Page 1 Summary.

40. Surveys of 1600 respondents between 21 and 24 April 2017 of people eighteen or older from 137 population points of 48 regions. Margin of error regressive as normal from 3.4 percent. See: "Санкции и контрсанкции," (In English): "Sanctions and

Counter-Sanctions," *Levada Centre*, 15 May 2017, Retrieved 28 May 2017, http://www.levada.ru/2017/05/15/sanktsii-i-kontrsanktsii-3/.

41. Kelly, Lidia, "Russia dips into pension fund in about-turn for Putin," *Reuters*, 20 June 2014, Retrieved 13 April 2017, http://uk.reuters.com/article/uk-russia-economy-spending-analysis-idUKKBN0EV1A720140620.

42. Suslov, Mikhail, "The Production of "Novorossiya": A Territorial Brand in Public Debates," *Europe-Asia Studies*, Volume 69, Issue 2, p. 202, (pp. 202–21).

43. Kononczuk, Wojciech, "The Failure of Integration. The CIS and Other International Organisations in the Post-Soviet area, 1991–2006," *CES Studies*, Centre for Eastern Studies, Warsaw, Poland, May 2007.

44. For one, see: Terry, S. "Thinking About Post-Communist Transitions: How Different Are They?," *Slavic Review*, Vol. 52, Issue 2, 1993, pp. 331–37.

45. Though none, bar the Baltic countries, succeeded in fully joining the alliance.

46. This is on top of the recurring theme prevalent in Russian society that money was and is the driving force for Russia's supposed manipulation at the hands of foreign powers.

47. Those cited over the course of this book, and others.

FOUR

The Skill of Russia

INTRODUCTION

From the time long before I first arrived in Russia almost twenty years ago, I've heard all about the skills of Russians, their abilities to persevere and innovate and so on. Regardless of the near-constant media focus on Russians' skills, in everyday life, Russians are reminded of the skills of Russia in almost every place they go. Roads, universities, organizations, and you-name-it have a named appropriately-skilled patron, and indeed, Russia has accomplished much of practical and theoretical use over the centuries.

In dealing with rampant corruption and an overbearing state, this often extends to the dynamic conduits through which ordinary Russians operate to figure out solutions to problems by sometimes exceeding the restrictions of the state, that is, by extension in the 2000s and 2010s decades, the Putin regime.

Such is the epitome of what might be called "normalized skill-set application," where the education, prowess, and intelligence of the Russian people are both constricted by and surpassing the boundaries of the Putin regime's mismanagement of Russia. I've always greatly admired the abilities of ordinary Russians to exceed the strictures of the state and the hobbled economy to achieve great, and unexpected, undertakings and accomplishments.

Certainly the "skills" of Russia are a much-discussed aspect of the present-day Russian social sphere, comparatively-speaking, to any other expression of nominal importance in Russia of the 2010s. I can attest to the fact that Russians are proud of their skills and scientific acumen. Skills can mean those skill-sets which figuratively get you through life, and, in the case of the Russian people and in view of this book, by aggregate. Skills can also mean technologies and continued pragmatic development(s). In greater specificity, skills can further mean the powers and innovations needed to get past normal obstacles and impediments to financial and economic prosperity, up to and including regularized avoidance of the Russian state.

By "skill" in this case, there needs to be a deliberation on the abilities and developing services and technologies that Russia, and Russians, have been able to accomplish in the past, present, and prospectively in future.

Except for some minor examples from my personal experience, I will not discuss so much in this case the unique abilities of the ordinary man or woman, extensive and of course impressive in capability, and certainly no less than compared to any other nationality, in favor of a broader examination of what Russia has brought to the world and to progress as we consider Russia's modern technological modality. I also focus on modus operandi of the Putin regime and its destructive influence on the Russian peoples' ability to improve on the status quo that they find themselves in today.

Politically, more than one observing expert and non-expert Westerner[1] doubted the production of Russia, and in the post-Soviet era, due to failed policies and Western sanctions, Russia has lagged, technologically-speaking,[2] thereby lacking the "cutting-edge" of all technologies yet investigated by our human species. In response, Russia has been dependent on medium-level technology descendant in part from Soviet-era research and development anxiously supported by high oil prices, which by the way also keeps the economy going.

Further, and as to be covered, in response to Western sanctions, the Putin regime has sought to design and build domestically what it has been unable to acquire from the West, with varying amounts of success.

Many Westerners, including myself on occasion, point most drastically at the lack of general infrastructure, which is true particularly outside the major cities. Despite all of Russia's very impressive accomplishments in innovation, those same Westerners, also including myself, doubt Russian-developed technologies, as it systemically lags behind some Western countries both in military and non-military applications.

Russian technology has long been a source of pride for both ordinary and elite Russians, however, as it has notably been a leader in science for long years through the Soviet and post-Soviet eras. Everyone knows the adventure of the first man in space, Yuri Gagarin; however, in the modern era, serious problems and accidents involving Russia's space program undermine its activities even in this area, as it has aimed towards commercial use with a smaller budget than America's NASA.[3]

Turning an eye towards the military, every observer knows the AK-47 and its successors, and Russia's tanks and high technology aircraft including drone development. Russia has invested in science, in research and development and in practical usage over time, even when the economy and asinine political experiments have failed to provide a fertile petri dish in which to "grow" these achievements.

Additionally, general science has continued some progression: new elements discovered first in Russia are added to the Mendeleev table of elements on occasion. Although not as popular as Boeing and Airbus, Russia produces commercial aircraft as well, which are perfectly capable of doing almost everything their Western counterparts are able to perform, short of range and fuel economy perhaps.

As referenced above, when American President Barack Obama said in December 2016 that Russia produced nothing that anyone would want beyond weapons and natural resources,[4] he was, in worst case, absurdly wrong, and, in best case, exaggerating more than a little. In process, it was a political gesture that Obama meant to convey parallel to and in the wake of bad Russo-American relations due, in equitable parts, to Russia's physical interference in Ukraine, American sanctions policy, and Russia's yet-to-be-fully-publicized cyber interference in the 2016 American Presidential election. While Russia's trading position has always been somewhat agricultural in nature, even more so hearkening back to pre-Soviet times when the Russian empire was Europe's "breadbasket," statements such as that were and are rather narrow-minded.[5]

As such, Russia has produced much that can be offered to the world, but unfortunately if one only looks at current headlines, one would not be amiss in thinking that Russia is somehow conquering the world in information and has only produced a bevy of computer hackers to foment global chaos.[6] To that extent, the Putin regime is using the "tools" at its disposal, that is, social media, in an information campaign against America's electoral system in order to forward Russia's interests. As former Associate Director for Science and Technology in the Office of the Director of National Intelligence and Director of Research at the National Security Agency, Eric Heseltine, maintained in a seminar given in October 2017 at the think tank, Center for the National Interest:

> Russia's use of platforms like Facebook and Twitter is a "showing of the flag" in the social media cyber space. Moscow's aim was to divide the United States on multiple levels by targeting specific groups and specific "hot button" topics. Overall, Russia wanted to create dissent inside its American adversary using the tools Russia's government had available. Haseltine argued that, because Russia has a GDP roughly equal to that of Texas, it cannot engage in traditional warfare with the United States.[7]

The eagerness to address this problem not only with the justified reinforcement of security in America's electoral system, but also with aggressive sanctions beyond those already imposed on Russia is a central hallmark of treating Russia as a lasting principal enemy in America's foreign policy. This argument further mirrors the "confrontational" analytical viewpoint espoused by many analysts who seek to put Russia, rightly or wrongly, in its "place."

While I myself am very confrontational on many aspects of the Russian-Western relationship, any potential Putin-inspired expansionism like Crimea must be checked, on the question of sanctions, they should be carefully chosen and applied (and not permanent), being vigilant to degrade the Putin regime and organization as much as possible, and not to drive the Russian people closer to authorities.

More questions present themselves. Internally-speaking, how do Russians examine the allegations that foreign countries are being attacked by highly skilled computer and internet hacking and thereby subversion by elements of, and loyal to, the Putin regime? When (not surprisingly) foreign governments and peoples counter negatively to such attacks, how do Russians interpret these reactions?

Once again, this book in totality examines the views of the Russian people and how they perceive their social, cultural, and predominant place in the universe that is the world we know. Furthermore, as discussed in the introduction, I will not seek to "prove" any specific criminal allegations that might be referred to are true.

There is no doubt Putin-backed organized hacking does take place, it is international state-sponsored criminal activity, but I will leave others to do investigatory analyses of all the hacking and subversive attacks that the Putin regime is accused of doing.

I am predominantly concerned with Russian society, customs, social policies, and public opinion and how they perceive these eventualities. Insofar as it is important for this study here, the "skills" prevalent in those mentioned attacks are of concern and is a prominent issue here.

So where to begin? In this chapter, I will begin with an examination of the all-important necessary of top-level education and inspired technological achievement that is one of the most characteristic constructs of post-Soviet Russian society.

EDUCATION, TECHNOLOGY, AND MARKETS

As a general population, Russians, it must be mentioned, are some of the most highly educated on Earth. The literacy rate is one of the highest; beyond that, Russians are infinitely proud of their literature and cultural contributions to the world. Almost every Russian can quote lines of Pushkin, Tolstoy, and other famous native writers, or even whole stories, to an extent that would be unthinkable for Americans and British in even trying to remember more than two lines of Shakespeare. (For just one example, "to be or not to be," it can be asked of an American where that quote is from; countless will have heard the quote but will have no idea the source.)

Further, Russian universities are among the best in the world, although they are far from the top of public ratings[8] which are dominated mostly by Western universities that do cutting-edge research. Just to name one or two, Russians take great pride in Moscow State University and St. Petersburg State University, alongside with the inclusion of some others, to show that they indeed have a large role to play in the development of future technologies, that is, the future "skills" of Russia.

There is also the reputed issue of "brain drain" from Russia in the post-Soviet era, that is, the departure of trained researchers from Russia (Russia's "brains") for better paying jobs in the West and elsewhere. However, analysts studying this subject have posited that, concerning Russia's researchers, perhaps this is not as bigger problem as the previous stereotype of a mass exodus might have led you to believe, instead pointing to Russian researchers' lack of connection to the outside:

> Meanwhile, the figures provided in our research indicate that contrary to the popular stereotypes, the major problem for Russia remains the small scale of intellectual exchanges and labor migration of the Russian scientists while the majority of those leaving the academy permanently move to non-academic jobs within the country. Of special concern is the lack of contacts between a large number of the Russian regions with the outside world, preventing their effective inclusion into the international academic community.[9]

Many Westerners of the 2010s decade point out Russia's numerous flaws in its science production and application. It is true that, even when Russia has faced a problem for a great long time, Russia's technological infrastructure has in many cases been unable to find a solution to the problem in question. It is very popular for opinionated Westerners to point out that Russia has so much, yet so little; again, Russia has vast quantities of oil underlying its northern realms, yet only Western technologies can effectively drill and pump in those climates.

By extension, Russia can produce weapons but, less popularly, toothbrushes. Russian cars are not particularly well-known or efficient; having studied Russia for more than fifteen years, I've never heard a single soul there dream about buying a Russian Lada. Everyone wants a German BMW or some fancy Italian brand, or maybe even, in one case or two I distinctly remember, a Chevrolet convertible. On a personal note, one of my good Russian friends always wants a German car (doesn't matter what kind of German car, mind you, just German). In short, although Russian toothbrushes and cars do exist, people still run to the shop and buy well-known (and prestigious) Western brands.

As such, the Russian elite's desire for foreign products, in the post-Soviet era with foreign culture, movies, and merchandise achieving prominence after the fall of the Soviet Union, even as of the mid-2010s, there was (and is) no lack of respect for all things foreign in Russia.

On that basis, at least in high-end purchasing, Russian industries are necessarily hamstrung by their Western counterparts that have already, on good reasons of quality, availability, and brand-knowledge, monopolized certain markets across Russia. In some areas of high luxury demand, there is simply no equivalent Russian brand or source in which to balance the influx of Western brands on the market. As far as consumer electronics go, gaming systems, smartphones (although semi-ally China does ok with its Huawei brand), televisions, vacuum cleaners, microwaves, you name it, if Putin thinks that he can replace the market, then he is crazy. There will never be an updated Russian domestic equivalent, Putin can forget about it.

This is not to say that Russian sources don't exist in many other markets, but Russian production does not provide a furtive qualitative opening for them. When someone wants a computer, every brand is foreign. Pretty much everyone knows that this cannot be easily countermanded; no amount of advertising capability on Earth, at least in my own opinion, could make a Lada equal to a BMW.

In addressing the Putin regime, despite your supposed best efforts, including the long-held dreams of say, Russia's 2000 to 2011 Finance Minister Alexei Kudrin,[10] I must break this to you harshly. You lost a long time ago in many industries.

That said though, it can be argued that this is the case in every country on many points. Does every country really need its own globally-popular brand of toothbrush? Does every country need its own brand of hairspray? A counter-argument here that is common among ordinary Russians is that Russia has what it needs when the "going gets tough," as it were.

Parallel to that, as with the previous quote by American President Barack Obama, various analysts, including those at well-known financial magazine *Forbes*,[11] argue that Russia is "not important" (i.e., not the "next big thing") on global trade for many major purposes. What does it mean however to be "important" or "not important" for any major market when speaking about a foreign source or actor?

For Russia as an actor of innovation, this has some basis for concern. The price of not producing your own consumer goods is both foreign dependency and export marginalization on the global market. Being constantly on a war footing, that is, being able to produce only what can service your economy in a situation of great stress and pressure, for those who want to develop the skills of Russia, this is a major ongoing problem that cannot be easily remedied.

For a recent example of this aspect, I refer to a question posed from a major analytical organization. The organization asked: "How important will Russia be in a post-sanctions environment for European Union trade?" A friend of mine answered that Russia will be of the same level of important as it was before the sanctions, that being "not much." Stressing

Russia's dependence on a natural resources-based economy (a "one-trick pony"), Russia will be the same as before sanctions, that is, not be very important for the EU in any real way even after sanctions. Russia will hence import all things and export nothing sans oil, gas, and whatever else Russia can dig from the earth that can be burned for power; as such, the one-trick pony at issue.

This narrow-minded view of the country possesses, however, elements of being a patently false argument, as it only looks at Russia through a negative lens that any Russian, supporting the "skills" of Russia discussed in this chapter, would know to be at best simply anti-Russian and at worst openly antagonistic.

Sanctions do have at least one friend, it must be said. As discussed by Polina Popova for Fair Observer, the Putin regime benefits most by the continuing sanctions regime. Putin can dutifully and reliably deflect Russia's problems onto the backs of Western countries, and he can score points on most issues when it comes time to tighten the belts, as it were.[12] A report by Rebecca M. Nelson for the Congressional Research Service advising the U.S. Congress in 2017 can, at best, even after several years of sanctions, say that:

> The effectiveness of the sanctions in inducing a change in the behavior of the Russian government remains to be seen. Although the Russian government continues to face a number of economic challenges, many which are unrelated to sanctions, economic forecasts suggest that the Russian economy is stabilizing and there is some evidence that investor sentiment towards Russia may be improving.[13]

Further, when you make a patriotic issue out of it and it does specifically from the perspective of the average Russian, Russia has a certain level of hidden economic reception far beyond the viewpoint of those who try to force change in this fashion. Thinking with the glass half-full instead of half-empty, as any Russian often does, Russia is a huge market full of highly-skilled consumers with a substantial, but not huge, amount of money in their pockets.

Regardless of sanctions, Russia remains what Paul T. Christensen rightly calls a "semi-periphery state" in most regards as an economy that remains outside the core economic values of world trade.[14] The strategic economic environment being what it is, Russia is still important, but it is all relative. For some businessmen (and women) in some industries, Russia is not important; for others in other industries, Russia is very important. In the end, it depends. For necessities, Russia can get along, too big to ignore or to fail, but not big enough or creative enough at the policy level to drive innovation or commerce. For consumer items, it is much the same. What kind of widget are you trying to build or sell and where do you want to build/sell it?

Consequently, for Westerners friendly to a confrontational outlook, it is easy to look at the situation with Russia as a "glass half-empty" state. They look at Russia's defects and dwell on them. This is not, and never has been, the Russian way, of course. Russians urge, as they have to me on more occasions that I can remember, that one must be inclined towards the "glass half-full" diagnosis when one looks at such a question.

PRODUCTIVE CAPABILITY

Russia's productive capability in manufacturing, functionality, and innovative technology is based in the major cities, and there's nothing much special or unusual about it. Transporting manufactured materials between cities, now that's a problem. To best understand Russia on this point, one must understand the role of productive capability outside the biggest cities and its relationship to the peoples' skills.

Russia is necessarily hobbled by its poor infrastructure, transportation between towns is poor and not getting better. Some towns are entirely dependent on train lines for goods, transport, and limited for common transport otherwise. There are holes in many side roads that could fit a car or even a swimming pool, trust me I've seen them, but there are many more issues that involve this problem as well.

Russia still suffers from the aftereffects of the Soviet Union from aspects of the Soviet tendency of central planning, which duly led to the formation of a great many single production towns (or so-called "mono-towns") spread across the span of Russia. To maintain these towns, Russia has had to subsidize them, which is expensive and draining from the federal budget, as that much money is much needed elsewhere.

These towns in some ways represent the skill of Russia every bit as much as the dynamism of central Russia and St. Petersburg. The problem, of course, is that they are inefficient and ever so slowly falling behind in any technological usefulness that they might have originally had. The Soviet Union benefited greatly from some of these towns in the times of mid-twentieth central planning, when you needed a million tank treads, a town dedicated to producing a million tank treads could be useful, assuming that quality control was basically looked after (the threat of being buried with the refuse kept some workers in line in the Stalinist era; other towns used their share of forced labor by enemy prisoners of war).[15] Nevertheless, many of these towns kept in gear far into the Soviet period, and a great many of them, too many,[16] exist today, again completely dependent on state finances to stay in existence.

As of 2017, according to Prime Minister Dmitry Medvedev, addressing the problem of Russia's mono-towns will take years, as some of them struggle to keep state money to support them.[17] Indeed, the mayors of these towns push and use their connections to keep mono-town status, which includes their own cash flow coming to keep their towns from disappearing.

The dangers of these mono-towns to the state are a question of efficiency, however, the dangers of these towns to the Putin regime is more complex. From my research and repeated visits to a great many of them, these mono-towns are full of Putin voters (and the parties allied to Putin); supporters who could be relied upon in past years to trot out and bring up the vote tallies. These towns have also in some cases been the first ones to protest the current regime as they have seen their towns being endangered.[18]

As I spoke on before, and will again, Moscow has become increasingly out of touch with what was once considered the Putin heartland in the regions, even though that heartland still reliably votes for him. What will happen once state support starts to cut into these towns, corresponding to the steadily increasing hit that sanctions have put on the budget? Beyond this, those truck strikes I mentioned in chapter 3 might have a further impact here; many of the towns are connected by rail-line, but that's not always the best way to go, and airplanes are not taking care of business that far in Russia. Will these towns and mono-towns diversify and stay, or will they close, and the inhabitants wonder towards the central cities where jobs of equal productive level may not be instantly available?

For the near-future, some of the towns are still viable, though the word "necessary" is highly questionable, and the state is attempting to diversify them to a limited extent. These towns have experts in certain fields and skilled workers, and my experiences is them show that some would resist getting up and moving to the major cities. As mentioned at the beginning of this section, Russia needs to invest in infrastructure and improving road and rail access in certain cases, but that can only be done however at not some small expense. Some of the industrial, resource collection, and manufacturing materials from these places are still needed, but it is an open question as to how long and to what extent the Putin regime will continue to finance them.

What will always be a factor is how long that centralized subsidies can bolster industry and manufacturing across Russia. Also, what will the people of these towns do when their towns are obsolete? Again, they are mostly all Putin voters, so he might have a problem.

THE CONNECTIONS OF RUSSIAN TECH TO THE WEST

The skill of Russia is a very difficult thing to pin down in more abstract and broad-scope terms; one can talk about education, market, technology, and small-town life in Russia forever, but still not fully understand the "trans-pollination," if you will, involved in many of Russia's technological and skill-based achievements. Fundamental to any discussion here is the fact that the "house" of Russia must have the imagination, the innovation, and the viability of hope for the future, and that there must be a certain level of these prospects for future applied usage. As a side note, technologically-speaking, every day there is something new under the microscope in Russian history, past, present, or future that makes Russian technologies even more interesting. It is also useful to examine here, as compared to how Westerners perceive some things of the future, is how the Russian people can (and do) see these things completely different.

It is a distinct part of my argument that, whatever the case may be, in civilian technologies, Russia is forever connected to the West, and even Putin cannot escape this fact, even when he is conducting policies that openly alienate the Western powers. As remarked on before in previous relevant sections, but also useful here when talking about how we contemplate Russia's skills and technologies both past and future, foreign analysts tend to see Russia distinctly in a practical light or in a confrontational light. Some give more heed to Russia's real achievements in innovative technologies; opposing that view, others are quick to point out that many of Russia's achievements were based on espionage and stolen designs and, as such, this may continue to be the case. Soviet-era advancement and key achievements (the nuclear bomb, the space program, and so on) were indeed based on similar blueprints and familiarized copies (through whatever means of acquisition), if not openly stolen, from the West.

Furthermore, as for civilian technologies, there is no such thing as a Russian smartphone, but that, and technologies of that nature, are far beyond any hope for Russia "catching up" or some such.

Whatever the case may be, Russia's future lies with connecting domestic technologies with the technology and skills of the West; one day, when humans explore the stars (I am a hopeful person after all), I have the definite feeling that Russia will have a role to play, and there will be native Russian technologies among those explorers. You can never overlook Russia's knowledge of space exploration as natural and key to technological evolution, including of course Yuri Gagarin and so on, first man in space etc. etc. Albeit short-term, as for now (2017), with the retirement of the American space shuttle, Russian Soyuz rockets[19] (and Russian engines, namely the RD-180s and RD-181s on other rockets[20]) have the only capability for maintaining and resupplying the International Space Station (ISS).

On the negative side, however, there are still indications that new Russian military technologies are heavily indebted to, if not using, Western technologies.[21] By extension, there are some who still question the adequacy of domestic Russian technology in general and ask whether even Russia's newest weapons use Western tech.[22] I will not deeply engage these questions here, instead I will focus on a key issue here, in that the Russian people do not necessarily see their advancements, civilian or military, in such a light, nor should they. I've interviewed and talked to innumerable Russian people who rarely if at all acknowledge their technologies as being based to any degree on Western designs, but rather in a competitive approach to such achievements. They see the future of skills and technologies in Russia as being bright, despite the relative limitations of their domestic budgets and applied sciences.

In lightly defending some of Putin's foreign adventures, my interviewees have professed, even when Russians are acknowledging how American aircraft carriers roam the seven seas, that Russia can yet do more with less, and anyway the idea continues that the Russian military is only for "defense" anyway. Russian battlefield drone technology is battle-tested and has been developed somewhat extensively.[23] Further and again concerning civilian domestic production, or so I've been told, what does Russia need a native smartphone or, say, a car, anyway? Other people make them (figuratively-speaking) "sexier," or something to that effect, as told so eloquently by one of my (generally pro-Putin) English students in Moscow, when I inquired about what Russians think about Russian technology.

Nevertheless, the idea that the Putin regime has only used the military for defensive purposes is something of a strange concept for those who know something about world events, but I will discuss those elements in the chapter dedicated to looking at Russia's allies in the world.

Back about semi-civilian uses of technology, which sanctions have tried to limit as well, most critically, Putin has attempted to address technologies in areas such as in oil extraction where once upon a time Russian oil companies had sought Western partnerships and associations to support machinery where Russia itself fell short.

Russia still has vast quantities of oil lying underneath the Siberian plains yet to be tapped, and before the Ukrainian adventures, far northern Russian-state supported oil companies had been seeking Western infrastructural technology to bridge the gap between what Russian oil pioneers could do alone and what could be achieved with help.[24] You see, digging and sucking up oil in the freezing far northern fields has always been something quite stressful on machine parts and technologies. After sanctions, many of these partnerships fell apart as Western oil conglomerates could not any longer afford to be associated with or give added technologies to Russian oil companies. As explained by Forbes here: "Russian banks and Gazprom's ability to secure long term funding in U.S. dollars have also largely been blocked. Adding more pain, the U.S. and EU also banned exports of services and technology to Russian state oil firms engaged in Arctic and deep-water and unconventional oil and gas exploration and production."[25]

In this absence, Putin and his regime asked Russian companies to come up with ideas to substitute Russian alternatives for Western technologies.[26] The results of this request(s) have been decidedly mixed in the past and will be in the future. While some parts and construction has been possible, substituting for Western iterations, other technologies have been very difficult to reproduce domestically. Faced with this, Russia can invest hard-saved currencies but beyond that can only wait and see what its own scientists can come up with. Some fields have had to be surrendered to inaccessibility for the time being during this attempt at making a politically-inspired technological "jump."

Just for a bit of commentary, while anything is possible in mid-2010s Russia, the chances of a significant technological achievement(s) are, I think, remote, just because the Putin regime says so.

Another aspect that many observers, both foreign and within Russia, are quick to point out and which I will cover in the next section, is an examination of the technologies and skill-sets supporting military technologies and capabilities, and, again, how they, at least in their own propaganda, have done more with less and the supposed admiration of the Russian military that can, say, interfere in such far afield places as Syria during that civil war. Again, the argument of the defensive nature of the Russian role in the Syrian civil war (although I will touch on that) is of contradictory issue, but anyway, I digress.

MILITARY

Russia is well-known for its military skills and technological advancements, but the degree to which it is independent of Western influence is worthy for debate. Not only has Russia's military technology been bolstered by reverse engineering Western technologies, espionage, and licensed collection, but as soon to be covered, many technologies and unique skill-sets developed in Russia are de facto responses to opposition technologies. The Putin regime has been quick to bolster and allocate money towards financing domestic military research, but limitations on military-related technological and skill-based advancements have been prevalent because of Russia's longstanding international political problems. While, as mentioned before, Russia has made notable developments in areas like drone technologies and weapon systems, because of difficulties concerning sanctions, in some areas of R&D, Russia's procurement of new technologies is significantly degraded.[27]

The military of Russia is talked about endlessly by the Western intelligence agencies. While the influence of the Russian military is formidable indeed, it is not, and never has been, the greatest promoter of technological innovation in Russia. The Russian military has been much more technologically sluggish, reliant on mass production and numerical advantage, rather than on innovation. Yet, Russia has done well when necessary with what resources that it has in some (but far from all) areas of technology and skill-set usage. Even many more pessimistic observers fail to disagree on that aspect, although at the same time they laugh at certain systemic problems of Russia's military.

Acknowledging at least some technical achievements, I've been present myself when officers in the American Navy openly laughed at some of the rusty ships of Russia's Black Sea fleet. Anyone taking only one look at Russia's single Admiral Kuznetsov "Heavy Aircraft-Carrying Cruiser" would know what I was talking about.

Reflecting a desire to bolster Russia's image, the military of Russia has had a fervent promoter in the form of the Putin regime as well. Despite tragedies and deaths related to Russia's military especially concerning its foreign adventures,[28] propaganda and domestic media outlets, up to and including international outlets (both foreign- and Russian-owned), often bounce back to refer to the skills of Russia in research, development and production of military hardware as a demonstrative adjunct of Russian ingenuity.

Internationally, Russian state-owned and operated media outlets like Sputnik and Russia Today[29] and internet promotion, almost constantly show off the newest brands and technologies of Russia's military accomplishments, concerning how they match up to, and can address, rival Western technologies.[30]

Although such media outlets would love to say otherwise, as is well-known, American defense spending dwarfs Russian spending by leaps and bounds (and this is before recent American President Donald Trump's defense increases),[31] and even Putin's media cannot easily ignore that fact. Russian defense production must then emphasize how Russia is the under-dog when discussing the possibility of any military confrontation between the West and itself.

For just one example, Russia's development, production and distribution of its new fifth-generation fighter plane to rival new fighter development in the United States always has a front-page influence within and outside Russia. America's new F-22 Raptors and F-35 programs can and must be countered from the Russian point-of-view. However, while quick to attempt to match them and their stealth technologies, Russia's fighter programs have met a sizable number of snags. The development of composites durable enough, light enough and capable of minimizing the radar cross-section of Russia's new fighters has been to slow to come to fruition, although Russia is nevertheless moving its Sukhoi T-50 PAK-FA program to production and deployment with all available speed.[32]

For another example, and made much of an example by Putin himself, Russia's nuclear arsenal has been touted and received heavy investment,[33] of course from the insecurity that Russia's other force elements do not always match up with their Western counterparts. Putin is no stranger to saber rattling with nuclear arms anyway, not that it gets him anywhere.[34]

Russia's nuclear submarine fleet receives the best training, manned by those with the best skill-sets (no draftees allowed), and the best types of military research and development. To maintain Russia's nuclear forces on which much Russian prestige has been based upon, the RSM-56 Bulava Submarine Launched Ballistic Missile (SLBM) has been heavily promoted as keeping Russia's nuclear fighting capability well-intact. Nevertheless, the Bulava program since its nominal deployment has been ripe with failures when tested[35] from its submarine launch platforms, including the new Borey-class submarines of which, as of 2017, three such submarines are active.

Russia's military has always been known for its air defense systems. Throughout the Cold War, the Soviet Union made air defense a high priority, ranking those forces second only to sustaining nuclear capability and the Army. In post-Soviet Russia, while the best models are kept at home, Russia sends its second-level forces far afield. Following the shoot-down of a Sukhoi-24M in November 2015 in the Syrian civil war theater, pro-regime Russian media, notably TASS, boasted about the three levels of air defense provided to the Russian Hmeymim base in Syria.[36] Also famously, more subtle boasts were made about the shoot-down of Malaysian Airlines flight MH17 in 2014 over eastern Ukraine by Russian-backed (or Russian-trained, if not actually Russian soldiers) fighters in the Donbas region using a Russian-made Buk-9M38 air defense missile/launcher.[37] (The ease of shooting down a slow-flying heavy passenger aircraft notwithstanding.)

While these incidents are mentioned from other facets in other chapters of this book, the central point here is the training, skills, research, and development to build these air defense systems.

Yet how does the Russian public regard this continued focus on Russia's military when, as covered before, services dedicated to the Russian people, to Russia's infrastructure and health care, are intermittently failing? Those whom I've talked to and interviewed are proud of their military and proud of the fact that Russia can defend itself from the Western threat, meaning that a great deal of Putin's rhetoric focuses on a strong defense and a less-publicized aggressive foreign policy has indeed gotten through to the people.

The Russian people are also aware, from my experience, of Russia's shortcomings even in the realm of technology, the military, and Russia's most prominent skill-sets, as to be discussed in the next section. Also, Putin used military spending to bolster the flagging economy as well, so that certainly helps relations.

Many know, although it is a subject that Putin attempts to hide with some effectiveness, that some Russian soldiers and countrymen have not come home alive after going to Syria (or going wherever they went) in eastern Ukraine.[38] This includes contractors as mentioned before.

However, as long as the numbers of those dead are (relatively) small, as long as Putin keeps a limit on the information available, and as long as he does not attempt too much, and given that the opposition is nationalist to some extent, there is little prospect that developments in this area, in and of themselves, could be the beginning of the downfall of the Putin regime. I remember a talk with a middle-aged guy in Moscow, we'll call him "Alexey," who vented at me quickly and often that Russia has its interests just like the United States has, and Russia has the skills to do what Russia needs to do, although he still, of course (as is usual), professed about the corruption of, quite literally, everything.

HUMAN FAILINGS AND DETERRENCE TO RUSSIA'S SKILL

It is an all-too-saddening fact that, while Russia has one of the most highly-educated, highly-skilled, and highly-trained work forces on the planet, it is also true that Russia is held back as it is by the substantial vices and disabilities of its human population. Never the healthiest population in history anyway, Russia's continuing epidemics of AIDS, alcoholism, high drug use, and poor health care in the regions outside the major cities (and even in many cases within) build a toxic maelstrom that impedes Russians from improving their productive and economic situation.

Traditionally, and perhaps more than a little according to stereotype, vodka has been the vice of choice for Russians. For one extensively-researched unfortunate example, long reports[39] issued by Russia's monitoring agency, Rospotrebnadzor, paint a grim picture of an environment where, among other issues, Russians are willing to drink pretty much anything which contains any sort of alcohol. A December 2016 tragedy in Irkutsk killed more than fifty people after a group drank what some describe (media sources use different descriptions here) as a cosmetic product containing methanol.[40] In response, the Russian government of Prime Minister Dmitry Medvedev has suggested banning the sale of the base product in question, but it is little doubt that that will make the problem worse; it will make Russians simply turn to other sources of alcohol to get their fix.

Perhaps not so different from other countries but acute in Russia as well, drugs are a widespread problem. The use of opium and heroin, relatively recently including the morphine derivative Desomorphine Krokadil (which can be produced from easily available over-the-counter codeine), take a big chunk out of the health of the youth of Russia. Some estimate 100,000+ users in Russia to inject the drug, which causes surfaces of the users' skin to turn similar to crocodiles.'[41] While drugs have been a global terror worldwide, the conditions of post-Soviet life have brought drugs and their harsh results more strongly to the Russian population. The Russian government, as with other governments, has attempted to stymie Krokodil production through the banning of over-the-counter sales of codeine, and this has had some effect, yet overall the problems of drugs in Russian society is extensive and unlikely to lessen in today's social climate. I myself have seen the effects of the uses of many such drugs in Russia, including Krododil, and the many of the effects are ghastly, leading to lost education, broken homes, and houses full of addicts who spend their days getting high. Russia's hospitals on the edges of society are filled with the remnants of those who have experience with this and other drugs and they represent a serious impediment to a progressive society in Russia.

HIV and concurrent AIDS are also terrible strains on the society of Russia, having been fueled by that just-mentioned intravenous use of drugs that spiked tremendously in the post-Soviet era.

As explained by the Russia & Eurasia Program at the Center for Strategic and International Studies (CSIS), which does in-depth studies of HIV in Russia: "Until the mid-1990s, Russia and Eurasia had relatively few cases of HIV/AIDS." Now, again quoting CSIS's materials, "these states [of Eurasia, including Russia] are experiencing the highest rate of new HIV infections in the world."[42]

In interviews with Western journalistic sources, the head of the Russian state's HIV Center, has made various statements over the last few years about how the HIV epidemic is only getting worse,[43] with some 90,000 being infected "last year" (2014) only to be countered by the Russian state-backed, "Russian Institute for Strategic Studies (RISS)" (Российского института стратегических исследований (РИСИ), which says that everything is under control, and that Russia (including programs in Moscow[44]) is a world leader in HIV control.

RISS also publicizes blatantly homophobic articles such as this one, which says that gays are not more than 2 percent of the population and have 55 percent of the HIV infections.[45] With this bipolar approach to HIV/AIDS and given the high level of stigmatization of high risk groups in the Russian population, there is little doubt that the HIV infection rate in Russia will continue to skyrocket. RISS and the Putin regime, aiming to maintain the backing of the Russian Orthodox Church (which routinely opposes condom use), will continue to do little to stop the rates of new infection which have led to high levels of HIV infection in that favored class of Russian citizenry by Putin, the heterosexual population.

Furthermore, there exists a large population of Russia in its prison system, which remains a haven for many of these alcohol and drug abuse problems and HIV and other disease distributions. Russia's modern-day Gulag suggests that that terminology should not be retired as of yet, and, according to some reports, is worse than the Soviet-era Gulag, although of course this is a difficult comparison.[46] Russia's prison population further degrades its skill-set as well, with an unknown number of political prisoners held.[47]

Overall, many of these problems are societal and nevertheless generate a substantial deterrent to the productive expansion and advantageous use of the knowledge of its human population. Russia's declining population will continue to decline, due to these problems of low birth rates and high levels of alcoholism, drug use, and HIV (not even mentioning the other diseases and killers of Russians, and there are many).

The reasons for this, as has been explored in previous sections and will be explored further, stem from cultural traditions, from circumstances, from past authoritarianism continuing until today, and indeed from Russia's difficult history, where a stiff drink was what little solace that ordinary Russians could get from an overbearing government.

They also however come from Russia's current issues in trying to both improve its economy and find its purpose in the post-Soviet world, where Russia as a construct has been unable to get rid of a corrupt status quo, achieve financial stability (partially, but not only, because of Western sanctions), and improve the quality of life of its citizenry.

In the absence of said stability, analysts are left to ponder what could have been. What could Russia have been like if reforms had been more successful in the 1990s? What would Russia be like if civil society had been better established in the 1990s and 2000s decade? Indeed, through the good skills of its populations, could Russia have achieved a better level of stability in the world, in which it could operate more like a friend of nations, and less like an antagonistic element in an increasingly volatile world of the 2010s?

For one, I like to think that Russia would have become a leading innovative power, exactly what it is not, if a stronger democratic civil society had been able to establish itself in the post-Soviet era; where drinking, drug use, and other vices would be a lessening necessity for a population to get through the day.

Of course, these are questions that we will never know. Perhaps, as many Russians have told me, Putin has been good for Russia, and Russia is the harbinger of Putin himself. Again, it is likely for obvious reasons that we will never know such things, but who knows, for the future, even given all the things I have spoken about here, I will remain an optimist.

POLITICAL AND TECHNOLOGICAL DETERRENCE TO RUSSIA'S SKILL

The political reasons for Russia's current technological situation cannot be understated. Russia's post-Soviet state of technology, continuing to use legacy elements from the Soviet period instead of diversifying, improving, and acquiring Western support and technologies, perhaps taking advantage of a more conciliatory approach towards other technological powers instead of near-constant opposition, has been a key deterrence to Russia fulfilling many of its short- and long-term goals. Additionally, Russia of the Putin era has been noted for its inability to expand and make progress upon many of the technologies that it does have. This can be blamed only in part on Western sanctions; distinct choices by the Putin regime also have been significant factor which have seriously slowed any attempts to take advantage of Russia's strengths while lessening Russia's weaknesses.

This I would refer to as political deterrence at the domestic level. One of the foremost manifestations of Putin's political interference in Russia's development has been the attempt to control that great resource, or even revolution, of the twenty-first century, the spread of information primarily through the internet.

As has been discussed by just about everyone in all realms of human technological interest, the internet is in some ways the present and future of humanity's life on Earth. Coinciding with serious drawbacks, the interconnectivity and power of the internet has brought humanity both closer together than ever in human history and compartmentalized human-group relationships/thought more surely than ever before (in some cases at the same time); this cannot be overstated or doubted. Before the twenty-first century, the chances that someone in one corner of the world could find out information or pictures on or about peoples in the farthest opposing corners of the world was highly unlikely, excepting the limitations of travel journalism and some such. However, although sometimes overstated, limited or focused information is a key enemy to the control of thought and peoples.

The manipulation and possible self-isolation of and in the internet by select populations can make the internet overall a dividing force just as easily as it could bring peoples together. One only cursory glance at the proliferation of false and fake news stories under the guise of respectability which the Putin regime used, and uses, against other peoples is one manifestation of the possible manipulation of the media. Further, the self-tailoring tendencies of many individuals and populations to "only read the news they agree with" is representative of the self-isolation possibilities of the internet.

Together, combining focused internet manipulation and the self-isolation principle, when used by a hostile government such as Russia against foreign electoral activities (as previously referenced, the Internet Research Center in St. Petersburg), can breach opportunities for creation of a devastating tandem approach for agents, like for example the Putin regime, to exacerbate problems for the regime's possible enemies and to elect weak or dissonant administrations in countries which could pose a threat to the Putin regime or its allies (see Trump et al.).

Focusing still on Russia's internal questions, not surprisingly, authoritarian and hybrid regimes like Russia's have struggled long and hard in coming up with ways to deter their citizens to rightfully have access to unlimited information such as that afforded by the internet. As Carolina Vendil Pallin has discussed in an article, one way that the Putin regime has sought to impose control on the internet was through ownership of domestic resources, and through new laws and regulations.[48]

As pointed out by Pallin: "Many of the infrastructure companies were already either state owned or owned by someone who was close to the Kremlin by 2013."[49]

The number of laws, regulations, and attempts to stop the internet have been of multiple variety, many of them appealing to conservative thought in Russia, including the need to save children from venturing into "evil" internet places and so on. Referring to Pallin, it is largely true that the Russian Orthodox Church has often been on the cutting edge of alleging the detrimental nature of certain internet websites for "good people" to have access to. Porn sites have, perhaps not surprisingly, been the first to have bans placed against them.

More aggressively, the Putin regime, in practice through the Federal Security Service (FSB) and legally through laws passed by the Duma, has been at the forefront of attempting to regulate the internet. Its need to control political space on the Russian internet is practically insatiable. Through the work of Roskomnadzor, the Russian state agency that controls the blacklist (albeit with unclear authority), some elite- or politically-oriented social networking sites which refuse to localize data (as prohibited by Russian law) and/or which have end-to-end encryption, albeit ones with low-use in Russia, have been banned, including most namely, for those Westerners familiar with it, LinkedIn and, recently (as of 2018), Telegram.[50]

In my interviews and conversations in Russia (perhaps unlike more gullible foreign populations, which shall remain here nameless), ordinary Russians have been largely cognizant of the fact that the regime is trying to stop them from seeing certain websites. Unimpressed by such artificial attempts at control of information, those Russians who are familiar with computers, and who want to see banned websites, of course find ways around such imposed guidelines, sometimes using proxy servers and other methods of which there are many.

This dynamic of attempting to control the internet relates to issues of a social and cultural nature, far beyond traditionally "simple" pornography however. Reflecting the increasingly closed social environment at the Putin regime's behest, the Russian government has recently passed laws which use obsolete, backward, and openly anti-LGBT rhetoric to further stigmatize latent non-traditional thinking and which are supposedly meant to "deter" homosexuality through the banning of anything which, the state says, "promotes" homosexuality, including the seeing, hearing, and reading something can "turn" somebody "non-traditional."[51]

Not only are such laws backward, discriminatory, and may well promote anti-LGBT violent behaviors in society, such as was discussed in the second chapter, but they also significantly degrade the employment of skills and education in society. Any such openly discriminatory rhetoric, especially when supported by the state, leads to a less free and open society and, while other countries successfully integrate and incorporate the differences recognized in all human societies to the benefit of their working classes, Russia will continue to fall behind and further become a society where not all are accepted and which cannot therefore reach its own full potential.

Through these facets, the Putin regime's attempts to limit the internet and (as discussed more in chapter 3 but mentioned here) attempt counter sanctions by developing domestic technologies and find substitutes for specific technological processes are doomed to failure. Putin is trying to degrade the knowledge of Russia's people and skill-sets while at the same time asking them to think of better ways of doing things without outside help. This fundamental paradox cannot be resolved, and so Putin's choices in foreign policy have in many cases created a politically-charged deterrence undermining his plans for renewing his regime. Only by resolving sanctions can Russia be brought back to the future, if you will, and that is of course not likely in the near-future.

"FOREIGN" DETERRENCE TO RUSSIA'S SKILL

While it is in-line with the Kremlin's propaganda, it is nevertheless regrettable that we must acknowledge that there are foreign deterrents to Russia's technological and skill-based expansion. I've already pointed out on more than one occasion that foreign sanctions and limitations on technological distribution to Russia have prevented Russia from making sizable expansions to its own technological competency and economy.

However, the effects go deeper than that, towards perhaps some unacknowledged places. Russia's aggressive foreign policies and their deep opposition in Western and allied countries, including some countries which are nominally "friends" with Russia, have led to increasingly hostile acceptance of Russian money in foreign banks, the failure for Russian companies to get needed loans and foreign investment, failed business dealings with Russian figures, and indeed discrimination against the Russian people themselves for travel through resistant visa regimes.

As I will discuss in more detail in a chapter dedicated to Russia's money, Russian government figures, elites, normal people, and their monies are treated with great suspicion, their property is threatened by sanctions, and this too leads to a degradation of Russia's skills, in so being that Russians and people tied to Russia in various ways sometimes suffer under strict limitations, if technologies and monies are wished to exit from and then be returned to Russia. A great many foreign police and military organizations, including the American FBI and the British MI5 are rabidly on the lookout for any potential for money laundering or shady dealings from Russia, which is, as I've much discussed, a country under a bevy of sanctions.

It is indeed further true that Putin has brought this both on his ruling class and the Russian people at-large. In the Yeltsin period before 1999–2000, so much was hoped for in bridging the gap between a newly-free post-Soviet Russia and its former adversaries in the West. It is true that the financial policies of Yeltsin did not bring prosperity immediately, and International Monetary Fund (IMF) loans to Russia were very poorly implemented. However, in time, I would argue that, if the free market (as promoted) had been maintained as a key goal in the next administration of Putin (or perhaps someone else, had Yeltsin chosen him/her), then Russia would have been markedly better off.

Even despite the financial crisis of 1998, there could have been bright days ahead for the skills and technologies of Russia if only a keen eye had been kept on the idea of a free and fair civil society which could promote a potentially burgeoning economy. Yet this is another of those "what-ifs?" which are sometimes discussed among observers of Russia and its government. We will never know what could have been possible if Russia had turned away from policies antagonistic to its neighbors and continued to push for skill-set and economic reforms.

CONCLUSIONS

As we have seen over the course of this chapter, Russia's technological potential and skill-sets are being damaged by failure of reform and by Western sanctions in service of the Putin regime's aggressive foreign policies and its will to stay in power.

In turn, we have found that, regarding Russia's educational systems, technologies, and productive abilities, Russia is at times strong, but in the last sections, I analyzed the limitations, disadvantages, and obstacles to Russia's full potential as a skilled nation, particularly with Vladimir Putin in charge.

Perhaps most strikingly, I reflected on how, on one hand, the Putin regime has instituted laws and domestic policies to degrade the Russian people's access to information, principally through the internet. On the other hand, Putin is asking the Russian people to develop new innovative technologies and to find substitutes for machinery and services that can no longer be acquired because of sanctions.

Further, Putin is asking natural resource specialists to do much more with far less, and without access to information; this is a nonsensical policy of the highest rank. The Putin regime is also trying to diversify and improve military technology while yet still having and using legacy Soviet weapons. This too marks a kind of nonsensical policy that only an authoritarian could understand. Yet, these are but two such aspects of Putin's current technological policies; the list goes on and on in which the people of Russia are put in a vice grip by the effects (some unintended) of sanctions on Russia and the right desire of foreign governments to encourage democratic change in the Russian government, or at least to support a less aggressive and/or less antagonistic government to come to power in Russia than the Putin regime.

Therefore, as an artifice of the "house" first discussed in the introductory chapter, the skill of Russia is a fanciful thing, especially since so much has been accomplished before. The skill represents the workmanship of that house, as Russians attempt to build something better in the post-Soviet era yet are held back both by their own faults and by the faults of their not-always-entirely-freely chosen leader.

The questions forwarded are: how do we understand the skill of Russia? Is Russia a great nation deserving of respect from other countries? Or is Russia a lost cause descendant from Soviet times? Is the glass half-empty or half-full?

Russia, it can be held, on the notable subject of its skills, is half-*something*.

These examinations necessarily lead us to the next chapter of this publication, in which there will be a discussion of the Putin regime heading Russia as an ally of a few and as the antagonistic enemy of many nations. A country and a people, as will be argued in the next sections, can only be as good as the peace that it and they keep with their neighbors.

NOTES

1. This is represented by professional analysts and academics on Russia, not to mention those who make/made policy, like, for example former American President Barack Obama. See: "Obama Dismisses Russia: It 'Doesn't Make Anything,'" *Reuters*, Huffington Post, 3 October 2014, Retrieved 13 April 2017, http://www.huffingtonpost.com/2014/08/03/obama-russia_n_5645953.html.

2. Though, as will be discussed, not in all areas.

3. Carroll, Oliver, "Russian space programme close to collapse as latest failure exposes its fragility," *The Independent*, 6 December 2017, Retrieved 7 December 2017, http://www.independent.co.uk/news/world/europe/russia-space-programme-collapse-soyuz-2-1b-rocket-cosmodrome-launch-failure-latest-news-a8094856.html.

4. Obama's words: Russia "doesn't produce anything that anybody wants to buy, except oil, gas and arms." See: Vielma, Antonio Jose, "Obama says Russia is a smaller, weaker country than the US," *CNBC*, 16 December 2016, Retrieved 13 April 2017,

http://www.cnbc.com/2016/12/16/obama-says-russians-cant-change-us-or-weaken-us.html.

5. See: Assessment Series, "Trading Profile: Russia Guards Against its Vulnerabilities," *Stratfor*, 9 January 2018, Retrieved 11 January 2018, https://worldview.stratfor.com/article/trade-profile-russia-guards-against-its-vulnerabilities.

6. The now-famous Internet Research Agency based in the Olgino district of St. Petersburg in Russia is representative of this, in that the computer troll farms there seeded a highly-debated level of unrest in the United States and probably did contribute at least some to the Trump Presidential victory in 2016. This has been extensively covered by the New York Times and other in other formats and has at least some bearing on what I discuss here. See: Chen, Adrian, "The Agency," *New York Times*, 2 June 2017, Retrieved 23 November 2017, https://www.nytimes.com/2015/06/07/magazine/the-agency.html.

7. "Russia's Information Efforts," *Center for the National Interest*, Retrieved 22 November 2017, https://cftni.org/recent-events/russias-information-efforts/.

8. Probably the most prominent is the Shanghai "Academic Ranking of World Universities" (ARWU) system which has three Russian universities in its top five hundred. See: ARWU, Ratings, Retrieved 13 April 2017, http://www.shanghairanking.com/.

9. Korobkov, A. V. and Z. A. Zaionchkovskaia, "Russian Brain Drain: Myths vs. Reality," *Communist and Post-Communist Studies*, Volume 45, 2012, p. 336, (pp. 327–41).

10. Kramer, Andrew E., "Russia Plans to Promote Technology Innovations," *New York Times*, 4 February 2010, http://www.nytimes.com/2010/02/04/business/global/04ruble.html.

11. Rapoza, Kenneth, "Russia's Three Biggest Problems," *Forbes*, 24 January 2013, Retrieved 23 November 2017, https://www.forbes.com/sites/kenrapoza/2013/01/24/russias-three-biggest-problems/#3df9f2235c86.

12. Popova, Polina, "Sanctions Have Only Increased Putin's Support," *Russia Insider for Fair Observer*, 28 November 2014, Retrieved 13 April 2017, http://russia-insider.com/en/ukraine_business_opinion/2014/11/27/05-04-14pm/sanctions_backfire_theyve_only_increased_putins.

13. Nelson, Rebecca M., "U.S. Sanctions and Russia's Economy," *Congressional Research Service*, CRS Report, R43895, 17 February 2017.

14. Christensen, Paul T., "Russia as Semi-Periphery: Political Economy, the State, and Society in the Contemporary World System," *The Political Economy of Russia*, ed. Neil Robinson, Lanham, MD, Rowman & Littlefield, Inc. 2013, pp. 169–90.

15. It is useful to note here that single-production (-company) towns are not a uniquely Soviet/Russian phenomena; they were in fact common in many other countries including the United States. The dynamic here is that the continued lack of even-attempted diversification caused extreme stagnation in Russia, and, due to lack of infrastructure thereby isolating these towns, Russia suffers more than many other countries, including the United States, in having people solely dependent on these towns.

16. The number of such towns vary by source; I've seen estimates at around the three hundred mark of such mono-towns, with ninety to one hundred of them being in some level of critical condition, that is, without subsidies from the state, they would disappear within months.

17. "Медведев: преодоление проблемы моногородов в России потребует долгих лет," "Overcoming the Problems of Single-Company Towns Will Take Years," *RIA Novosti*, 6 February 2017, Retrieved 20 March 2017, https://news.rambler.ru/economics/36020912-medvedev-preodolenie-problemy-monogorodov-v-rossii-potrebuet-dolgih-let/?updated=news.

18. Luke Harding has also researched this phenomena in the past in-depth. See, for one such article: Harding, Luke, "Protests Against Putin Sweep Russia as Factories Go Bloke," *The Guardian*, 6 June 2009, Retrieved 23 November 2017, https://www.theguardian.com/world/2009/jun/07/russia-putin-policies-protests.

19. "Russia Progress Spacecraft," *NASA,* Undated, Retrieved 14 April 2017, https://www.nasa.gov/mission_pages/station/structure/elements/progress.html.

20. As the Russian state-supported mouthpieces are quick to point out. See: "Sanctions Be Damned: US Becoming More Dependent on Russian Space Rocket Engines," *Sputnik,* 15 October 2016, Retrieved 14 April 2017, https://sputniknews.com/business/201610151046374565-russian-space-rockets-us-dependence/.

21. Weinburger, Sharon, "Hacked Emails Reveal Russian Plans to Obtain Sensitive Western Tech," *The Intercept,* 28 May 2015, Retrieved 14 April 2017, https://theintercept.com/2015/05/28/u-s-cyber-firm-alleges-hacked-emails-reveal-russian-front-operation/?utm_content=bufferc679b&utm_medium=social&utm_source=twitter.com&utm_campaign=buffer.

22. Gady, Franz-Stepan, "Is Russia's "Deadilest Tank" Using Western Technology?" *The Diplomat,* 6 June 2015, Retrieved 14 April 2017, http://thediplomat.com/2015/06/is-russias-deadliest-tank-using-western-technology/.

23. Le Miere, Jason, "Russia Developing Autonomous 'Swarm of Drones' in New Arms Race With U.S., China," *Newsweek,* 15 May 2017, Retrieved 28 November 2017, http://www.newsweek.com/drones-swarm-autonomous-russia-robots-609399.

24. Chazon, Guy, "US Sanctions Not Mere "Trifles" for Russia's Oil Industry," *Financial Times,* 10 August 2014, Retrieved 13 April 2017, https://www.ft.com/content/99ef756c-1d50-11e4-8b03-00144feabdc0.

25. Daiss, Tim, "Western Sanctions Rip Into Russia Energy Projects, Japan Comes to Help," *Forbes,* 5 September 2016, Retrieved 13 April 2017, https://www.forbes.com/sites/timdaiss/2016/09/05/western-sanctions-rip-into-russia-energy-projects-japan-comes-to-help/#3e5673802b1e.

26. From one of the Kremlin's own mouthpieces, see: "Russian Firms Urged to Develop Technology in Case New Sanctions Imposed," *Sputnik,* 7 December 2016, Retrieved 14 April 2017, https://sputniknews.com/science/201612071048286142-russia-technology-sanctions/.

27. In corresponding thought, this is not to say that the regime of Russian President Putin has not had, and does not have (as again Christensen urged before when talking about Russia's status as a "semi-peripheral" state), a substantial positive impact on the skills, internal outlook, image, and past/present/future defense production of Russia, it definitely has; however, at the same time, the regime has continued to rely on past military policies preserving bureaucracies, aspects of corruption, and reforms which have not touched key areas beneficial to the regime elites themselves, therefore these have been necessarily obstructionist obstacles to true innovation.

28. "Putin—War," *Open Russia,* May 2015, Retrieved 13 April 2017, https://openrussia.org/post/view/4803/.

29. See *Sputnik* in English, https://sputniknews.com/. See also: *Russia Today,* http://www.rt.com.

30. "New Russia Armor 30% Lighter, Make Soldiers Intellectual Fighting Machines," *Sputnik,* 16 September 2016, Retrieved 13 April 2017, https://sputniknews.com/russia/201609161045382928-russia-body-armor-production/.

31. "U. S. Defense Spending Compared to Other Countries," *Peter G. Peterson Foundation,* 18 April 2016, Retrieved 13 April 2017, https://www.pgpf.org/chart-archive/0053_defense-comparison.

32. See: Majumdar, Dave, "Russia's New PAK-FA Stealth Fighter Has A Big Problem," *National Interest,* 10 March 2017, Retrieved 14 April 2017, http://nationalinterest.org/blog/the-buzz/russias-new-pak-fa-stealth-fighter-has-big-problem-19734. See also: "Trials of Second-Stage Engine for Russia's 5th Generation Fighter Jet to Begin in 2018," *TASS,* 1 March 2017, Retrieved 14 April 2017, http://tass.com/defense/933350.

33. "Шойгу: оснащенность Российской армии современным оружием и техникой за год выросла на 7%," In English: "Shoigu: Russian Army Weapons and Technical Equipment Grew by 7," *TASS,* 19 December 2014, Retrieved 22 March 2017, http://tass.ru/armiya-i-opk/1660936.

34. "Nato condemns Putin's nuclear 'sabre-rattling,'" *BBC*, 16 June 2015, Retrieved 14 April 2017, http://www.bbc.com/news/world-europe-33153703.

35. "Залп двумя ракетами «Булава» оказался успешным лишь частично," In English: "A two-rocket Bulava Launch was Only Partially Successful," *Vzglyad*, 27 September 2016, Retrieved 22 March 2017, http://www.vz.ru/news/2016/9/27/834979.html.

36. The English language version of this article is here: "Three Layers of Russian Air Defense at Hmeymim Air Base in Syria," *TASS*, 12 February 2016, Retrieved 22 March 2017, http://tass.com/defense/855430.

37. Sterling, Toby and Anthony Deutsch, Malaysian Flight MH17 Downed by Russian-Made Missile: Prosecutors," *Reuters*, 28 September 2016, Retrieved 22 March 2017, http://www.reuters.com/article/us-ukraine-crisis-mh-idUSKCN11Y0WN.

38. Reports compiled by Mikhail Khodorkovsky's Open Russia organization estimate that some two hundred Russian soldiers have been unaccounted for the eastern Ukrainian conflict as of May 2015. See the report by assassinated Russian political actor Boris Nemtsov on the Open Russia website: "Putin—War," *Open Russia*, May 2015, Retrieved 13 April 2017, https://openrussia.org/post/view/4803/.

39. As of 21 December 2016, this report issued for 2015: On the State Sanitary and Epidemiological Welfare of the Population in the Russian Federation in 2015: State Report, Federal Service for Supervision of Consumer Rights Protection and Human Welfare, 2016—(<состоянии санитарно-эпидемиологического благополучия населения в Российской 0едерации в 2015 году: Государственный доклад> Федеральная служба по надзору в сфере защиты прав потребителей и благополучия человека, 2016), 200 с.

40. "Трагедия в Иркутске может ускорить введение акцизов на спиртосодержащие средства," *NKK News*, 20 December 2016, http://gnkk.ru/news/the-tragedy-in-irkutsk-can-accelerate-the-introduction-of-excise-duties-on-alcohol-containing-means.html, retrieved 21 December 2016.

41. Grund, Jean-Paul C., Alisher Latypov and Magdalena Harris, "Breaking Worse: The emergence of krokodil and excessive injuries among people who inject drugs in Eurasia," *International Journal of Drug Policy*, Vol. 24, 2013, pp. 265–74.

42. "HIV/AIDS in Russia & Eurasia," website, Russia and Eurasia Program, Center for Strategic and International Studies, Retrieved 23 March 2017, https://www.csis.org/programs/russia-and-eurasia-program/russia-and-eurasia-past-projects/hivaids-russia-eurasia.

43. "Russian HIV-Aids epidemic worsening under Kremlin policies, says expert," *The Guardian*, 15 May 2015, Retrieved 23 March 2017, https://www.theguardian.com/world/2015/may/15/russian-hiv-aids-epidemic-worsening-under-kremlin-policies-says-expert.

44. "ВИЧ: эпидемии нет! Что особенного в столичной программе по борьбе со СПИДом," (In English: "HIV: no epidemic! What is special about the capital's program in the struggle with AIDS"), *Argumenty I Fakti*, 20 June 2016, Retrieved 23 March 2017, http://www.aif.ru/society/healthcare/vich_epidemii_net_chto_osobennogo_v_stolichnoy_programme_po_borbe_so_spidom, Article publicized on the RISS website here, retrieved 23 March 2017: https://riss.ru/smi/31792/.

45. "Геи составляют не более 2% процентов населения и 55% среди ВИЧ-инфицированных," (In English: "Gays constitute not more than 2 percent of the populations and 55 percent of them are infected with HIV"), *Russian Institute for Strategic Studies*, 25 August 2016, Retrieved 23 March 2017, https://riss.ru/demography/demography-news/33341/.

46. Akirama, "ГУЛАГ Путина страшнее ГУЛАГА Сталина," (In English): "Putin's GULAG is worse than Stalin's," 6 May 2017, Retrieved 9 May 2017, http://www.akirama.com/2017/05/06/3565/. See also: "Публицист Ибрагимов заявил в суде о пытках током," (In English): Publicist Ibragimv spoke in court about electric shock," *Kavkazskyi Uzel*, 6 May 2017, Retrieved 9 May 2017, http://www.kavkaz-uzel.eu/articles/302255/.

47. *World Prison Brief*, Russian Federation, Prison Studies, Retrieved 9 May 2017, http://www.prisonstudies.org/country/russian-federation.

48. Pallin, Carolina Vendil, "Internet Control through Ownership: the Case of Russia," *Post-Soviet Affairs*, Volume 33, Issue 1, 2017, pp. 16–33, DOI: 10.1080/1060586X.2015.1121712.

49. Ibid., p 17. Another excellent book on the matter, as Pallin points out: Ledeneva, Alena V., *Can Russia Modernise?*, Cambridge: Cambridge University Press, 2013.

50. Mak, Aaron, "What's Happened Since Russia Banned Telegram," *Slate magazine*, 25 April 2018, Retrieved 26 April 2018, https://slate.com/technology/2018/04/russian-internet-in-chaos-because-of-telegram-app-ban.html.

51. "Vladimir Putin signs anti-gay propaganda bill," AFP, *The Telegraph*, 30 June 2013, Retrieved 13 April 2017, http://www.telegraph.co.uk/news/worldnews/europe/russia/10151790/Vladimir-Putin-signs-anti-gay-propaganda-bill.html.

FIVE

The "Allies," Friends and Family Life of Russia

INTRODUCTION

Not much different from other countries, most (if not all) Russians believe that, and Putin would probably agree, Russia needs allies, needs to be "friends" with, and needs to be an "ally" to, like-minded иностранцы (foreigners), nominally meaning people outside of Russia and/or in foreign countries.[1] Naturally, insofar as the second principle studied over the course of this book, the theme of Independent Russia, which is held near and dear to segments of Russian society, this element is contradictory. It is precisely this contradiction that must be examined here and which I have found to be abstractly fascinating.

By extension and in turn, and contradictory to the Independent Russia theme periodically professed, it has been one of Putin's longstanding goals to be a "leader" to some degree of a coalition of countries in addressing world, or at least regional, problems and crises.

Corresponding to the limitations of other chapters of this book, I will not seek to excessively spend much time talking about foreign policy revolving around and in Russia and the unique issues that Russia must address; believe you me, many people have spent a lot of time covering that type of material and I cannot really add to that on a critical geopolitical level.[2] However, as I have said before, I will seek to provide my own take on how foreign policies and the alliances and "friends" of Russia relate specifically to the people of Russia, and not to the Putin regime (although I will certainly mention Putin and his regime more than once).

Likewise, I will only consider the regions closest to Russia and the former Soviet Union and not, say, those allies of the Putin regime in the Middle East like Syria and, on occasion, Iran which have very little direct relationship with the Russian people. Although I will mention Syria periodically (and that country's limited role in Russian public opinion) as I have done before in this book, I consider the Syrian War for Russia to be primarily an issue of adventurism for the regime (as opposed to the Russian people).

Alliances in the modern era, for the purposes of this chapter, are the agreements between states and peoples (though not always the same) for common defense or coordinating goals for military or civilian purposes. There are myriad alliances and agreements of coordination between modern day states, for military defense or nuclear waste disposal; mostly what I will talk about here is those agreements of meaningful context in the post-Soviet era that have some degree of wide-reaching and serious political and military purpose regarding Russia's population. Far from all agreements will be covered; such an endeavor of trying to understand every signed agreement between every country and Russia in the modern era would be a book by itself.

Russia leads or co-leads its own fair share of political and/or military international organizations, some of which I will cover in this chapter, including most prominently the Shanghai Cooperation Organization (SCO, founded in 1996), the Eurasian Economic Union (EEU, founded ultimately in 2015, but having serious problems[3]), and the Collective Security Treaty Organization (CSTO, founded in 1992 by extension of Russia's initial post-Soviet organization, the Commonwealth of Independent States, CIS).

Representing the veritable political and/or military "opposition" to Russia, or at least its most important neighboring alliances of which Russia does not belong, they are the North Atlantic Treaty Organization (NATO), led by the United States, and the European Union (EU).

As in part addressed previously, Putin's desire for modern-day alliances of relative convenience and beneficence to Russia fits historical norms; at the same time, Russia in the Soviet era, and long previous, had some level of constant conflict on its periphery as the struggle for control and friendly puppet states continued. "Among Russia's deeply rooted behavioral patterns a fundamental one was formed by four centuries of territorial expansion."[4]

From the center outwards in the post-Soviet-era, the desire for influence and leadership of some bloc of countries includes Russia's complex relationships with its former post-Soviet partners, i.e., the other fourteen former Soviet republics. For the Putin regime, though not so much for the people, this also includes as is relevant now, (again) Syria and Iran, and various others globally. Finally, we should also not forget of course Cold War and post-Soviet Russia's love-hate relationship with China (a member of the SCO) and the United States and the many countries of Europe, now most of which are members of the European Union and NATO.

Multi-national surveys on friendship, of "who has who's back" as it is characterized in part in the subsequent article, have been taken in the last quarter of 2016 by WIN/Gallup International and publicized by Bloomberg and the results are somewhat surprising.[5] While not unexpected given its superpower status and position as de-facto leader of NATO, the United States is the majority "go-to" country when many countries' security is at stake, but Russia has its own adherents in the survey, including those polled in four NATO countries: Bulgaria, Greece, Turkey, and Slovenia. China in some respects supposedly has Russia's "back" as well.

In other spring 2017 surveys conducted by Pew Research Center in some Middle Eastern countries including Israel, Russia is seen as more important than the United States in influence and is gaining prominence in the region.[6]

While the WIN/Gallup survey took place spanning the time period of America's 2016 presidential election, the results show, I believe, two things: (1) the changing dynamic of world security vertices, with countries that share Russia's cultural influence (not overlooking propaganda from Russia) and Christian Russian Orthodoxy religion paralleling Russia's general world view, but also the self-portrayal by Putin's Russia of Russia as an alternative sphere of reliable security to the American status quo and (2) the lack of trust in an America led by President Donald Trump and his questionable pronouncements of security correlated to America's allies. Likewise, the Pew study shows the effects of Trump's erratic foreign policy on the critical Middle Eastern theater of operations.

Additionally, Trump's implied announcements both during and after the presidential election that even NATO countries would not be completely secured based not on simple membership in NATO but on their individual contributions to NATO's funding have inevitably taken their toll on trust in America's fundamental friendship and treaty obligations, once so solid but now perhaps less so, for the present and for the future.

As for Russian public opinion, as seen by Figure 5.1, Levada polling data[7] generally shows that, except for Belarus, many countries are consistently rated badly in their relationship with Russia, although good and bad (again, generally) come together over time:

Over the course of this chapter, I will discuss this aspect concerning the principle diagnostics of Russia's and Russians' traditional relationships, including how Russia and Russians relate to foreign citizens and concerns. After a short section about Russia's and Russians' allies, I will discuss Ukraine, Russia's closest relationship.

Next, I will discuss Russia's friendship with the West and with the United States. As an American who has long lived in Russia, I have seen how Russia and Russians deal with individuals who visit from the West and from America. I will go into more detail later, but I've found that Russia and Russians have a love-hate (mostly general liking) friendship

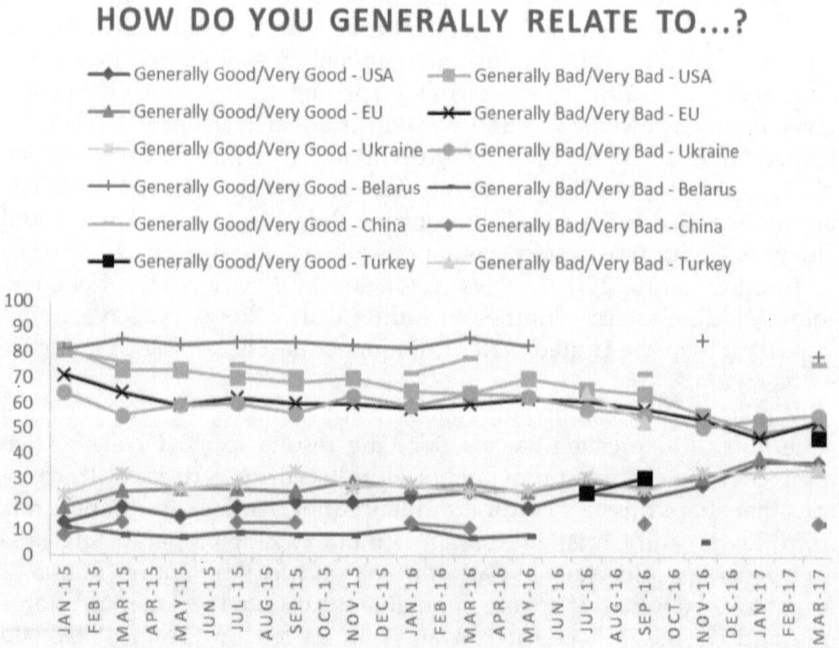

Figure 5.1. Opinions of Russia's relationships with other countries in Russian society. Data courtesy of Levada Centre.

with me and usually a helpful relationship involving my long research in the country.

Thirdly, I will discuss in broad terms how Russia and Russians deal with the Caucasian lands, its (and their) wars there in Chechnya and later Georgia.

Fourthly, I will discuss how Russia and Russians see its (and their) friendship with Asia and China, in specific.

As each section progresses, using my research and myriad interviews, I hope to apply a separate, more individualistic, account for an examination of the treatment of Russia's (and Russians') friendship with foreign citizens and countries. As for while Russia and Russians profess to love the visitors to the (their) country, the situation is not always so clear-cut in practice. In the following parts of this chapter, I will hone these ideas down to the level of friendship and family life in Russia. In substance, this chapter is firstly written to detail and discuss the application of how Russians see allies perceiving to deal with Russia and how Russians consider themselves a collective ally of any other country. Lastly, we will discuss how Russians see family life in Russia and what this adds to our overall understanding of this country.

Questions to be covered include: what does this tell us about what Russians "want" from the global community, from their neighbors and family, and from where do Russians perceive Russia as coming from and where should Russia be going in future? This is important for the "house" of Russia as it can be said that how a "house" is treated can be determined by the views of, and views on, "neighbors," if you will. Every person needs help at some time, and the giving of and acceptance of help can be a unique commentary on a person's house or, in the case of Russia, a country's position in the world at-large.

How Putin has dealt with these countries in the 2000s and 2010s decades has been a great matter of discourse both inside and outside of Russia, for both observers and citizens of Russia, although for the latter group it is still most important to put food on the table and to have full stores of meat, fish, fresh vegetables and those Western products of which Russians have become accustomed to.

Russia's alliances have evolved much in the post-Soviet era. Ultimately concerning Russia's changing stance with the West and its potential allies, as Dmitri Trenin wrote for *The Guardian* in late March 2017 in response to the "Don't Call Him Dimon" anti-corruption protests of 26 March 2017: "[Putin] first tried to fit Russia into an enlarged west, as a senior ally of the US in NATO and a close partner of the EU within a "greater Europe." When his efforts failed, he steered Russia away from the western orbit, rebuilt the country's military power and used it to protect Russian security interests in Ukraine."[8]

In detail in previous chapters and sections, I have already discussed how Russia and Russians seek to gain and hold respect for Russia, however this chapter seeks to deal with how they maintain friendship with other peoples of the world. Russia being the great, but somewhat regional, power that it is in the 2000s and 2010s decade, I will discuss Russia's friendship and alliances and what this means for Russian citizens.

SO, WHO ARE RUSSIA'S, AND RUSSIANS', ALLIES?

Answering the question of who Russia's allies are, and ordinary Russians' (not to mention elite Russians', to the extent they are separate from the Putin regime et al.) allies, it should be a simple question, but yet a valid one, however, because for Russia, and for Russians', as with a great many other things it must be said, it is fairly complex.

Firstly, to answer the question of who Russia's allies are, one must separate the question accordingly. Strictly speaking as a country, one must talk about who the friends of Russia and Russians are, and one must talk about who the friends of the Putin regime are, because the two are far from synonymous.

Russia (separate from the Putin regime), and Russians, have many friends; I count myself as one of them. There are few countries and peoples on Earth who truly have a bone to pick with a more peaceful Russia and the desires of Russians to improve their country through legal avenues of international commerce and finance.

Then, however, you come to discussing the political system, and you see that the Putin regime has correspondingly few friends and a lot of enemies, as to be discussed in detail here.

The Putin regime has a friend of several right-wing parties across Europe who want to dismember the European Union and acknowledge Russia's sphere of influence, as Putin very much wants. Indeed, representatives of Putin's United Russia party have been meeting with those parties in recent times.[9] The Putin regime is allied with several authoritarian regimes, including, as mentioned before, the Syrian Assad regime in its bid to keep Bashar Hafez al-Assad in power during the destructive Syrian civil war. Russia has "representatives" in Nicaragua again for the first time since the Cold War, likely conducting electronic espionage.[10] Through the Russian intelligence services, the Putin regime secretly has its representatives sneaking around making friends with sympathetic elites in foreign countries, including the United States. The American Donald Trump presidency has had dealings with the Putin regime; whether Trump and his people knew about the connections to Russian intelligence are, at the time of this writing, unknown.[11]

The Putin regime has friends in former Soviet countries that want to foment separatism and rebellion, including the direct support of rebels in eastern Ukraine, in Moldova's breakaway Transnistria, and possibly secret support for covert agents in the Baltic States. That last point is denied strongly in Moscow (even more so than the first point), but it is a mainstay of maintaining a confrontational (and sometimes justifiable) analytical attitude towards Russia, and I suggest it should be kept in mind.

As Anatol Lieven wrote in April 2017 on the much-hyped question of Russian covert ops in the Baltic states:

> Thus the Baltic States have been presented by much of the Western media and policymakers as likely next victims of Russian media. It is fascinating however in this context to do an internet search for Russian official threats to the Baltic States or Russian actions aimed at provoking internal conflict in the Baltic[s—Ibid] in recent years. There are none. All that the search turns up are thousands of western (and of course Baltic) articles and interviews stating that such a threat exists.[12]

By inclination or desire, the Putin regime (as separate from Russia) can be understood to have four (4) categories of friends outside of Russia:

1. Those who desire, openly or covertly, to help the Putin regime under unclear circumstances, i.e., as alleged by some analysts to be the American Trump administration.

2. Those who receive funding from the Putin regime, i.e., (allegedly) at least some of the far-right parties in Europe.
3. Those who receive direct military assistance in regional altercations, i.e., Syria, eastern Ukraine, Georgia, and others less publicized.
4. Those who (perhaps) are not really friends with the Putin regime, but which are open to alliance with a scheming authoritarian regime, i.e., the American Trump administration (if it does not fall under category 1), or, to say it another way, like two ships running parallel in the night to gain the advantage of joint protection.

We should remain cognizant of these influences as the Putin regime holds these "friends," to be principal.

At this point, I will discuss Ukraine because it is the first step in such a discussion, since Russia and Russians share its (and their) closest history with that of Ukraine and the Ukrainians. Reflecting Russia's origins, I believe that any such examination merits first looking at Ukraine and Ukrainians as separate from all other countries of the world.

THE RELATIONSHIP FOR THE RUSSIAN PEOPLE, AND FOR THE PUTIN REGIME, WITH UKRAINE

Perhaps not surprisingly, given the long and complex history between Russia and Ukraine, the most predominant of all of Russia's relationships in the post-Soviet era has been Russia's relationship (or lack thereof) with Ukraine. Representing the origin and birthplace of the Russian idea,[13] Ukraine throughout history has been paramount to understanding how Russia is seen, how Russia sees itself, and how Russians deal with friendship and shared history.

Many self-considered Russian individuals themselves originate from Ukraine, have dealings with and educational periods in Ukraine, vacationed in Ukraine, and more than a few have family members still in Ukraine; likewise, the opposite is true, with Ukrainians having relatives in Russia, visiting Russia for whatever purposes, and so on.

Nevertheless, in the eyes of more than one Russian whom I've spoken with, according to their own words, Ukraine has always been a predominant source of insurrection and was the "rebel" republic of the Soviet Union, discounting the Baltic states which, or so I've been told, were not really ever a part of the shared Soviet past and space in the first place (something many Baltic citizens would have no problem with, I'm sure).

The separation of Putin vies-a-vie the people in the section title emphasizes that Russia and Ukraine as countries or governments are not really "friends" anymore, if the two countries/governments ever were in the first place in the post-Soviet era, but as two peoples are bound as ever before.

However, for both the Russian people and the Putin regime, the series of events and evolving geopolitical factors in the two countries have had repercussions in both all the same, particularly following, in succession (1) the rise of Russian president Vladimir Putin, (2) the fall of pro-Russian Ukrainian president Viktor Yanukovich, (3) the Russian invasion of Crimea and eastern Ukraine, (4) the subsequent attempts by Russia to normalize these pronounced aggressive foreign policies, (1–4) the battle over the flow of gas and fossil fuels and payment, (5, etc.) and so on. Given the rise of authoritarianism in Russia, the progression of these occasions was in some way predictable, even from the very beginning with the post-Soviet fall and concerning any successive alliance. Concerning the 1990s-decade, academic Roman Wolczuk wrote back in 2002: "From the very outset of discussions on the successor to the Soviet Union, it was apparent that the views of Russia and Ukraine were incongruent. Ukraine was adamant that participation in any successor institution was, at best, a temporary exercise to bring about a "civilized divorce."[14]

On-going domestic (for each side) and international aspects are however paralleled by the relatively-peaceful views of many (though far from all) Russians and Ukrainians on a personal level. Indeed, no matter how hard that the Putin regime has tried through controlled media to demonize the Ukrainian populace, there is, at least in my own studies, interviews, and fifteen years of research, still a generally substantive view in Russia that Ukrainians are at least good people on a fundamental level.[15]

Likewise, separate studies and, not to mention, my own experience, has shown that Russians as a people are not disliked by most Ukrainians,[16] although survey results by, say, Pew Research Center can give a more muddled, albeit pro-Western, view on such aspects as joining NATO, and concerning the Kremlin-directed invasion of Ukrainian territory:

> [in Ukraine] the security situation on the ground posed a serious challenge to safely surveying the public. Pew Research Center was, however, able to interview in all regions of the country except Luhans'k, Donets'k and Crimea. The areas covered by the survey represent roughly 80 percent of the Ukrainian population. Among those surveyed, a majority of Ukrainians (67 percent) support becoming a member of the EU. They also favor joining NATO by a 53 percent-to-32 percent margin. At the same time, a plurality (47 percent) expresses support for negotiating with the rebels and Russia. Roughly a quarter (23 percent) says using military force to fight the separatists is the best way to end the conflict in the east, and another 19 percent volunteer either both or neither.[17]

As stated over the course of this book, the Russian people and the Putin regime are separate with oftentimes divided goals, loyalties, and outlooks, though the Putin regime panders for support (often successfully) when at all possible. This is complicated also by the Putin regime's emphasis on "sovereignty," or the non-interference of third parties in the affairs of states, while at the same time de-emphasizing sovereignty by recklessly invading and annexing parts of other states. As such, this is an inconsistent lie propagated by the Putin regime. Indeed, and in turn, my first book argued that the culture of lies in Russia produces antipathy among the Russian people against the Putin regime as often as in favor (and vice versa).

However, what does the Putin regime want from any friendship with Ukraine? That is easily apparent. I would consider that Putin wants Ukrainian abeyance to the Russian "sphere of influence" preferably in the form of a weak Ukraine that will join whatever alliances that Putin comes up with, including the SCO and others. The Putin regime has done that by giving Ukraine headaches in any way that it can, by taking Crimea, by introducing Russian troops to eastern Ukraine, by disrupting gas flow to Ukraine, the list goes on and on.

In fact, as argued by Professor Andrew Wilson in a December 2017 report for American Enterprise Institute, and further from his 2014 book on the subject,[18] the Putin regime wants chaos in Ukraine pure and simple, so that Putin can pick and choose his preferred partners and interlocutors in Ukraine. Consistently working on where Ukraine is "weakest," and Ukraine has more than its share of weaknesses in its political system, Putin harbors policy such that: "the cumulative intent is to create a failed-state scenario as a consequence of, rather than a justification for, Russian intervention."[19] This "scenario," to make Ukraine into a failed state is a brazen tactic that, as Wilson considered earlier in that report, extends from non-consideration of Ukraine as a "real" state, and that is one real factor seen in my work here as well.

To take a step back however, now necessarily focusing on the Russian people's views of life and alliance with Ukraine on this point,[20] beyond geopolitical considerations and what niceties stated previously, what do Russians really desire from Ukraine and how would they see the relationship between Russia and Ukraine?

The answer to that question can be expressed in a series of words, I posit, and it would be something along the lines of: peace, but on Russia's terms.

Again, a sense of dissatisfaction has always dogged this relationship. To an extent, on one hand, it has been my experience that Russians sometimes see themselves as the aggrieved party in the post-Soviet era. In pre-Soviet times, Ukraine was often a disquiet, to say the least, section of the Russian empire. In Soviet times, the distribution of resources, technology, and aggregate economic beneficence between the two countries was extremely complex. The two peoples, Russians and Ukrainians, had always been intertwined, but during Soviet times, disagreements of any substantial nature were papered over.

Nevertheless, the question of distribution of land was always a concern, even in the Soviet Union; land is and has always been a foremost concern for Russians and Ukrainians, and this stands true even to this day. In 1954, the Soviet Union under Nikita Khrushchev transferred Crimea to Ukraine, as Khrushchev: "saw the transfer as a way of fortifying and perpetuating Soviet control over Ukraine now that the civil war had finally been won. Some 860,000 ethnic Russians would be joining the already large Russian minority in Ukraine."[21]

Analyzing post-Second World War Ukraine, Soviet authority tried to stabilize itself through a variety of ways. Citing other studies as well as his own, as academician Martin Blackwell writes concerning housing distribution cities of post-war Ukraine: "By the mid-1940s, scholars agree, the Soviet Union's fundamental problem at home was a paradoxical need to stabilize a new regime noticeably strengthened by the Second World War. One way the Kremlin undertook this stabilization was through acceptance of anti-Semitism in places like Kyiv."[22]

Still, over time, at least for Russians, Soviet control and the parallel Soviet "family of nations" concept did become somewhat ingrained. When the Soviet Union fell, my research has shown that for many Russians, including Mr. Putin himself it seems, they felt betrayed by all of this. For many Russians, some of which have complained to me as if I could rewrite history, why did the Ukrainians have to make the breakup of the Soviet Union so disingenuous?

As such, the current love-hate relationship that ordinary Russians have with Ukrainians was renewed. Yet Ukrainians have much right to be distrustful of Moscow; that is beyond question. By extension, the Putin regime takes advantage of this love-hate relationship between Russians and Ukrainians just like it takes advantage of every other conceivable opportunity available.

Furthermore, for the Ukrainian side, some international actors[23] still indirectly, and sometimes unknowingly, insult Ukraine and express doubt as to whether Ukraine is separate from Russia. The most often manifestation of this is use of "the" before Ukraine, i.e., "the Ukraine," which is how Ukraine was referred to in Soviet times.[24] Many Ukrainians, quite rightly if they believe in a separate Ukrainian sovereignty and culture, consider this a lack of sympathy for a separate Ukraine and as something close to heresy.

Part of this idea, that of a Greater Russia without regard for a real separate Ukrainian culture, is also suggested by evidence that the Russian Orthodox Church is making use of its Ukrainian branches and clergy (the Ukrainian Orthodox Church-Moscow Patriarchy, UOC-MP) in holding loyalty in Ukraine to Moscow,[25] as well as aiding the cause(s) of pro-Russian rebels in eastern Ukraine,[26] but it is further rooted in the idea that Ukraine is eternally part of "Holy Rus'," which has been spoken about earlier in this book.

As of the mid-2010s, and as discussed in chapter 3, these feelings of grievance always lie just under the surface, but percolates to the top whenever Putin engages in aggressive foreign policy against Ukraine, including the invasion of Crimea and eastern Ukraine and the annexation of Crimea. Crimea, again as I've been told by more than one Russian, is, and always has been, a part of Russia, no matter what Russian leaders have agreed to in the past and no matter what took place during Soviet times. The supposition does exist that maybe Ukraine owes even more to Russia, but Russia will not ask for more (unless Ukraine continues to be annoying, and then all bets are off).

From a second purview, from my research I posit that ordinary Russians do not at all see themselves as an aggressive people towards Ukraine, even from the perspective of the previously-discussed grievances (that they, supposedly, should have every right to have) towards Ukraine/Ukrainians.

Before the Putin regime's 2014-on aggression towards Ukraine, this was a much more common outlook on the relationship towards Ukraine and with Ukrainians. Post-Crimea and east Ukraine, now many Russians feel the need to say up front that they have no problems with Ukraine. Anyway, as discussed previously, in the post-Soviet era, at least on a social level, Russians have for the most part a brotherly outlook towards their Ukrainian counterparts, and in a great many cases, this includes real familial ties. In that respect, a great many Russians have relatives in Ukraine and so on that they worry about, cousins, aunts, etc.

From this perspective, the aggressive policies of Russia in Ukraine are entirely elite-inspired, for the benefit of Putin elites and regime supporters, and furthermore entirely Putin regime-based for the most militaristic policies against a Ukrainian nation determined to be free. Russian allegations that the Ukrainian government is fascist and domineering against the Russian and Russian-speaking populations of Ukraine are purely a figment of the Putin regime's rhetoric, although the Ukrainian army and the militias fighting against pro-Russian rebels do have their fair shares of fascist and Nazi-inspired adherents; this should not dismiss or lessen the substantive Ukrainian desire to maintain and protect its borders against pro-Russian invasion.

Also, one must always account for the real cultural, civil, and sovereignty separation between Russia and Ukraine, and pay real heed to the real horrors that have been visited upon Ukraine in the pre-Soviet and Soviet past.

As mentioned earlier, but again it needs to be said, Ukraine has suffered no small bit under Russian rule, including an artificial famine in Soviet times, the forced deportation of sub-sets of Ukraine population, such as the 1944 deportation of the Crimean Tatars[27] (who eventually, for the most part, returned), the restrictions on Ukrainian language, and the overall destruction or repression of Ukrainian symbols, people, ideas, and culture that have been prominent throughout history, pre-Soviet, Soviet, and post-Soviet times. The list of atrocities that are involved in the traditional Russo-Ukrainian relationship is quite long and my research on Russian public opinion has found that many, if not most, Russians don't even want to acknowledge even the half of them. Also, Crimean Tatar identity has become a "lodestone" for determining the idea of "Eurasianism" for Russia as well, indicative of the competition over defining national identities for all involved.[28]

At the same time, Ukraine's dealings with the West perhaps bother many ordinary Russians and elites, including Putin, the most. Ukraine's and many Ukrainians' desire to become part of the European Union, NATO, and a general ally to Western organizations and government institutions at the expense of Russia's Eurasian institutions and defense alliances. Perhaps out of all the foreign policy dealings of the Putin regime and out of all the relationships to "allies" that concern Russia, these desires of Ukraine and Ukrainians gall Putin and some Russians the most.

Relative to the introduction of a potential visa-free regime between Ukraine and the EU in 2017 (although as of this writing, that had not been formalized), this annoyance is even more heightened. Minutes after professing brotherhood, many Russians I've met continued with "surprise" that their Slavic "brothers," the Ukrainians, would "betray" Russia in such a way, but here we are.

Many Ukrainians I've talked to, as with many non-Russian former peoples of the Soviet Union, don't believe a word that Putin says, and subtly question the words of Russians in general, and no amount of influence can or will change that. This concept of friendship between Ukrainians and Russians, while still holding for familial reasons, is almost completely lost for Ukrainians, and from experience perhaps in some ways as well it should.

This point-of-view will be referred to over the course of this section, as I analyze in the next section, Russia's relationship and "friendship" with the generalized West.

LOVE, HATE, AND THE WEST

As has been explored earlier in this book and as is well-known, Russia's love-hate relationship with the countries of the West, almost all of which are now democracies but of course have not always been, is a recurring feature of international foreign policy. While it does not come close to rivaling the amplified love-hate relationship between Russia/Russians and Ukraine/Ukrainians, the Western consideration is significant in and of itself.

It is precisely this angle from which the theme of "Independent Russia" is most focused on in Russian society. While one cannot overlook the firm foothold that some American firms have in Russia,[29] in contrast, many times I've been told by ordinary Russians, rich and poor, young and old, etc. etc., that Russia does not do what the West tells it to do. As a side note, I cannot ever recall anyone across the vastness of Russia saying that Russia does not do what *China* tells it to do, and this cultural opposition is precisely the important tangent on which Russia itself can be most observed.

Much as with other governments including their own however, ordinary Russians separate Western peoples from their governments.

On one hand, with the ever-present pro-Putin media machine to point things out, the fundamental conflict in Western societies between military intervention and non-intervention are made light of. With great enthusiasm, pro-Putin media tries to show how those same Western countries which are always the first to say they want peace on Earth, goodwill to man, negotiate peace treaties, find common cause with neighbors, such and so on, then continue to lead wars in the Balkans, in Afghanistan, in Iraq, and on and on. This perpetuates the view in Russian society that Western countries are decadent and divided, etc.

At the same time, Russians in my experience reject that rhetoric on an individual level. Russian people, in my opinion, are some of the kindest when it comes to Western visitors. Similarly, Russians desire friendship with their neighbors, including their western counterparts.

Again, you would never know this from watching much of the news in Russia; the magnanimous view is rarely prevalent in the propaganda from the Putin regime and as portrayed by strongly nationalist groups within Russia.

By the "West," I also must stress that many usually (but not always) group together all those countries of the West and including those of Eastern Europe which were formerly in the Soviet sphere, but which are now independent; many of them (but not all) are quite prosperous now as members of the European Union and of NATO. Oftentimes, again though not always, I will be generally focusing on the primary rivals and influences of Russia in the West when I use that term, those of the United Kingdom, France, Germany, and, of course, that "main opponent" (Glavnoye protivnik) the United States and *including* their altogether necessary alliances with Eastern Europe thereby also taking account of Eastern Europe's concerns and problems. As Ariel Braun writes on Eastern Europe as concerning any potential alliance with the large eastern mass that is Russia:

> Eastern Europe is not at the center of Russian foreign policy concerns, but it is nonetheless profoundly important. When we examine the relationship between Russia on the one hand and Eastern Europe on the

> other, we can see ambition, hope, potential, risk, as well as fear in the latter region. [. . .] Moscow's definition of national interest becomes less comprehensible and reassuring along Europe's eastern periphery. Not surprisingly, the counterpoint to Russian ambitions is Eastern European fears, ultimately diminishing security for everyone.[30]

Nevertheless, given this attention but inattention to Eastern Europe, the Putin regime, as will be the argument, is inclined towards looking to the largest countries which it recognizes as the "West," both by the regime and by ordinary Russians, while at the same time having that "evil eye," if you will, planted towards Eastern European countries, some of which will be duly discussed here.

By the West, I also mean even those former Soviet republics which were appropriated, many say criminally, by Moscow into the Soviet Union and which now clearly define themselves as part of Europe, those being: Latvia, Lithuania, and Estonia. These countries so clearly define themselves as part of Europe that it is impossible to consider them otherwise; they are part of the European Union, NATO, and some myriad other alliances with Europe. Their difficulties are substantial in dealing with Moscow, for they have quite probably the most experience therein, addressing the fear that the Putin regime might take advantages of their, in some cases, large ethnic Russian populations and try to divide them up as Russia did with eastern Ukraine, or even attempt to take them over like Ukraine's Crimea.

The Baltics' fears, again quite probably justified, have led them to ask for added and more visible defensive support from NATO, which NATO has duly provided at a non-threatening (to the Russian military) but still substantial few brigades worth of western power deployments. It is arguable but worthy, in my opinion, that this support should be visibly and markedly introduced and enhanced, while making sure (by stating it over and over again) that they are no offensive threat to Russian lands.

As a counter-point, my consideration of the West does not include Belarus, run by the former Communist heavyweight, the overt authoritarian Alyaksandr Lukashenka. His regime continues to keep Belarus locked in the past, a Soviet nightmare (if you will) that Belarus has not been able to wake up from, and a polity clearly focused on staying in Moscow's (i.e., Putin's) "orbit."

Lukashenka's relationship with Moscow and with Putin himself has not always been shiny and full of roses, however, but Belarus has been a reliable marker for Moscow's development of its own sphere of influence, which Putin has so strongly manifested. Recent protests and strikes in Belarus have however endangered this rather fragile set-up. Lukashenka's recent law against unemployment has angered his people to no end, and he might just actually be in real trouble.[31] It is unclear as to how much longer the Lukashenka regime will last, if the regime could survive his disappearance from the scene, and if Belarus could, in fact, have a European future ahead of it.

Back to addressing Russia's and Russians' relationship with the West as a whole, my own research and experiences are also relevant here. I have met a great many Russians who desire peace and prosperity with the West, though with the nationalist overtone that they sometimes proclaim themselves not to be European and/or that they will oppose the will of the United States.

A burly Russian once told me near one of the metro stations in Moscow that he disliked America and Americans in general but I, personally, was a very good person. I took that as rather cold comfort, and I understood the insult (and took it as such, though I am not easily offended, especially in view of keeping a calm demeanor and environment), but I here acknowledge the general point-of-view. I've also met Russians who had good jobs in Russia, but who disagreed with the outlook there to such an extent that they would rather be unemployed in Europe than continue to live in Russia. All these point to and contribute to the, as mentioned before, lesser love-hate relationship to the West that is of issue here.

How does this contribute to the discussion here? One way to look at it is seeing the latent attraction of the West to many Russians. Much has been written about the "brain-drain" in Russia, that is, of an outflow of the skilled and knowledgeable labor force in Russia for perhaps greener pastures in Western countries.[32] I've found that this exists but, at least in my research, it is not quite so strongly the case as many would profess (there is no veritable stampede underway), especially for elites and those close to the Putin regime. Much of my research agrees with the general paradigm in fact, although again there are still a fair number of remaining professional Russians who still consider Russia home.

The question therefore when looking at the "house" in the consideration of Russia versus the West: can the Russian skilled and educated population feel loyalty to Russia and can Russia replace or renew the loss of knowledge and labor that is filtered outwards? About this section, how does this affect Russians' view of the West, that is, the temptation of the West?

My research has found that, though the West is seen as a potential possessor of valuable expertise (see chapter 4) and full of good people, in the end, there are still many Russians who agree with Putin that Russian friendship with the West is desired but not "necessary," despite all the help that a peaceful Russia could receive from the West. Not to make this sound too much like a street fight, but Russia has its own "will" to exist "Independent" (again that theme) of all others. Putin makes this position into something that he can maintain his political stranglehold on, and it does work after a fashion.

On this level, Russian public opinion and culture towards the West has taken the form of several exigent features in Russia's relationship with the West, its relationship with its own citizens, and, in turn, the relationship of Russia's citizens with the regime.

Firstly, and notably (and especially annoying to the opposition), in substantive collision with the West, ordinary Russians have little to no problem with Putin's adventures in Syria, therein the deployment of the Russian air force to support the Syrian Assad regime, or with the use of Russia's armed forces in Ukraine's eastern Donets'k and Lugans'k regions. To also be of note, the opposition's nationalism and sometimes support for the Crimean annexation does complicate matter a little for those looking to wholly support Russia's opposition and oppose both Putin and his assertive foreign policies.

Alternatively, these could be seen in the matrix of alliances; in the first case with an old international ally, the Syrian Bashar Hafez al-Assad regime despite the consequences (i.e., annoying the West, if that was not part of the point anyway); in the second case, with presumed Russians living in east Ukraine (though not necessarily devoted to re-joining the "homeland"), again perhaps despite the consequences, as the economy will blatantly suffer from sanctions.

These strategies are nominally seen as part and parcel with the need of Russia to support friends in difficult places, with the separate reality that the Putin regime is only hoping to reinforce itself and its stature, and many ordinary Russians are pacified with aspects of these plans, though most all ordinary Russians know that Russia can ill afford such endeavors.

Again, this is also not to mention the fact that, as with the case of casualties among Russian troops in Ukraine, the steady drip-drip of Russian casualties in the Syrian theater of operations is also endangering Putin's little Middle Eastern adventure.[33] As Putin well knows, reminiscent of 1980s Afghan adventure in the Soviet era, Russian public opinion can only accept a limited number of casualties from such operations.

While ordinary Russians are aware that these policies create antagonism with the West, the Putin regime successfully interconnects the regime's friendship with the Syrian Assad government with a friendship with Russia. Thereby, the Russian public sees the need to support "friends" like Syria, especially as depicted by pro-Putin Russian media to a high extent, outweighing the need to be friends with the West. If the Russian opposition wants to divide the Russian public from the Putin regime, maybe the opposition could just start with asking (or maybe chanting), simply: why are Russian troops in Syria? It's a valid question that needs a good airing.

Secondly, ordinary Russians tend to have no problem with the abrogation of numerous treaties by the Putin regime, including those Cold War-reliant "stepping stones" that attend to management and deployment of Russia's nuclear arsenal(s). This is for more obvious reasons: these treaties, though they mean much in the West, have hardly impacted the outlook of ordinary Russians in any real way. There has been no real anti-nuclear war movement in Russia in post-Soviet history and, at least from those Russians I've spoken with, there is no real reason to believe that one is going to start now.

Thirdly, none of this significantly impacts the views of ordinary Russians concerning individual Westerners who live and work in Russia. While foreigners may have many difficulties with the Putin regime concerning visa issues, no matter the case, few Russians will have any problems with the foreigners in question. While they may not like your government, reflecting the excellent nature of the Russian home and family, they will welcome you, and, depending on the case, will be glad to share their love of Borscht and vodka with you at will.

Regardless of the Russian media's usual anti-Western angle, I can attest to this myself, the Russian home, as I have covered before, is a warm and accepting place.

All these considerations are part of the post-Soviet "house" that has been built, it seems downwards, especially in the case of Russia's difficulty with addressing the West on mutually beneficial terms. In parallel, Russians' respect for foreigners from the West is unparalleled, and it is my findings that those who profess outright nationalism even on a personal level have little support and constitution beyond slogans and maybe some graffiti on rarely-glimpsed walls.

RUSSIA AND THE CAUCASUS

Russia and the Caucasus, between Russians and the peoples of the Caucasus, have a far more ancient historical relationship than the equivalent between Russia and the West. In fact, calling any relationship here a friendship is a stretch by any definition of the word, perhaps a better designation is as a collection of "selectivized" friendships. The Russian empire long sought to subdue the Caucasus, and, in turn, the peoples of the Caucasus, under a variety of leaderships, long opposed the Tsarist armies.

While the peoples of the south Caucasus, Armenia, Azerbaijan and Georgia, were by and large considered peoples that had more consequential dealings with the Ottoman and Iranian empires until they were conquered by the Russians in the nineteenth century, the peoples of the north Caucasus, Chechens, Ingush, Dagestanis, and so on (under the broad Russian generality of "Kavkazians"), had primary dealings with the Russian armies long before, As such, they were more subject to rule from Moscow, brought about by a string of Russian armies seeking to bring them to the most brutal heel. With the help of the "hosts" of Cossacks, who were usually self-governing allies of the Tsar of neighboring Caucasian territories, Russian rule was forced, or imposed, on the regions more than it was ever to be accepted, and many a times, principles of "divide and rule" had been used by the Russians Tsars to maintain its foothold across the Caucasus.

As such, in response, among others, particularly the Chechens and Ingush, known as the Vainakh or as Nakh peoples, and organized into clans, fought to preserve their nation throughout history with uprising after uprising. Differing from Russia's predominant Orthodox Christianity, these were Muslim peoples practicing the Shafi'i school of Sunni Islam. Their beliefs were egalitarian, and they strongly supported personal freedom, but also dedication to their teips, or clans.

As such, befitting this traditionally antagonistic relationship between peoples of the North Caucasus and Russians and their strikingly different origins, of raids and rebellion, both ordinary and elite Russians oftentimes had, once again, a love-hate relationship with the peoples of the Caucasus. The Caucasian peoples both mystified and confounded their Russian neighbors, with stereotypes abound for each side towards the other. From the approach, as discussed by other social analysts,[34] said Caucasians in some ways have a certain mystique in that they are seen as being unable to be tamed; in that context, their women are mysterious, their men are vicious and ready to fight and die for their honor.

This parallel continues into present-day post-Soviet Russia. In addressing predominant conflict, Ukraine (arguably) notwithstanding, perhaps first and foremost for the Putin regime, elites, and ordinary people, is the relationship between larger Russia and the most restive region of the North Caucasus, Chechnya. Well-known are the two Chechen wars of 1994 to 1996 and 1999 to 2006 where Russia has once again tried to tame, with varying levels of success, specifically the Chechen region. President Putin himself came to power in 1999–2000 saying that he would bring Chechnya safely to Russian rule and reinforce Russia's territorial integrity, which was a constantly debated issue of the earlier Chechen war and, more broadly, the entire 1990s decade for Russia.

In this endeavor, as mentioned before, Russia has had broadly mixed results. The stability of the "house" of Russia has been entirely dependent in the 2010s-decade on the relative peace following the 1990s and 2000s wars in Chechnya. Having put so many people and so much treasure into fighting the wars in the Chechen region, Russia is in a position where it cannot be perceived to attempt a "reset" (to use that wonderful President Barack Obama et al. terminology) without completely endangering the entire structure of Russia's current political and territorial boundaries. Therefore, Russia is wedded to Chechnya, and indeed, aspects of Chechnya are wedded to Russia, which brings us to Putin's man in Chechnya, Ramzan Kadyrov.

Russia's support for the son of an earlier warlord, Ramzan Kadyrov, the young Chechen pro-Russian leader of the region has been the linchpin of the Russian strategy for most of the 2000s and 2010s decades. Kadyrov became Putin's "man" in Chechnya under rather violent circumstances; to again mention his father, Ramzan took power after his father, Akhmed Kadyrov, was killed in a football stadium explosion in May 2004. Under the circumstances of today's modality of Russian power in the Chechen territory, being Putin's man there, Ramzan can get away with quite a lot in his region. This is in fact something that Kadyrov is proud of and which has been, it must be said, quite tough and at least a little impressive. In modern day Russia, where governors serve at the whim of Putin's rule, Kadyrov's power in his area, and even perhaps out of it on occasion, is unmatched.

Purportedly, many of Kadyrov's policies do not align with Russian law and the Russian constitution, much to the dismay of many across Russia who (not surprisingly) believe that blatantly unlawful exceptions to the Russian constitution should not exist. The laundry list of such policies is long and varied, including the allegation that he has his own private army.[35] [36] [37] [38] [39] [40] [41]

Yet, for all the serious allegations and supposed breaches of the Russian constitution, given Kadyrov's alleged "army," his influence, and his hold over Chechnya, President Putin remains beholden to the younger vital leader of that potentially restive region. As suggested, many of Kadyrov's policies, if true, contradict Russian constitutional law, but acknowledging Russia's dependence on his ability to keep Chechnya quiet, the Putin regime is not eager to broach the subject of dismissal, some other type of punishment, or pass legislation that would upset the young Chechen leader. As of late 2017, only Kadyrov himself, seemingly much to the distress of the Kremlin which denies any such possibility, can speak of his own resignation from his post.[42]

The Russian people at the same time recognize the potential restiveness of Chechnya and, in my research, are necessarily standoffish about how Russia deals with the region, and the North Caucasus in general. Ordinary Russians are concerned about those regions but are understandably hesitant to speak on the subject.

For example, I asked one Russian guy of whom I respect about what he thought about Chechnya's unique position in Russia; he shrugged and told me that as we were in public, we shouldn't speak openly about such things. Later, he told me that I should watch my back traveling around Russia and avoid "Kavkazians" in general. I've found this reluctance to discuss the issue as being quite common in many parts of Russia outside the North Caucasus.

As such, Caucasians are somewhat feared, according to their reputation and looks; parallel to this, said peoples are often checked constantly when police are around. I myself have witnessed darker-skinned people regardless of origin being routinely picked out of crowds by the police in metro stations and train stations across Russia. Regarding workers' and living equality, it is still common for vacancy advertisements across greater Russia to ask for "Славянская внешность," or "Slavic appearance," when hiring or renting respectively, which I posit is blatantly directed against the hiring of Caucasians and/or Muslims in general. Though the North Caucasus is (almost) quiet as of the late 2010s, for ethnic Russians, any confrontations with Caucasians in general society inspire further fear; a fear which is indicative of the overall nature of Russo-North Caucasus relations of the mid-2010s.

On the matter of Russia's and Russians' "friendship" with the peoples of the South Caucasus, the Armenians, Azerbaijanis, and Georgians, they are treated much more as foreign citizens are, but with the influx of immigrants coming from those regions to make money in somewhat-richer Russia to send home or to make a life there. Many of the markets across Russia that were once a haven for sellers from those countries have been shut-down, but in fact many of them are still in Russia, although not so prominently as they once were. Further, and much like the north Caucasians, they are subjected to enhanced document checks and to forced bribery more so than non-Caucasians.

On a country level, Georgia's desire to join Western institutions such as NATO, and following the Russo-Georgian war of 2008 which caused them to lose the pro-Russian regions of South Ossetia and Abkhazia to Russian occupation, has caused a focus of anti-Georgian verbiage and policies in their direction, namely the banning of many Georgian products from selling in Russia. On the other hand, Russia has a close friendship with Armenia thanks to Armenia's willingness to date to stay in Russia's "orbit," and to Russia's help with Armenia's war against Azerbaijan in their conflict over Nagorno-Karabakh. Correspondingly, Azerbaijan's relationship with Russia is less positive, although not to the extent of Georgia's.

All in all, the dynamic of Russia's relationship with the Caucasian peoples and countries is tenuous at best. To call them allies or "friends" with Russia is to invite profound overstatement, yet this is a significant sector in which Russia, and Russians, must engage relative to promoting stability within and on the edges of Russia's current borders.

THE EASTERN POWERS

In the modern era, Russia has had two preeminent foreign policy relationships of highest importance to its east. These are of course Russia's relationship with China and the same with Japan. As mentioned in in earlier chapters with the formation of early Russia, Mongolia once had a lot of influence on how Rus' came into being a long time ago, but that was another time and will not be covered so much here. South Korea is an economic power also, but not a predominant actor insofar as Russia's people go; North Korea and surrounding issues with the Kim Jong-Un regime are worthy of mentioning in time.

Bearing on the subject of this book, and especially in the western 60 percent (the far more populated part) of the country, ordinary Russians have minimal interpersonal and intercultural contact with Japanese culture or people and even less so with their Chinese counterparts. Nevertheless, these relationships should at least be covered here, given how important each are to Russia's general future.

Particularly concerning Russia's vast fairly-empty far eastern territory, as potential or current regional and/or world powers themselves, China and Japan are predominant. China is well-known for being an economic powerhouse, as well as its large population of over 1.3 billion people, compared to Russia's population of around 140 million. Japan is also well-known for being an economic powerhouse, and for its technology.

Today, Russia has an alliance with China within the context of the organization known as the Shanghai Cooperation Organization (SCO) and a contentious, but usually civil, relationship with Japan, revolving in part around claimed islands and continuing trade which has usually been equally beneficial.

Japan did not necessarily suffer enormous destruction, get invaded, or lose wealth at the hands of Russia (then the Soviet Union) during the Second World War, but Japan did lose a series of islands, the Kuriles, which remain an old point of some contention to the present-day. Levada Centre polling generally shows that the Russian people are against giving the islands to Japan, and additionally the Russian regimes, Soviet and post-Soviet, have held them as bargaining chips over the years in certain diplomatic discussions of note.[43]

Regardless, in the post-sanctions environment, Russia has sought to maintain a friendship with Japan, and Japanese goods are of great interest in modern-day Russia. Quite notably in my studies around the major cities, in recent years, even Japanese culture and cuisine have become, to a small extent, part of Russian society.

While maybe another could argue that it's just part of globalization coming to Russia, but non-Russian cuisines have come somewhat into vogue, particularly in the biggest cities, and I've notably met some big (Russian) fans of Japanese cuisine. While not being something I might have expected in my early years in studying Russia, the number of sushi places has exploded, with such chains as "Sushi Wok" and others making serious competition against American brands like McDonalds and Burger King.

From the opinions of a great many Russians I've known, although there is a sizable minority who hate such things; there is also a sizable percentage who indeed love the taste.[44]

The sushi phenomena, I believe, is one aspect that has added to a certain, albeit limited, degree of multiculturalism in Russian society which otherwise might not have existed, although it is difficult to develop an analytical structure on the subject. I would argue, strongly in fact, that in the wake of Russia's difficult relationship with Western countries, the rise and fall of McDonalds, if you will, the application of certain popular elements of Japanese culture within Russian society have been a notable departure and, perhaps, improvement on the normalized anti-Western depression in Russian cultural life. Again, other analysts could argue that such things are a "fad," that they have no roots in Russian culture and its popular everywhere, however, I do believe that anything is better than nothing.

On the question of China, cooperation in that sphere, in the grand scope of today's geopolitical atmosphere, has been Russia's only prevailing "acceptable" ally. As Marcin Kaczmarski wrote in April 2017: "China has been Russia's key political partner in the region. Similar views on international politics and similar interests form the basis for Sino-Russian political cooperation. [. . .] China remains Russia's only partner in the sphere of security and defense cooperation."[45]

For the Putin regime, the part about sharing similar views and interests when looking at how to deal with territorial issues parallel to Western powers has been of utmost importance.

Comparatively, China's role in the Russian view of allies, alliances, and friendship is a relatively new thing. While during the Cold War, they were semi-rivals for promoting Communism, Russia's and China's disagreements have been softened recently through negotiation and, as stated before, now the two have formed the Shanghai Cooperation Agreement (SCO), including several military agreements focused on the arms trade and mutual training exercises.

Further on the point, Russia is now betting rather large sums of money on China being a pivot of oil and gas (and natural resource development) consumption away from Western exports. The construction of Gazprom's wonderfully-named "Power of Siberia" pipeline aiming at supplying gas to China is epic in scope and equally wondrous in the likelihood of corruption involved in the mega-project.[46]

The predominant implication of all this in the modern era is centralized Eurasian security; that the two will watch each other's backs, possibly as a "defensive" military alliance, should one of the two take a step too far and engage in some military application that the Western powers really do not like.

In Russia's case, this has been in favor of Russian military conflicts with Ukraine, Georgia, potential the Baltic States, and over the skies around Europe/NATO. Also, in Russia's case is the use of nuclear and chemical weapons to assassinate people in the United Kingdom. In China's case, this has been in favor of China's maneuvers and aggressive actions against Taiwan and in the South China Sea, attempting to extend its territory through "building" new islands for military landing strips in the area.

The reality in this "cooperation" has however been far from strong. Continued disagreements have plagued the Sino-Russian relationship; some of them have been more complex than either would like to admit.[47] In fact, despite all the public statements, it is far from assured that either would seriously support the other in any future military scenario against the Western powers.

On the level of the ordinary Russian citizen however, and contrary to the Putin regime's periodic pronouncements of great Sino-Russian friendship, in my experience, very little of this has any lasting purview. Many Russians look on with some concern, perhaps not unjustified, as more Chinese settlers take residence in the east, and in eastern Russian cities like Vladivostok and others. Notably, at least in my research, Chinese culture has had less impact, especially in western Russian cities.

Overall, one must ask how all of this impacts the relationship of China and Russia, insofar as, for example, the Shanghai Cooperation Agreement and other such agreements between the two (relative) powers? It would be an overstatement to call the two "allies" per se, but they are not enemies either. It is in China's best interest to secure their broad border with Russia, should it decide to make a more serious "play," as it appears to be doing as of the mid-2010s, in the west Pacific.

It is in Russia's best interest to secure that same border, particularly because the eastern Russian frontier is so sparsely populated and little defended. It is also in Russian interests because of Putin's aggressions in the West and Russia could never dream of fighting a multi-front war in any case.

Associated with the relationship with China, but also very important as far as world peace is concerned, is Russia's relationship with North Korea. Indeed, North Koreans have representation in Russia's educational institutions and universities, and Russians I know from Moscow State University (amongst others) associate North Koreans in Russia with the students there. Also, in my own experience, there are North Koreans working in localized groupings around Russia, although I rarely met a great many of them personally. As studied by Alexander Gabuev of the Carnegie Moscow Center, and citing American State Department statistics, some estimated 50,000 North Koreans worked in the shadows (i.e., avoiding sanctions with Russian help) in Russia.[48]

As a long-term problem as of the late 2010s, the North Korean development of nuclear weapons is a continuing source of regional instability for all countries concerned. On the other hand, the continued six-way dance (sometimes two-way dance, sometimes no dance at all with the rise of U.S. President Donald Trump's own love-hate relationship with the North Korean leader) that China, Japan, South Korea, Russia, the United States, and North Korea engage in gives Russia an opportunity to appear as a peacemaker in some circumstances, and at other times as a disinterested observer. North Korean labor, on a small scale, also allows Russia to passively support North Korea, as much of the laborers money goes home, to circumvent and short-circuit any attempt at open regime change against North Korea, also giving Russia added sway in its regional foreign policy position. Nevertheless, while this whole issue causes much tension in the region, for Russia, it is oftentimes a side-note to Russia's larger relationship in the Far East.[49]

In substance, the Russian and Chinese peoples are far from natural allies, and their governments struggle to maintain any sort of alliance even in already established economic and military frameworks. China's powerful economy can only view Russia's as a comparative backwater; the true opportunities for large-scale trade are elsewhere. So then, there is a nervous alliance, on paper and in some actual, albeit very occasional, demonstration, between the two neighbors, where talk is very cheap, and the future is relatively-speaking a serious question mark.

CENTRAL ASIA

Caught in between the Russo-Chinese dynamic, and to a far lesser extent, the Russo-Japanese modern dynamic, lie the many countries of Central Asia. They no doubt predominate Putin's view of Russia's "sphere of influence," and Kyrgyzstan, Kazakhstan, Tajikistan, and Uzbekistan are current (as of 2017) members of the SCO as well. They however come under pressure from powers like Iran and China also, as well as Turkmenistan which represents a prominent "crossroads" in the region.

American intrusion into Central Asia in service of the American-led war in Afghanistan and its aftermath has brought more than a little hand-wringing to the Kremlin. Even India has its singular extra-territorial military base in Tajikistan, at Ayni. The Russians are not happy about this Indian base, by the way, and, as can be seen from the referenced article, they have made that feeling clear.[50] Useful to also note that Turkey has its own influence in the region though, via the many Turkic peoples there.

Further complicating all these security and economic arrangement, Kazakhstan, Kyrgyzstan, Uzbekistan, and Tajikistan are all members of the Collective Security Treaty Organization (CSTO), which has its own security structure and has agreements with the SCO.

Surely to the dismay of the Putin regime, with its fingers dipping in everything, the Kremlin holds a surely diminishing dominance over a fair amount of decision-making across Central Asia, and it is unclear how long even this limited positioning can last.

Russia still maintains a significant military presence in the Central Asian states, including military bases in Kyrgyzstan and Tajikistan.[51] One could call these countries to be allies of Russia, I would probably agree, but although, again to point out the difference, I doubt their friendship with Putin and his regime except on the most conciliatory level.

In the post-Cold War environment, for the Western "powers," America, Britain, France, Italy, et al., Asia and the Middle East have been where "the action is," such as it is. Focus on the rising countries of Asia, China and India, plus the complicated maelstrom of the Middle East, has occupied the defense, political and economic establishments of the West to no end, during and after the rise of radical extremism and Islamist terrorism's greatest singular demonstration of effect, the September 11, 2001 attacks in the United States. As of the twenty-first century in general, America wants to change the view of Central Asia away from that of what was once known as the Great Game: "The government of the United States, in particular—the leading player in this game—likes to downplay the continued validity of the idea of a game and pretend that the hectic shuffling for position among states and companies has no geopolitical significance."[52]

In opposition, the Putin regime no doubt sees the struggle in Central Asia as a "game" and as one that it intends to win. Such is the case also even outside Central Asia, as the regime has focused much of its attention on Ukraine, China, and on highly-questionable endeavors like the Syrian Civil War, on which the Putin regime has used as its own demonstration of Russian military technology and, to some degree, Russian military prowess.

Yet, for Russia, it is obvious that much of Asia's dynamism remains largely a mystery in some key ways. As mentioned at some points previous, concerning its distribution of friendship and alliances (if you will), Russia still uses its military and technologies as a carrot much as it did during the Cold War. While it is true that in military technology, Russia is still considered a global leader, this however ignores the economic argument of Asia. How Russia acts as an economic and financial ally in the region, to the degree it can, instead of as some kind of abstract wannabe-great power which the Putin regime still wishes to be, would be most impressive in gathering the friendship that the regime voices as necessary.

Put another way, for Russia, as like the predominant Western powers, Eurasia and the Middle East will continue to be of prime importance for the foreseeable future. The true test of Russia will be how best to build and take advantage of these potential friendships, both internally and externally, to improve the Russian position, without falling back on simply being a source for military technologies.

Further, concerning the people of Russia, the peoples of Central Asia inhabit the internal Russian landscape as well, with many Central Asians occupying the same space in Russian culture as south Caucasians (Georgians, Armenians, et al.), belonging but not fully "belonging." Many Central Asians are Islamic and suffer discrimination from that as well, and there is some evidence originating from a 2015 report by International Crisis Group that Islamic State (IS) has made inroads in those populations as well.[53] Traditionally the Central Asian republics were the poorer parts of the Soviet Union, and now as independent countries, they are somewhat poorer than modern Russia. As peoples, Central Asians were and are suffering from restrictive measures in Russia, but they have relatively more opportunities there than in their home countries.[54]

In parallel, I've had the great honor of being able to survey and interview a fair share of Central Asians living around Russia, but particularly in Moscow. In general, from my informal contacts among these groups, I've been told that life in Russia is difficult but bearable, much like many Russians told me all the time.

Again, this is not to say that there are no elements of discrimination, racism, religious bias, and/or ethnic dominion of Russians against Central Asians, like with many of the other nationalities discussed, indeed there are, it is instead to say that the positions of Central Asians in Russian culture are unremarkable as separate from other equivalent nationalities trying to live in Russia; many Central Asians, as with Caucasians, make money in the major cities and send it to wherever "home" is, and this is unlikely to change despite the Russian government's attempts to bulldoze and change their markets and other financial nexuses of living in-country.

THE "FAMILY" OF RUSSIA

Having examined and analyzed the both the Putin regime worldview of friendship and alliance abroad as well as the views of the Russian people on the same, consequently, for the Russian people, I will briefly break this down to what it means at the micro level, as opposed to the macro-level of talking friendship between states and peoples. For myself, this section is more personal than many of the previous; I have some great experience with the Russian family and have it to be one of the kindest in practice amongst all others.

Further, and last but far from least, it is worthy to at least mention that, insofar as this chapter goes, the family in Russia is of paramount importance, and that has not been surprising in my studies as it is characteristic of all cultural, ethnic, religious, and social boundaries which I have examined.

The geopolitical relationships, for most civic and ethnic Russians, are entirely secondary to the importance of domestic affairs. I cannot overemphasize this within any specific cleavage at issue.

For many ethnic Russians themselves, Russia is in the home, with Russian meals and Russian drink, much like many other peoples on the Earth. The same is true in view of the "other," non-Russians similarly share culture, food and drink, and any examination of the friendship and allies of Russia cannot forget to mention this.

There are stereotypes nonetheless, some of which have an element of truth. It has been my experience that in the views of ethnic Russians, as mentioned in the previous sections, the families of the Caucasian peoples are considered strong, also hostile when Russians recount strange, dark stories of how the people of the Caucasus deal with rival families (and clans, in that parallel relationship), "steal brides," and so on.

Non-Russians are equally dark when they recount the tendencies of Russian families, at least in my experience. An Azerbaijani-Russian man in Moscow told me some years back something to the effect that all Russian men get drunk and beat their wives. Of course, this is nonsense but as with many stories, it perhaps does have at least a grain of truth, as some such stories do. According to a recent report by the human rights organization, Stop Violence Against Women (StopVAW), "women in the Russian Federation experience domestic violence at an exceptionally high rate."[55]

Whatever the case may be, except for improved academic and cultural understanding, it is best to avoid such stereotypes and focus on the real issues within Russian families crossing all mentioned ethnic, religious, and social boundaries. Russian life revolves around the family, and Russian families are moderately large (at least traditionally). As with individuals, Russian families struggle with life against the "other." As I detailed in my first book, trust is a rare concept in Russian society; individuals lie to the government much as the government lies to the people. Also, however, individuals lie to each other making a cycle, and trust is only established between perhaps the closest family members.

So how does one characterize the "Family" in Russia? I, for one, characterize the concept as the closest bond possible in the context of the constant rhetoric and propaganda radiating from the state. The individual must battle the state and recognize the corruption therein; yet, if he or she is to prosper in modern Russia, some semblance of understanding and support must be granted the state, or more pointedly, the Putin regime. This is not a democracy except in the vague sense; instead it is an "electoral regime."

RUSSIA'S AND RUSSIANS' FRIENDS AND FAMILY—CONCLUSIONS

This section has examined the existential relationships and factual aspects of Russia as a global "ally," what Russia and the Russian people seek to "be" in the context of Russian friendship, of alliances made to other countries and to the western powers, and what Russia hopes to accomplish through these avenues of friendship. This section has also emphasized the differences between the ideals of friendship as concerning the Putin regime and, in somewhat opposition, towards Russians as a people. In some of the sections, I briefly examined the familial relationships and stereotypes of the civic and ethnic Russian family. As such, as I mentioned, I have nothing but the greatest respect for the Russian family, and the friendships that I have made with many a Russian.

The results of this study have not been pretty. The Russian state continues to attempt to establish friendships and alliances through old-world ideals. Russia believes that it should support allies in predominantly old-school methodologies, using hard treaties and military support, while emphasizing and de-emphasizing (sometimes at the same time, if that's possible) a concept of "sovereignty" according to its own will and desire (see the section on Russia's infiltration and annexation of Crimea). While this is antagonistic to the Western powers, these hard concepts are of primary importance to the Putin regime in its bid to be a global "player," if not a power.

In the meantime, as covered in many of the sections, Russians and the Russian family could not care less about such world power dogma, wishing only for a stable economy while at the same time supporting, as covered in other chapters, a Russia that could command respect. These concepts are complicated absolutely in the Russian case, and when discussing the Russian "house," many a times the external view is much more stable and perhaps even more impressive than the internal view. In this way, today's Russia cannot avoid being like the Soviet Union.

In few places can these concepts be clearer, and no greater demonstration of these vertices, than the Russian deployment of military forces to the Syrian civil war theater of operations. Russians, in my opinion, support and don't support this foreign adventure, again oftentimes at the same time. They support the venture in so far as Putin can present it as supporting stability and a world ally of Russia. Russians do not support it insofar as any possibility that Russian treasure or, more importantly, large numbers of Russian soldiers come home in body bags.

The people of Russia, that most important of resources of Russia, will support Putin because they still believe that Russia should be a capable friend and defender of the Russian "family" (or the regime's own concept of it as transposed by the Putin regime and state) abroad. Ordinary Russians, I posit, will not support Putin at that point in the future when too much is on the line and the future of the Russian family is not clear.

On this basis, in the next chapter, I will discuss the money of Russia, and how it is a great determiner of how the Russian people deal with the state and Putin regime, how the Putin regime deals internationally on financial issues, and how all of this can prop up, or bring down, the post-Soviet "house" of Russia.

NOTES

1. This is so common a sentiment that it is strange even to repeat it but given some of Russia's more confrontational policies of the last few years, I suppose it bears repeating here.
2. My own personal favorite is: Richard Sakwa's *Russian Politics and Society*, 4th edition, but he is criticized as being too much of a Russophile by fellow academics. See: Sakwa, Richard, *Russian Politics and Society*, 4th edition, Routledge, New York NY, 2008.
3. Galstyan, Areg, "Is the Eurasian Economic Union Slowly Coming Apart?," *National Interest*, 29 March 2017, Retrieved 16 April 2017, http://nationalinterest.org/feature/the-eurasian-economic-union-slowing-coming-apart-19947.
4. Fedorov, Yuri E., "Continuity and Change in Russia's Policy Towards Central and Eastern Europe," *Communist and Post-Communist Studies*, Vol. 46, 2013, p. 316, (pp. 315–26).
5. Poll conducted by WIN/Gallup International ~1,000 people in sixty-six countries globally, October–December 2016. Margin of error: +/-3.5 to 5 percent. Champion, Marc, "Four NATO Nations Would Pick Russia to Defend Them if Threatened: Poll," *Bloomberg*, 17 February 2017, Retrieved 18 February 2017, https://www.bloomberg.com/politics/articles/2017-02-17/melania-trump-s-slovenia-would-pick-russian-over-u-s-protection.
6. Fetterolf, Janell and Jacob Poushter, "Key Middle East Publics See Russia, Turkey and U.S. All Playing Larger Roles in Region," Pew Research Center, 11 December 2017, Retrieved 20 December 2017, http://www.pewglobal.org/2017/12/11/key-middle-east-publics-see-russia-turkey-and-u-s-all-playing-larger-roles-in-region/.
7. Survey of 1600 respondents, eighteen or older, from 137 population points of 48 regions of Russia. "Россия и мир," (In English): "Russia and World," *Levada Centre*, 10 April 2017, Retrieved 21 May 2017, http://www.levada.ru/2017/04/10/rossiya-i-mir-3/.
8. Trenin, Dmitri, "Russia is the house that Vladimir Putin built—and he'll never abandon it," *The Guardian*, 27 March 2017, Retrieved 27 March 2017, https://www.theguardian.com/commentisfree/2017/mar/27/russia-house-vladimir-putin-built-never-abandon.
9. "German Nationalist Petry Met With Putin Allies," *Newsmax*, 20 February 2017, Retrieved 29 March 2017, http://www.newsmax.com/World/Europe/EU-Germany-Russia-Nationalists/2017/02/20/id/774610/.
10. Partlow, Joshua, "The Soviet Union fought the Cold War in Nicaragua. Now Putin"s Russia is back.," *The Washington Post*, 8 April 2017, Retrieved 16 April 2017, https://www.washingtonpost.com/world/the_americas/the-soviet-union-fought-the-cold-war-in-nicaragua-now-putins-russia-is-back/2017/04/08/b43039b0-0d8b-11e7-aa57-2ca1b05c41b8_story.html?hpid=hp_hp-more-top-stories_centamrussia6pm%3Ahomepage%2Fstory&utm_term=.ead3f1c5168e.
11. I will not here discuss the Trump administration's dealings with the Putin regime during the 2016 American presidential election or during the transition after Trump won. I will leave that to the American Federal Bureau of Investigation and its

investigators. The only thing that I will say is to state the fact that multiple former and current members of the Trump administration are under scrutiny.

12. Lieven, Anatol, "A Poisonous Giant Russian Squid Ate Trump's Brain," *Valdai Club*, 7 April 2017, Retrieved 26 April 2017, www.valdaiclub.com/a/highlights/a-poisonous-giant-russian-squid-ate-trump-brain/?sphrase_id=64690.

13. As discussed in detail in previous chapters.

14. Wolczuk, Roman, *Ukraine's Foreign and Security Policy: 1991–2000*, RoutledgeCurzon, New York and London, 2002, p. 52.

15. The levels of personal animus towards Ukrainians as a people in Russian society, I've found, is very low, having conducted hundreds, if not thousands, interviews and informal conversations across Russia.

16. Based on my own research, the same is true with Ukrainians versus Russians.

17. Simmons, Katie, Bruce Stokes, and Jacob Poushter, "NATO Publics Blame Russia for Ukrainian Crisis, but Reluctant to Provide Military Aid," Pew Research Center, 10 June 2015, Retrieved 15 April 2017, http://www.pewglobal.org/2015/06/10/nato-publics-blame-russia-for-ukrainian-crisis-but-reluctant-to-provide-military-aid/.

18. Wilson, Andrew, *Ukraine Crisis: What It Means for the West*, Yale University Press, New Haven CT, 2014.

19. Wilson, Andrew, "Russia's Unfinished Business in Ukraine," American Enterprise Institute, December 2017, p. 6, (pp. 1–7).

20. Again, for the Ukrainian argument, see, amongst others, see: Wilson, Andrew, *Ukraine Crisis: What It Means for the West*, Yale University Press, New Haven CT, 2014. [and] Wilson, Andrew, *The Ukrainians: Unexpected Nation*, Yale University Press, New Haven CT, 2000.

21. Kramer, Mark, "Why Did Russia Give Away Crimea Sixty Years Ago," "The Transfer of Crimea from Soviet Russia to Soviet Ukraine, 1954," Wilson Center, 19 March 2014, Retrieved 27 March 2017, https://www.wilsoncenter.org/publication/why-did-russia-give-away-crimea-sixty-years-ago.

22. Blackwell, Martin, "The Housing Question and Anti-Semitism: Soviet Authorities in Kyiv after World War II," *Krytyka*, December 2017, www.krytyka.com/en/articles/housing-question-and-anti-semitism-soviet-authorities-kyiv-after-world-war-ii. Further to: Blackwell, Martin, *Kyiv as Regime City: The Return of Soviet Power After Nazi Occupation*, University of Rochester Press, NY, 2012.

23. Not the least of which, pre-American presidential candidate Donald Trump (a fair amount of time before his presidency) in an interview in 2015. See: Walker, Shaun, "Trump discusses Ukraine and Syria with European politicians via video link," *The Guardian*, 11 September 2015, Retrieved 14 April 2017, https://www.theguardian.com/us-news/2015/sep/11/donald-trump-ukraine-video-link.

24. For a decent English language explanation of the different between "Ukraine" and "the Ukraine," see: Steinmetz, Katy, "Ukraine, Not the Ukraine: The Significance of Three Little Letters," *Time Magazine*, 5 March 2014, Retrieved 28 March 2017, http://time.com/12597/the-ukraine-or-ukraine/.

25. Wilson, Andrew, "Russia's Unfinished Business in Ukraine," *American Enterprise Institute*, December 2017, p. 5, (pp. 1–7).

26. Higgins, Andrew, "Evidence Grows of Russian Orthodox Clergy's Aiding Ukraine Rebels," *The New York Times*, 6 September 2014, Retrieved 6 December 2017, https://www.nytimes.com/2014/09/07/world/europe/evidence-grows-of-russian-orthodox-clergys-aiding-ukraine-rebels.html.

27. Ozcelik, Sezai, "Analysis of the Crimean Tatars Situation During the Occupation of Crimea by Russia in 2014 with the Conflict and Peace Studies Approach," E-Journal of Law, January 2015. See also: Williams, Brian Glyn, *The Crimean Tatars: The Diaspora Experience and the Forging of a Nation*, E.J. Brill Academic Pub, Leiden, 2001.

28. Wilson, Andrew, "The Crimean Tatar Question: A Prism for Changing Nationalisms and Rival Versions of Eurasianism," *Journal of Soviet and Post-Soviet Politics and Society*, Volume 3, No. 2, 2017.

29. R apoza, Kenneth, "American Companies Thriving In Russia: Is There Something To Be Ashamed About?," *Forbes*, 3 August 2016, Retrieved 5 April 2018, https://www.forbes.com/sites/kenrapoza/2016/08/03/headline-halah-t/#2cbe6885f991.

30. Braun, Ariel, "Resetting Russian–Eastern European relations for the 21st century," *Communist and Post-Communist Studies*, Vol. 45, 2012, pp. 397–98.

31. Yalowitz, Kenneth and William Courtney, "Belarus: Between Russia and the West," *National Interest*, 29 March 2017, Retrieved 16 April 2017, http://nationalinterest.org/blog/the-buzz/belarus-between-russia-the-west-19943.

32. Holodny, Elena, "Russia's Brain Drain is Astounding," *Business Insider*, 2 December 2014, Retrieved 15 April 2017, http://www.businessinsider.com/russia-brain-drain-putin-ukraine-crimea-2014-12.

33. "Российский военный погиб в Сирии в результате нападения боевиков," (In English): "Russian soldier died in Syria as a result of militant attack," *Interfax*, 20 April 2017, Retrieved 25 April 2017, http://www.interfax.ru/world/559326.

34. See: de Waal, Thomas, *The Caucasus: An Introduction*, Oxford University Press, Oxford UK, 2010.

35. In the newest (as of 2017) version, Kadyrov's men (the "Kadyrovtsi") are involved in the setting up of the Putin regime's new National Guard. See: Shlapentokh, Dmitry, "The Kremlin's Last Resort: Kadyrovtsi in Russia's National Guard," *Central Asia-Caucasus Analyst (CACI)*, 03 March 2017, Retrieved 15 April 2017, http://www.cacianalyst.org/publications/analytical-articles/item/13430-the-kremlin-last-resort-kadyrovtsi-in-russias-national-guard.html.

36. Souleimanov, Emil, "Nemtsov's Assassination and the Chechen Trace," *CACI*, 18 March 2015, Retrieved 15 April 2017, http://www.cacianalyst.org/publications/analytical-articles/item/13164-nemtsov%E2%80%99s-assasination-and-the-chechen-trace.html.

37. Souleimanov, Emil, "Chechen Units Deployed to Eastern Ukraine," *CACI*, 04 June 2014, Retrieved 15 April 2017, http://www.cacianalyst.org/publications/analytical-articles/item/12990-chechen-units-deployed-in-eastern-ukraine.html.

38. "Chechen Leader Kadyrov Denies Sending Troops to Ukraine," *BBC*, 28 May 2014, Retrieved 15 April 2017, http://www.bbc.com/news/world-europe-27599836.

39. Ferris-Rotman, Amie, "ANALYSIS-Sharia law threatens Moscow control in Muslim Chechnya," *Reuters*, 26 August 2010, Retrieved 15 April 2017, http://www.reuters.com/article/idUSLDE67O0S0.

40. "Russian Daily Denies Investigative Journalist Fled Chechnya After Threats To Life," *RFE/RL*, 15 May 2015, Retrieved 15 April 2017, http://www.rferl.org/a/russia-chechen-child-marriage-milashina/27018364.html.

41. Milashina, Elena, "Убийство чести," (in English: "Honor Murders,") *Novaya Gazeta*, 3 April 2017, Retrieved 15 April 2017, https://www.novayagazeta.ru/articles/2017/04/01/71983-ubiystvo-chesti. See also: Eleftheriou-Smith, Loulla-Mae, "More than 100 gay men 'sent to prison camps' in Chechnya," *The Independent*, 12 April 2017, Retrieved 15 April 2017, http://www.independent.co.uk/news/world/europe/chechnya-gay-men-concentration-camps-torture-detain-nazi-ramzan-kadyrov-chechen-russia-region-a7677901.html.

42. "Kremlin says head of Chechnya to remain despite talk of quitting," *Reuters*, 27 November 2017, 7 December 2017, https://www.reuters.com/article/us-russia-chechnya-kremlin/kremlin-says-head-of-chechnya-to-remain-despite-talk-of-quitting-idUSKBN1DR0ZA.

43. "Спор России и Японии вокруг Курильских островов," (In English: "Dispute Between Russia and Japan over Kurile Islands,") *Levada Center*, 5 August 2016, Retrieved 15 April 2017, http://www.levada.ru/2016/08/05/spor-rossii-i-yaponii-vokrug-kurilskih-ostrovov/.

44. This is a very informal conclusion, I know, but I feel it is reliable. My attempts at documenting what might be called the sushi phenomena in modern Russia have met with profoundly mixed results. While some more nationalistic Russians consider sushi to be inedible and unworthy of their attention, I've known at least an equal number of

Russians, including very close friends and associates who love the cuisine and are quick to ask for it when available. Many Russians, like on other subjects, simply shrug and don't see Japanese cuisine as anything special.

45. Kaczmarski, Marci, "Russia in East Asia: Ambitions Fall Short of Reality," *Intersection*, 6 April 2017, Retrieved 26 April 2017, http://intersectionproject.eu/article/russia-world/russia-east-asia-ambitions-fall-short-reality.

46. Foy, Henry, "Russia's $55bn pipeline gamble on China's demand for gas," *Financial Times*, 3 April 2018, Retrieved 3 April 2018, https://ig.ft.com/gazprom-pipeline-power-of-siberia/.

47. "China and Russia: the world's new superpower axis?," *The Guardian*, 7 July 2015, Retrieved 15 April 2017, https://www.theguardian.com/world/2015/jul/07/china-russia-superpower-axis.

48. Burrows, Emma and Matthew Chance, "Russia's Hidden World of North Korean Labor," *CNN*, 16 January 2018, Retrieved 17 January 2018, http://www.cnn.com/2018/01/15/europe/russia-north-korea-labor-intl/index.html.

49. Notably, Russia overall is actually one of the few countries in the far eastern region which has a significant interest in a lessening of tension on, as well as even unification of, the Korean peninsula, as a united Korea could be a noted source for future oil and gas development and pipeline construction, that being Russia's favorite subject in foreign, economic, and world financial polity. Comparatively, Japan fears the potential powerhouse of a united Korea, and China, despite North Korea's periodically annoying behavior, likes the military barrier that North Korea provides relative to American troops in South Korea.

50. Sharma, Rajeev, "India's Ayni military base in Tajikistan is Russia-locked," Russia Behind the Headlines, 26 October 2012, Retrieved 15 April 2017, http://in.rbth.com/articles/2012/10/26/indias_ayni_military_base_in_tajikistan_is_russia-locked_18661. Also see this article, which refers to the base at Farkhor, and not Ayni: The Hindu, "India to revive military base in Farkhor, Tajikistan," *The Hindu* (Indian Defense website), 20 July 2012, Retrieved 15 April 2017, http://indiandefence.com/threads/india-to-revive-military-base-in-farkhor-tajikistan.20385/.

51. Marat, Erica, "Russia Seeks Long-Term Military Presence In Tajikistan and Kyrgyzstan," *Eurasia Daily Monitor*, Volume: 8, Issue: 174, 22 September 2011, Retrieved 15 April 2017, https://jamestown.org/program/russia-seeks-long-term-military-presence-in-tajikistan-and-kyrgyzstan/.

52. Brauer, Birgit, "Central Asia: The Game Revisited," *The Impact of Asian Powers on Global Developments*, ed. E. Reiter et al., Springer, Berlin, 2004.

53. Tynan, Dierdre, "Islamic State Threatens Central Asia," *International Crisis Group*, 8 June 2015, Retrieved 9 December 2017, https://www.crisisgroup.org/europe-central-asia/central-asia/islamic-state-threatens-central-asia.

54. Oppelaar, Iris, "Central Asia and Islamic State: The Russian Connection," *The Diplomat*, 8 March 2017, Retrieved 9 December 2017, https://thediplomat.com/2017/03/central-asia-and-islamic-state-the-russian-connection/.

55. "Violence Against Women in the Russian Federation," *Stop Violence Against Women*, Last updated October 2014, Retrieved 14 April 2017, http://www.stopvaw.org/russian_federation.

SIX

The Money of Russia

INTRODUCTION

As Putin regime officials are apt to announce, Russians should keep their money in Russia to share in Russia's fate.[1] These statements often refer to Russian oligarchs with foreign holdings, state workers, rent-seekers, and those with money restricted through whatever processes internationally and by the Russian state, but the self-serving nature for the Putin regime is undeniable.

In few other highly developed countries of relatively-high standard of living, in view of the relative luxury of at least a very significant portion of the generalized population, does the bevy of state promises combine with a status quo where self-support and abeyance to the regime require an on-going balancing act more than in modern Russia. The Putin regime also promotes the theme of an Independent Russia insofar as the money of Russia is concerned, but there is much question as to whether this is tenable; most likely, it is not. Transparency in business is also a key factor in the limitation of Russia's "money," but that is clear for everyone who studies the subject.

Things are not looking especially brighter in future: according to Vnesheconombank (VEB) analysts, data from Rosstat, and additional interesting analysis from economist Anton Tabach, as of May 2017, Russians' disposable income fell by some 7.6 percent by year, falling backwards in real terms to the spring of 2009 during the previous financial crisis.[2]

Comparatively, Russia's economy is just behind the U.S. state of New York, according to Newsweek in 2016.[3] In regard to the Gross Domestic Product (GDP), adjusted for Purchasing Power Parity (PPP, "the sum value of all goods and services produced in the country valued at prices prevailing in the United States in the year noted"[4]), Russia ranks much better, behind the United States, but ahead of France and the United Kingdom.[5]

Whatever the case, despite all the promises of a varying form of welfare state, where the regime has at times effectively and traditionally guaranteed a viable social financial safety net, the Russian people cannot trust what their government says and individually must be self-reliant. I do not necessarily maintain that relative self-reliance is a curse, far from it in some cases—there is little wrong with having the wherewithal to provide for yourself. The overall paradigm does however create a society in these circumstances where those least able to protect themselves are routinely and quickly thrown under the bus in favor of adventurous elites and friends of the regime who seek to make money and pay few if any taxes. Those elites thereby have comparatively minor limitations placed upon them beyond supporting the Putin regime and maybe (maybe!) not being outspoken about their spending and property ownership (although few stick to the latter; the former is an absolute must): "The annual global wealth study published by the financial services group Credit Suisse says a mere 110 Russian citizens now control 35 percent of the total household wealth across the vast country."[6]

As I wrote in my first book, this was part of the culture of common lies that pervades Russian society, where the state lies to the people, and the people lie to the state, and to their fellow citizens to fight to get ahead and provide for daily subsistence.

The question over continuing economic reform has perhaps best been explained by Peter Rutland in detailing the struggle between modernizers, who believe in embracing Western market institutions, and nationalists, who think that such an embrace would denigrate Russian identity and cultural norms. Not to lessen Putin's role in this failure, however, Rutland further (and correctly) notes that, not unlike other countries such as India or Brazil in an indecisive phase of development and/or reform, Russia has failed to find any third-way between those two positions.[7]

For a country the size of Russia, with land and resources available, to not be able to find some way to spur economic growth without somehow perceiving to "lose" Russian identity (if this is even possible, I might add), that is an amazing part of the crux of Russia, a crucial failure of the Putin regime, and worthy of little short of amazement. Furthermore, the amount of rent-seeking on natural resource-related policy hinders any development on most (if not all) other progressive polity.

In line with the arguments presented in this book, the "house" of Russia in the post-Soviet era, I will posit, has been built economically on three relatively (but not completely) co-equal economic and financial pillars on which the country has been unable to diversify from. These pillars are (1) failed and incomplete privatization, (2) dependency on natural resource sales, and (3) the shadow economy, or, more specifically, state (and corresponding elites') financial and economic manipulation(s) in turn reliant on advantageous leanings in and against domestic and international holdings.

Most notably, opportunistic angles on all these facets keep much of Russia's population locked at subsistence level but enhances Russia's elite rich. Russia's still-prospering elites, as we discuss here, are dependent on these "pillars" continuing, and there is little that the people can do to affect them, short of a new revolution. The Putin regime has to play off its unstable popularity by ensuring that all the "pillars" are balanced. While the general population cares nothing about the elite rich and the oligarchs, they desire Russia to be treated with respect (as discussed in chapter 3). In this atmosphere, friends of the regime benefit; those that are not friends end up in exile or in prison, and so the status quo will continue for the conceivable future.

While Putin regime allies still make money, their capabilities are somewhat offset by new 2014-on sanctions against Russia enthused by the desire to punish those responsible for the horrid death of anti-corruption accountant Sergei Magnitsky in Russian prison and enforced by outside actors, such as the United States Congress, where oligarchs close to the regime (i.e., "significant senior foreign political figures and oligarchs in the Russian Federation, as determined by their closeness to the Putin regime and their net worth") are increasingly penalized and (theoretically) encouraged to separate themselves from the regime, the competitive arena among Russian elites is still a very rewarding place.[8]

Indeed, for those "oligarchs" which have already taken their money and owned property overseas, since around 2012 encouraging a repatriation or "re-nationalization of wealth," (referring again to Medvedev's quote at the beginning of this chapter) the Russian government is busy making it financially attractive to return their money to Russia.[9]

Uncle V. V. Putin will be more than happy to welcome those oligarchs' wealth "home" when they get tired of dodging investigators overseas.

Yet, and notably, sanctions, the beloved leverage of the West, do not necessarily deter all aspects of Russia's economic situation. As found by reportage by the Wall Street Journal, Russian-West trade increased in the years after sanctions started in response to the Crimea annexation.[10] Not surprisingly, the Putin regime is not eager to publicize that Russia's economic growth could be separated from sanctions-targeted pro-Putin interests, even overseas holdings, but the opposition has failed to make light of it either.

Indicative of these affairs, and the hazards therein, but still far above the heads of most all ordinary Russians and remaining reminiscent of the past, Russian elites still fight for position and influence as they revolve around Putin himself. In 2017, when former Economy Minister Alexei Ulyukayev, under highly questionable circumstances, was accused and convicted (and sentenced to eight years imprisonment) for allegedly taking an extorted bribe[11] from Putin friend (and oil company Rosneft head) Igor Sechin, an observer cannot help but remember historical occurrences of the Stalin era when equally high elites disappeared into penal colonies.[12]

Putting that aside, it also must be said that the three pillars of the Russian "house" are what drives Russia and the Russian state but do not necessarily represent the base-level economy in any functional order. Always, there are still relevant services and consumer goods markets for bread, cupcakes, milk, and baby food, but these do not underpin and source the Putin regime's efforts to keep itself in power, in that those factors do not pay the bills; no, that is done through maintaining financial reserve sourcing (the so-called "rainy-day funds," which have been looted in recent years) and accounts based largely on natural resource sales thereby subsidizing pensions and human services with enormous profits remaining expatriated. Stratfor groups the "rainy-day" funds into the "Central Bank Reserves," the (as-of-2017-defunct[13]) "Reserve Fund," and the "Wealth Fund." Beyond that, Russia is and will be borrowing more heavily internationally to keep the ship afloat.[14] Some lining of regime pockets is also in small part based on international niche markets in specific areas, such as the sale of weapons on ready markets.

All that said, as of 2017, Russia's individual taxation system is complex but not especially notable, with a 13 percent flat tax on residents and a 30 percent tax on non-residents of Russia; this system due to reforms that the Putin regime put in place early in Putin's terms and they too are used to support the Putin regime's policies. Seeking to bring home money held overseas to support Russia's financial situation, the Putin regime has taken to offering tax amnesty on capital levied for elites who would bring it back to Russia.

Concerning a new second amnesty (after a first around the time of the Ukraine invasion(s):

> Russia rolled out a similar amnesty program during the worst of the conflict in Ukraine, which coincided with a plunge in oil prices that triggered the country's longest recession of the Putin era. That 18-month initiative, the results of which haven't been disclosed, "didn't work as well as we'd hoped," Finance Minister Anton Siluanov said. Unlike that plan, this one waives Russia's 13 percent tax on personal income, according to Dmitry Peskov, Putin's spokesman.[15]

Also politicized, a Value-Added Tax (VAT) is paid at a now 20 percent rate, which someone living in Russia can see itemized on almost every store receipt they receive, though, wisely for the Putin regime, the VAT is less or non-existent on the basics, i.e., eggs, meat, fish, etc. While there is a constant push-and-pull between regions and localities concerning revenue, which is also predominantly centralized to Moscow through which taxation is collected (and no doubt a little disappears all along the way through this cycle, not to mention that Moscow is solely in charge of distribution to regions reinforcing Kremlin policy), this is all also, in my experience, far above the heads of many ordinary Russians. To say they are universally apathetic is presumptuous; instead, the importance of staying alive and feeding their families is more important than worrying about center-region tax distribution.

Yet, the Putin regime also can "enjoy" the perception that, in Russia, economics is seen as a "zero-sum game," in that the people subjectively understand that, for someone to "win" in Russia, someone else must lose. I've been told more times than I can begin to recall by ordinary Russians that "they" will lose regardless, while rich elites will gain; a sentiment not so different perhaps from other countries. However, this of course de facto aids in support for authoritarian regimes in general, and support for the Putin regime in this case: "in Russia this principle [that of sharp inequality] was embodied in very simplified utilitarian formula and became a typical example of a zero-sum game. Attitudes to reform were contaminated by the practices of privatization, the fall in output and in real incomes, and the chaos of the 1990s."[16]

Further, without the transference and hard currency production of the three pillars discussed here, the Russian state would be unable to maintain even the basic idea of a "social contract" that it holds with the Russia people. That social contract is, to put it most basically here: the Russian people shouldn't ask too many questions and the Putin regime should keep order and most social services going. Putin has already tried to manage and water down this contract, with far from certain results: "after a decade of welfare retrenchment during the 1990s, the Putin regime has re-constructed a narrower, more strategic 'market social contract' that shapes and constrains key areas of contemporary social and labour policies."[17]

Despite this contract though, which has been a feature of Russian political history from the first Soviet constitutions in which Soviet citizens had many rights and requirements—on paper—but (in reality) few if any at all, post-Soviet Russia is in many sectors failing its people. For example, although on paper, Russian citizens are supposed to have something approaching nearly-free health care, due to lack of investment and money, the health care system is falling into ruin and requires the purchase of private health care insurance, unless of course you have the personal money to pay or bribe your way into easy care.

The stories of abominable care are becoming widespread,[18] and is one representation of the pressure the Russian state is being put under by lower oil prices, having to inject money into the economy from "rainy-day" funds which in earlier times used to steady the bankers and all in all keep confidence in Putin that nothing was happening close to the "edge." When oil prices were closer to 100 dollars a barrel rather than surfing below 40–50 (although oil prices have rebounded somewhat as of

2017–2018[19]), that currency was fueling the social contract for him, thereby keeping the people happy; the oil drop also keeps in mind the parallel aspect of just how much the difficulties of continued Western sanctions are adding to the decrepit environment in Russia for its poorest citizens.

There is already polling evidence that shows that the Russian people are beginning to seriously doubt the Putin regime's ability to maintain the social contract. From April 2017 polling data by Levada Center and reported on by Interfax, almost 40 percent of Russians accuse the Putin government of failing to fulfill the state's duties to the people.[20]

In daily life, it has been my own experience that Russians perceive that their country is at its weakest by observing these failures in the social contract and through the rampant corruption of the state; these are the hints that drive opposition figure Alexei Navalny's days. The failures in health care and pensions create a potential wedge in public support that could potentially drive Putin into unpopularity, if not from power, one day.

One additional consideration is because the state derives its strength in the most part from oil, natural gas, and other resources sales, at the expense of trying to diversify Russia's aging infrastructure and change its poor economic management, which "turns off" foreign investment and the like.

RUSSIA'S GOVERNMENT BUDGET AND WHERE IT STANDS

Russia's budget in the post-Soviet era has been consistently underpinned by the sales of oil, gas, and other fossil fuels, as I have noted previously and on which I will talk directly about in a later section. This section is however dedicated to looking at how the people of Russia perceive the budget and Russia's finances, what Russia pays for, what Russia can afford, and perhaps, most importantly, how does Putin choose to focus discretionary spending in view of the sanctions that I have discussed many times previously in this book.

As would be unlikely to surprise no long-time resident of Russia, given the current financial and budgetary decisions of Russian policy makers, and with the Putin regime bent on policies that will almost certainly maintain and heighten sanctions on Russia for at least the conceivable future, the current budget does the people few favors. Further, as seen from the anti-corruption Dmitry "Dimon" Medvedev protests of March 2017, the youth of Russia is waking up to the fact that even the most public of officials in Russia is skimming significant resources off the top of Russia's finances and budget in order to have an array of palatial houses and, as Alexei Navalny made fun of Medvedev for, a duck house.[21]

True, the protesters are looking deep for reasons to parody Medvedev, birdhouses (even for ducks) are not shocking (this author's own mother who lives on a bare pension has a house where she feeds the various birds). Nevertheless, Medvedev is a big target following Alexei Navalny's "Don't Call Him Dimon" video where many of Medvedev's flashier assets were made prominent.

Yes, the budget is a consistent problem for those tasked in Russia with dealing with it directly, regardless of corruption by some. As the World Bank said as recently as 2015: "Weakening growth and sharply lower commodity prices, however, have narrowed the room for Russian policy makers to maneuver."[22]

Add to that continued sanctions, and the possibility of new ones targeting Russia's ability to borrow internationally, and the Russian people have little to hope for. Nevertheless, the Putin regime struggles to maintain significant budgetary resources for the defense establishment. While there have been cuts, those are not nearly as drastic as some have calculated, and Russia's military budget remains protected to support the Putin regime's continued foreign policy initiatives.[23] Further, as Mark Galeotti correctly refers to, Russia is pulling from social and domestic programs in order to support defense programs that may or may not come to fruition given all the cost overruns and so on associated with those types of military procurement.[24] As mentioned before, Russia can also "isolate" its economy and continue its ranging military stances by supporting some foreign policy initiatives as well: "Russia has spent much of its energy in recent years strengthening its relationships in the Asia-Pacific and the Middle East to mitigate pressure from the West. So expanded sanctions on Russian sovereign debt would be a hindrance, but not a burden heavy enough to change Russian behavior."[25]

All in all, this makes for a sad time for Russia's citizenry, not that it is altogether unexpected. Those who expect or hope for change are ready to protest, but as I have stated earlier in this publication, it is unclear if Alexei Navalny and his fellow opposition leaders are ready to not only inspire large protests in the street on a single day, but also to inspire Russia's people to think of Navalny (or someone else) as a potential president. Russia's budget is a failure, though not yet a disaster, but if there is no alternative, ordinary Russians, including the ones that I have spoken with in my research, are not confident in any future opposition administration either, and that bodes well for the Putin regime.

FAILED PRIVATIZATION, AND HOW RUSSIA GOT TO THIS POINT

The failure of privatization is well-known, not all but a fair amount of the "money" of Russia disappeared to foreign bank accounts, with some minority getting rich and most Russians . . . , well, of course not. This is what makes a "Russian oligarch," by the way, and how that creature is distinguished from a Western billionaire. A Russian oligarch takes advantage of closeness to the Russian state and, in almost every case, privatization to enrich itself. A similar Westerner doesn't.

To the degree that privatization has made many ordinary members of the Russian public "property owners," the Putin regime has been trying to roll that back too, duly calling it "renovation." The Moscow government of Sergey Sobyanin, with the blessing of the Kremlin, is trying to tear down all the "Khrushchovy," all those five-story apartment blocks of the Khruschchev era in Moscow, in favor of building yet more commercial blocks.[26] Of course, this means displacing all the owners of the flats within those apartment blocks, which, due to post-Soviet privatization, had made a great many families and individuals in post-Soviet Russia into "property owners." This shows yet more failed privatization even in the Kremlin's general polity and, combined with Moscow's (and other cities) policies to attack small kiosks and other such smaller establishments and markets, will make Moscow (and likely the other major cities) yet more controlled by rich elites who are, in turn, dependent on the Kremlin.

Indeed, some doubt whether the Putin regime wants economic expansion or not, and privatization is a good way of continuing corruption without causing a situation where the Putin regime would have to meet higher hopes. The Putin regime in fact has quite a lot of incentive to keep expectations decidedly low and dealings extremely opaque. Looking at Russia's economic situation parallel to continued privatization and, given post-Ukraine conflict sanctions and a weaker global oil market (as has been discussed throughout), Russia needs its people to have little hope and expect little in the way of future growth.

Mid-2010s deficits, projected at 3.2 percent as of 2017, in the Gross Domestic Product have economic advisers in the Kremlin reeling and looking for the most practical ways (i.e., through privatization) to deal with the situation that Russia finds itself in. Against high real interest rates (as of 2016 the second highest in the world) and a recession in manufacturing, Russian economic growth is steadily declining and not projected to begin at any point in the realistically definable future, and, again, the regime has arguably an interest in keeping it that way.

According to senior fellow at the Kennan Institute, Maxim Trudolyubov: "The Kremlin does not want to achieve economic growth by any means that would require softening its foreign policy stance, empowering the middle class, or unleashing a spending spree."[27]

Hence, with Russia's adventurous foreign policy, any economic growth would cause ordinary Russians to ask for more, but that "more" would of course not be forthcoming. Coupled with the need to keep the regime happy through corresponding corruption, Putin's people are becoming even more willing to resort to selling off the state's assets and properties, like those most-public natural areas and parks, such as the Khimki forest in northern Moscow where developers want to bulldoze an entire forest to make way for a highway.[28]

Privatization, therefore, is a good bait and switch deal where the regime can seem to be progressive, making the argument that state assets can be better run in private hands, while keeping the money coming in for the Putin regime and, at the same time, not having to worry about an unduly excited populace.

NATURAL RESOURCES

Natural resource sales have been the economic pivot on which the Russian state has relied on funding for all the post-Soviet era. As mentioned before, during good times of higher oil prices, Russia did save up a fair amount of money which has been used in the post-Ukraine invasion environment to prop up the regime. Plus, Russia, as mentioned, is trying to pivot towards China with the "Power of Siberia" pipeline and so on.

Indeed, much has been made by foreign analysts[29] of Russia's inability to maintain these funds in the hard times that are the mid-2010s (and which are projected to last for some years more). The Putin regime must make outlays for pensions and other social services based on petroleum sales and money saved in supporting accounts, for without them, it is highly unlikely that Putin can stay popular for an unlimited amount of time. Under the pressure of foreign sanctions, one can logically ask how Russia can maintain this.

The answer is that Putin must routinely return to aggressive geopolitics to hope to break the pressure against Russia, and thence save his regime. Every time the Putin regime has been in danger, it has used foreign policy and military might to reengage the citizenry in its support. When the Bolotnaya Square protests happened, the response was, almost as a natural occurrence, the Ukraine adventure(s).

For its part, the Putin regime rejects any restrictions on its freewheeling use of military adventures and Moscow-backed economic organizations by couching them in the nauseating repetitive accusation that the West is trying to surround Russia. In an interview with National Interest on 24 March 2017, the Russian foreign minister, Sergei Lavrov, refused the earlier Obama administration's attempts to reach agreements with Russia, referring to them as Obama's desire "to take over this geopolitical space around Russia without caring what Moscow might think."[30]

Whatever Putin or Lavrov might say, this does not however fix the long-term problems of Russia and how it funds itself. In the last few years, as is well-known, the price of oil has dropped precipitously (albeit with some rebound). Combined with that, the refusal of OPEC countries including Saudi Arabia to take steps to bring up the price of oil and petroleum puts Russia in a declining economic position.[31] Naturally, the Putin regime's mouthpiece Sputnik blames American "dominance" for OPEC's refusal.[32] Russia cannot rely on the sale of manufacturing or industry products, partly because of technological inferiority and partly because sellers in other countries have mastered or undercut the markets for anything that Russian factories might produce for the export markets.

As discussed in the earlier chapter on the skill-sets and technologies of Russia, the inaccessibility of foreign technologies and parts also preclude Russia from tapping into many of the broad petroleum fields of Siberia and around the Arctic Circle. Without partnerships with Western oil companies, Russia can have "possession" of many potentially lucrative fields, aided by an expansive military effort to declare for Russian primacy as much far-northern land and seabed as possible, but no way to tap those fields.

As such, likely for as long as Western sanctions last, Russia is both limited in versatility and in expansion; it is locked in a smaller "box," if you will, and there is little hope for an exit door in the conceivable future. In that way, albeit far from total, a confrontational attitude is dominant from Western quarters.

Many sanctions have been dependent on the return of Ukraine's Crimea to Ukraine, and, depending on Western elections, who could win them, and the fate of the American president Trump, more such restrictions could potentially be applied to that requirement. While, as justifiably pointed out by at least one analyst,[33] sanctions are limited in scope and while they do contribute to the Putin regime's "us-against-the-world," argument, sanctions do at least constrict Russia's economy to a limited degree, and these restrictions mean real difficulties for ordinary Russians.

So, therefore, Russia is given a choice of whether to give up land and/or ambition to gain land and/or ambition. Concerning Russia's need for access to more natural resources in the future and, given the fact that there is little evidence of something new or magical happening, for lack of a better phrase, the Putin regime is to some degree, "stuck."

Looking at the Putin regime's past behavior, of course it will not acknowledge this box that it is stuck in. So, barring a new sea change in the global political climate, and barring the possibility that Putin might actually "stare down" his foreign political opponents or (and it might be possible) find a practical ally in the new American Trump administration (given the restrictions that the U.S. Congress has put on Trump, this seems unlikely), it is more likely that Putin will decide to simply continue Russia's current behavior. That is, by saying that Russia will find new replacement technologies for Western ones (as discussed previously, unlikely) and continue to butt heads with the walls of the box that Russia is in.

MANIPULATION ON HOLDINGS, BANKS, AND THE SHADOW ECONOMY

Lastly, the Putin regime and the parallel elite sector relies on the constant financial movement and security of all types of currency and the laundering of money, both from domestic holdings (including the continuation of privatization as mentioned in that section, thereby kicking back myriad levels of currency to the regime) and from international holdings in offshore bank accounts (detailed in the Panama Papers scandal in 2015 on),[34] including the international shelf accounts as publicized most recently from the Papers-revealed Mossack Fonseca affair (although Russia seems at first glance to be less affected),[35] and also can be represented by the empty fancy office buildings owned by elite Russians in cities like London.[36]

These are all significant aspects in how Putin and his regime both hold power and seek to maintain the wealth of their inner circle(s). Once their wealth is gathered, insofar as it held domestically, the Putin regime's hold on banking in Russia and the transference through sympathetic and opportunistic trading outside Russia further secures their wealth far from the prying eyes of challenges to the regime's status quo.

Of course, the shifting number of banks in Russia, and each bank's constituency and how they connect to the global movement of money in service of Russia and its interests, is a matter of much discussion and investigatory journalism for the brave observer; some of the secrets of Russia's banking industry are closely held in Putin's Russia. Bloomberg's Evgenia Pismennaya and Gregory White count some six hundred banks across the expanse that is Russia, up to and including Russia's recent efforts to try to consolidate its banking industry while certainly serving the purposes of the state at the same time.[37]

It must be said that, through the Governor of Russia's Central Bank, Elvira Nabiullina, the Putin regime has to some extent stabilized Russia's economy and currency. This is helped by Putin's added military spending noted in chapter 3. As a leading figure, Nabiullina has maintained Putin's trust since the beginning of his presidency in 2000, and she has been a tough overseer of economic policies throughout Russia's difficulties in this period. As her four-year term is finished in June 2017, Putin nominated her for a new five-year term in March 2017.[38]

Some well-known outside critics, like Anna Nemtsova in 2015, even believe that she could be a threat to Putin's corrupt cronies in that she has been a somewhat liberal and fair-minded authority in a relative sea of swindlers and real and potential (Kremlin-backed) thieves.[39] This seems unlikely however, as Putin has always seemed quite confident in Nabiullina's outspoken but non-invasive activities and, in turn, no doubt some loyalty to the status quo of regime affairs was somehow earned (or forced).

Whatever the case, the free-flowing banking system, exiting and entering, legal and illegal, in Russia seems to be intact even after years of Western sanctions, which were touted at the time they were implemented to be a serious deterrent to Russia's economic well-being.[40] While some banks have been directly sanctioned, it seems safe to say that the movement of money on Russia's (including the elites' and regime's) global interests will continue.

This brings us to a key area on which the money of all Russia hinges, that of the powerful corruption interests:

THE GENERAL CORRUPTION

Corruption in Russia is probably the single most affliction on (and of) modernity in modern day Russia, which, although it has its roots in the Soviet era, has exploded in magnitude and in pervasiveness in the post-Soviet era and which represents the single most serious on-going issue that hold Russia back from a non-Putin regime prosperity. Recognizing that corruption is bad for the image, but not for the regime's wallet, Putin has attempted, usually on a truly false basis, to address the issue on some occasions. Most often seeing it as an image problem no less, the Putin regime since it began has sought to hide such corruption and accompanying behaviors through a variety of different ways and policies, many of them misdirecting the focus of the people towards easier rallying cries more conducive to the regime's own survival.

In response, as mentioned earlier in this book, leading opposition head Alexei Navalny, through his Open Russia group and his Anti-Corruption Foundation, has made a name for himself in Russia's polity, which has in turn led to protests in March 2017 following the release of a video detailing Prime Minister Dmitry Medvedev's many properties and holdings.[41]

The Putin regime's traditional response to addressing corruption has been to micro-manage the issue focusing on small-scale ordinary citizen encounters while completely skipping over the large-scale serious corruption inherent to his government. As such, when the Russian people focus on corruption, the regime usually focuses on case-by-case situations and broadcasts the regime's "hatred" of corruption on television shows. These periodic broadcasts are meant to show regime initiative; for example, one popular way of ordinary citizens expressing grievance has been through a "hot line" which has been set up where citizens can report corruption or bribery by individual police officers. Certainly, I've spoken to many a Russian who believes that these measures work; that you can call a phone number and complain about an individual police officer and something will be done.

Unlike in the past also, I've spoken to Russians who believe now that you can send a letter to the procurators office or talk to the police if you have some problem with an individual shop or establishment. In the 1990s and early 2000s, this was not always the case; some low-scale establishments could get away with pretty much anything, even making people sick from food or some other offering without any means for citizens to get back at the people in question. Now, according to public displays, this whole scheme of things is "over with," stores or restaurants seemingly cannot poison you and get away with it.

On top of that, through televised call-in shows and the like, Putin will answer questions from grandmothers and teenagers about broader questions in/about Russia, Russian policy, or who have some problem that he will, of course, speak to someone about fixing. Russian political scientist and Soviet dissident Gleb Pavlovsky referred to the whole call-in affair in a 2017 television interview with TV Rain as "какой-то праздник провинциального журналиста, ходока и просителя," ("some kind of holiday for the provincial journalist, walker, and petitioner") reflecting the "moment in the limelight" effect of the exercise.[42] If you should be one of the lucky ones who manages to land a question on these yearly (in December) call-in shows, then you are indeed in luck and whomsoever your grievance is against is truly in trouble.[43] By extension, in the eyes of ordinary Russians, this has been and is a good reflection on the Putin regime; it seems like the government has competence and will do something about personal grievances on some basis.

Nevertheless, the scope of these political pronouncements and/or investigations are tiny. Putting aside for a moment that even now, with these measures in place as forwarded by the government, in my own experience, there remains uncounted smaller occasions where corruption takes place. The responses to call-ins are "legend," you might say, and even in those cases, Putin and his regime have sought to pull such dealings as far away from the public as possible. Small-scale encounters are taken care of and forgotten; that is a key element of this projection on the part of the Putin regime.

Further though, this is not to say that there are at least some token large-scale investigations as well. Corresponding to the image that Putin has sought to project in his presidencies, there have also been a few large occasions where the media have gotten wind of a major "hit" on corruption.

One such incident was in mid-2016 when a committee deputy head of the Ministry of Internal Affairs (MVD) was caught, supposedly as part of a crackdown on corruption, with 123 million USD in his own house.[44] It is an attractive case, it seems. However, in Russia where corruption, especially at high levels, is rife, one wonders what else this senior MVD official did to warrant the attention of this supposed crackdown. It is possible also that it was perhaps someone else's turn to take "one for the team," as it were.

What all these skip, however, are the major criminal sins of the Putin regime, as is well-known, his Prime Minister's, Dmitry Medvedev's myriad houses, properties, and possessions, far beyond what could be afforded by his salary as Prime Minister of Russia. While Aleksey Navalny managed to get a grip on and calculate a long list of Medvedev's holdings, his are but one, albeit one very high, representation of the corruption at the highest levels of the Russian government. It would be difficult to accurately list all the various holdings of servants of the Putin regime, they change and expand every day mind you, but there are people out there dedicated to keeping running lists of these cases. One only must type a few keywords into a search engine to find the latest itemizations.[45]

Russia researcher Mark Galeotti, for one, recognizes this, pointing at corruption in "the industrial-scale theft of the great and the not-that-good: the sweetheart contracts for bridges and sports stadia, the government bailouts, the tax breaks."[46]

This serves however to emphasize the fact that all these aspects are of course far above the purview of the ordinary Russia seeking to make his or her way in life. The Russian people don't see the elites' palatial houses, of course, they see the holes in the road that can blow your tire easily if you hit them too hard. As I talked about in detail in my first book, the hopelessness against corruption is tangible. The Russian people have few means to monitor or deter corruption, in general large-scale, so they deal with the state almost mechanically, feeding authorities what they want to hear and operating on an antagonistic level with the state in all its forms when at all possible.

As such, corruption filters down to the bottom of the pyramid. Indeed, almost all work contracts operate on a dualistic basis regarding the state, people are paid under the table, and, despite all the work of the Putin regime towards "law and order," it is betrayed by the intelligence of the Russian people as a group. The Russian people are not stupid, they know what they are doing, at least as assuredly as the Putin regime thinks that it knows what it is doing.

This is the circle of lies in Russia.

CONCLUSIONS

The money of Russia has always been a frightfully disappearing thing; even back through the previous centuries, when elites, boyars, and monarchists took money from the common folk because of the peoples' lack of position to resist, because of law, and not least of which because of the backhanded desire for order. No different in some ways is the current period when elites are taking the money of Russia to what places where they can secure it free from taxes and responsibility to where they collected it from at the expense of the Russian people who work at the factories, stores, towns, and cities from where they need to "make a living," to use the American term.

Three pillars here were argued to be effective conduits from which modern elites have "robbed" Russia, quite accurate and simple, but for lack of a better and more inspirational word. They were: privatization, natural resources, and fast and covert movements of capital and current holdings/the shadow economy, and then the corruption of all three. A small number of elites are dead-set on maintaining their control on the money of Russia, and they probably will, as the Putin regime (or its successor over the years) is at the heart of the matter in seeking to support them, as well that the demonstration of the culture of lies would deem that it (and they) should.

At the top, they are all semi-friends, unless one of them endangers them all.

Nevertheless, Russia is a bright place, because the people to varying degrees fight for it to be so. The Russian people are in some ways the kindest and most generous people to their friends, but they are ready and willing to bypass and/or to correctly defend themselves when relatively-unknown people come to force more than they are prepared to give to the regime in situ. Over time, the Russian people will win, of this I have no doubt.

In the meantime, Putin uses the money of Russia to maintain the shell of the "house" that he himself had a significant part in building. It will likely not collapse as long as he is in power. It is still a strong house in some ways. Russia has a relatively strong economy, albeit declining if compared to some other parallel states. Russia still has reserve funds to steady everything. It can still borrow money and can seek to "build" bridges with the Asia-Pacific and the Middle East.[47]

Nevertheless, Russia as a country and a nation has a lot to worry about. Putin's aggressive foreign policies have brought even more trouble for the country. Western sanctions are slow, but they will take a toll. After a while, they will have an effect. It is inevitable.

Still, Russia is full of intelligent people, including, it must be said, Putin himself. He is not a stupid person, and he will not be taken down without a fight. The elites' money is a fickle thing. Unless they escape Russia, AND dodge sanctions which inadvertently drive them back, money can be taken away from any given elite at any time, should they decide to speak against Putin and his regime. Putin knows what he is doing.

Another question to ask is, do his opponent opposition figures know what they are doing? What will Navalny do if he is in charge, if he is President one day? Will he change all things? How will Navalny address the money of Russia if he is in charge?

To date, and I have been thorough in investigating this, he has been unsure of himself. One of Putin's main supporting arguments is that he can lead the country. Can Navalny? Can someone else? Those who wish to lead Russia need to convincingly prove that they can lead Russia, and get a grip on the pervasive money movement, laundering, and corruption which pervades the place.

Although he is something of a master of exposing corruption, as seen from his work against Medvedev and others, even Navalny needs to be forthright and decide on this question. If he were in charge, could he stop corruption as easily as he exposes it? Having seen him and his ilk for some time, I am not always sure, although he says he can and I readily acknowledge the difficulties of his opposition.

One thing about ordinary Russian people is that they hate a power vacuum; it will be the same case when Putin leaves office as when he took office. Someone must "win," and some will be rich. Someone, though, will lose also, and many ordinary Russians feel, with some justification, that they will be those who lose the most whatever the case.

NOTES

1. Russian Prime Minister Dmitry Medvedev, "They should keep the money in their [own] country so they share [financial] risks with it.," *Sputnik*, "State Officials Should Keep Money in Russia—Medvedev," 12 September 2012, Retrieved 9 May 2017, https://sputniknews.com/russia/20120912175920678/.

2. Tabach, Anton, "Индекс холодильника," (In English): "Refrigerator Index," *Vedomosti*, 31 May 2017, Retrieved 3 June 2017, https://www.vedomosti.ru/opinion/articles/2017/06/01/692435-indeks-holodilnika.

3. Perry, Mark J., "Economic Output: If States Were Countries, California Would Be France," *Newsweek*, 11 June 2016, Retrieved 17 April 2018, http://www.newsweek.com/economic-output-if-states-were-countries-california-would-be-france-467614.

4. "Russia GDP (purchasing power parity)," *IndexMundi*, Retrieved 21 April 2018, https://www.indexmundi.com/russia/gdp_(purchasing_power_parity).html.

5. "Russia GDP per capita PPP," *Trading Economics*, Retrieved 21 April 2018, https://tradingeconomics.com/russia/gdp-per-capita-ppp.

6. Synovitz, Ron, "Russia Has Highest Level of Wealth Inequality," *Radio Free Europe/Radio Liberty*, 10 October 2013, Retrieved 3 April 2017, http://www.rferl.org/a/russia-billionaire-wealth-inequality/25132471.html.

7. Rutland, Peter, "The Place of Economics in Russian National Identity Debates," *The New Russian Nationalism*, chapter 12, Edinburgh University Press, Edinburgh UK, 2016.

8. Aslund, Anders and Daniel Fried, "The list that's freaking everyone out in Moscow," *Politico.eu*, 18 December 2017, Retrieved 19 December 2017, https://www.politico.eu/article/kremlin-russia-donald-trump-the-list-thats-freaking-out-everyone-in-moscow/. Quote is by Aslund and Fried from the relevant statute in American law: H.R. 3364, the "Countering America's Adversaries Through Sanctions Act."

9. For a good recent overview of the campaign, see: Appel, Hilary, and Wendy Chuyui Sheng, "Putin's Renationalization Campaign: Fighting Corruption or Forcing Officials" Loyalty?," *PONARS Eurasia*, August 2017, http://www.ponarseurasia.org/memo/putins-renationalization-campaign-fighting-corruption-or-forcing-officials-loyalty. See also: Korsunskaya, Darya, Oksana Kobzeva, and Polina Devitt, "Russian

tycoons, fearing new sanctions, float new bond idea: sources," *Reuters*, 5 December 2017, Retrieved 24 December 2017, https://www.reuters.com/article/us-russia-sanctions-oligarchs-funds/russian-tycoons-fearing-new-sanctions-float-new-bond-idea-sources-idUSKBN1DZ0SH.

10. Thomas, Andrea, "Russia's Trade with the West Surges Even as Sanctions Mount," *Wall Street Journal*, 12 April 2018, Retrieved 12 April 2018, https://www.wsj.com/articles/russias-trade-with-the-west-surges-even-as-sanctions-mount-1523534781.

11. The circumstances of this "bribe" are truly laughable, involving a gesture during a game of pool and a basket of sausages. See: Kramer, Andrew E., "Fancy Sausages and a $2 Million Bribe: A Trial Uncovers Kremlin Infighting," *The New York Times*, 15 December 2017, Retrieved 22 December 2017, https://www.nytimes.com/2017/12/15/world/europe/russia-ulyukayev-bribery.html.

12. Carroll, Oliver, "Alexei Ulyukayev: Putin's ex-economy minister sentenced to eight years in prison colony for accepting bribe," *The Independent*, 15 December 2017, Retrieved 15 December 2017, http://www.independent.co.uk/news/world/europe/alexei-ulyukayev-guilty-vladimir-putin-russia-corruption-economics-minister-igor-sechin-a8111706.html.

13. "Минфин потратил в декабре последний триллион рублей Резервного фонда," (In English: "Ministry of Finance spent the last trillion rubles of the Reserve Fund in December,") *Gazeta.ru*, 10 January 2018, Retrieved 10 January 2018, https://www.gazeta.ru/business/news/2018/01/10/n_11031728.shtml.

14. "Russia Won't Sit Still for Additional U.S. Sanctions," *Stratfor*, 28 December 2017, Retrieved 30 December 2017, https://worldview.stratfor.com/article/russia-wont-sit-still-additional-us-sanctions.

15. Meyer, Henry, "Putin Tries to Lure $1 Trillion Home as Sanctions Fear Grows," *Bloomberg*, 26 December 2017, Retrieved 31 December 2017, https://www.bloomberg.com/news/articles/2017-12-26/putin-tries-to-lure-1-trillion-home-as-sanctions-fear-deepens.

16. Danilova, Elena, "Actual and Perceptual Social Inequality under Transformative Change in Russia and China," *Europe-Asia Studies*, Volume 69, Issue 1, 2017, p. 49, pp. 27–52.

17. Cook, Linda. J. and Martin K. Dimitrov, "The Social Contract Revisited: Evidence from Communist and State Capitalist Economies," *Europe-Asia Studies*, Volume 69, Issue 1, 2017, p. 18, (pp. 8–26)

18. Bennetts, Marc, "Russia's Bad Health Care System is Getting Worse," *Newsweek*, 21 November 2016, Retrieved 17 February 2017, http://europe.newsweek.com/dire-russia-health-care-523380?rm=eu.

19. See: Oil Price website, retrieved 16 April 2018, www.oilprice.com.

20. "Почти 40% россиян обвинили государство в неисполнении обязанностей перед народом," (In English): "Almost 40 percent of Russians accuse the state of failing to meet responsibilities to the people," *Interfax*, 25 April 2017, Retrieved 25 April 2017, http://www.interfax.ru/russia/559931.

21. Navalny, Alexei on Youtube (Also on Navalny's web site), "История о двух утках," (In English: "The Story of Two Ducks," 23 September 2016, Retrieved 10 December 2017, https://www.youtube.com/watch?v=3I6znZ60GaU.

22. "Russia Overview," World Bank website, Last updated 6 October 2016, Retrieved 1 April 2017, http://www.worldbank.org/en/country/russia/overview.

23. Galeotti, Mark, "The Truth About Russia's Defense Budget," *European Council on Foreign Relations*, 24 March 2017, Retrieved 1 April 2017, http://www.ecfr.eu/article/commentary_the_truth_about_russias_defence_budget_7255.

24. Gady-Franz-Stefen, "Is the "World's Deadliest Tank" Bankrupting Russia?," *The Diplomat*, 21 May 2015, Retrieved 1 April 2017, http://thediplomat.com/2015/05/is-the-worlds-deadliest-tank-bankrupting-russia/.

25. "Russia Won't Sit Still for Additional U.S. Sanctions," *Stratfor*, 28 December 2017, Retrieved 30 December 2017, https://worldview.stratfor.com/article/russia-wont-sit-still-additional-us-sanctions.

26. Yakovenko, Igor, "Renovatsiya." Deportatsiya. Revolutsiya?" Kasparov web site, 21 April 2017, Retrieved 24 April 2017, http://www.kasparov.ru/material.php?id=58FA25B24DA83. Thanks to: Goble, Paul, "Tearing Down the Khrushchoby—From Renovation to Deportation to Revolution?," *Window on Eurasia*, 23 April 2017, Retrieved 24 April 2017, http://windowoneurasia2.blogspot.ru/2017/04/tearing-down-khrushchoby-from.html.

27. See: Trudolyubov, Maxim, "'The New Normal': Why Kremlin Policy is Choking Economic Growth," *The Moscow Times*, 9 August 2016, Retrieved 9 August 2016, https://themoscowtimes.com/articles/russias-path-an-economy-that-didnt-want-to-grow-54891.

28. Cleek, Ashley, "Khimki Forest Defender Yevgenia Chirikova Is New Face Of Russian Civic Activism," *RFE/RL*, 29 July 2010, Retrieved, 16 April 2017, http://www.rferl.org/a/Khimki_Forest_Defender_Yevgenia_Chirikova_Is_New_Face_Of_Russian_Civic_Activism/2113306.html. [and] "Flurry of Moscow Activism Hints That Mood For Protest Is Very Much Alive," *RFE/RL*, 26 July 2015, Retrieved 16 April 2017, http://www.rferl.org/a/russia-moscow-protests-suggest-protest-mood-still-alive/27153373.html.

29. For one characterization, see: Chang, Sue, "Weak oil prices deplete Russia's sovereign-wealth fund," *Market Watch*, 27 October 2015, Retrieved 15 April 2017, http://www.marketwatch.com/story/weak-oil-prices-deplete-russias-sovereign-wealth-fund-2015-10-27.

30. Sergey Lavrov interview with Paul Saunders, "Sergey Lavrov: The Interview," *National Interest*, 29 March 2017, Retrieved 26 April 2017, http://nationalinterest.org/feature/sergey-lavrov-the-interview-19940.

31. "Why is OPEC refusing to cut oil production?," *Al Jazeera*, 13 December 2015, Retrieved 16 April 2017, http://www.aljazeera.com/programmes/countingthecost/2015/12/opec-refusing-cut-oil-production-151213090410559.html.

32. "OPEC Refusal to Fix Prices Signals New Oil Era," *Sputnik*, 19 November 2014, Retrieved 16 April 2017, https://sputniknews.com/business/201411291015293445/.

33. Movchan, Andrey, "How the Sanctions are Helping Putin," *Politico*, 28 March 2017, Retrieved 26 April 2017, www.politico.com/magazine/story/2017/03/how-the-sanctions-are-helping-putin-214963.

34. Harding, Luke, "Revealed: the $2bn offshore trail that leads to Vladimir Putin," *The Guardian*, 3 April 2016, Retrieved 15 April 2017, https://www.theguardian.com/news/2016/apr/03/panama-papers-money-hidden-offshore.

35. "Nothing to See Here," 9 April 2016, *The Economist*, Print edition, See on-line here: Retrieved 15 April 2017, http://www.economist.com/news/international/21696506-mossack-fonseca-leak-shakes-ukraine-more-russia-russia-finds-little-say-about-panama.

36. Smirnova, Olga, "Just who owns what in central London?," *BBC*, 21 March 2016, Retrieved 15 April 2017, http://www.bbc.com/news/business-35757265.

37. Pismennaya, Evgenia and Gregory White, "Russia's Central Banker is on a Tear," *Bloomberg News*, 14 February 2017, Retrieved 17 February 2017, https://www.bloomberg.com/news/features/2017-02-14/putin-s-central-banker-purges-100-banks-a-year-in-epic-crackdown.

38. Tanas, Olga and Stepan Kravchenko, "Putin Nominates Bank of Russia Head Nabiullina for New Term," *BloombergPolitics*, 22 March 2017, Retrieved 03 April 2017, https://www.bloomberg.com/politics/articles/2017-03-22/putin-nominates-bank-of-russia-head-nabiullina-for-new-term.

39. Nemtsova, Anna, "Is Putin Thinking About Changing His Ways?" *The Daily Beast*, 9 December 2015, Retrieved 3 April 2017, http://www.thedailybeast.com/articles/2015/12/09/is-putin-thinking-about-changing-his-ways.html.

40. I will say that sanctions have made a strong impression on the movement of Russian wealth globally, just not enough to warrant political or economic change on a strategic level in Russia.

41. One of many connections to the video, which is on youtube as well. See: Navalny web site, 2 March 2017, Retrieved 15 April 2017, https://navalny.com/p/5255/.

42. Nemzer, Anna, "Путин сдался аппарату»: Глеб Павловский о разгоревшейся войне кланов, показательной порке перед выбором преемника и тайных неврозах президента," (In English: "Putin gave out to the apparatus: Gleb Pavlovsky on the bourgeoning war of the clans, an indicative flogging before choosing a successor, and secrets neuroses of the president,"), TV Rain, 20 December 2017, Retrieved 28 December 2017, https://tvrain.ru/teleshow/politika_prjamaja_linija/pavlovskij-453359/.

43. I n my own opinion (agreeing with TV Rain analysis); see: "Собчак растворяет Навального в кислоте, руководство патриарха по выдаиванию денег, и легкий способ заработать на доносах," TV Rain,14 December 2017, Retrieved 19 December 2017, https://tvrain.ru/teleshow/panoptikum/sobchak_patriarh_donosy-452872/), these pieces of theater which are the call-in shows almost seem to be freewheeling, if you will, and Putin seems often to know what he's talking about, even though with "indifference" (as seen from the TV Rain analysis above). As such, I've never been convinced as to any real or deep meaning therein, although I've met many a Russian who watches the affairs almost as a reality show of sorts (and more than one Westerner analyst who reads and/or listens to the hours of dialogue with interest, maybe just to hear Putin spout his rhetoric or whatnot or hear the man himself make some narrow mistake, which will like clockwork be walked back politically in time).

44. Sims, Alexandra, "Senior Russian anti-corruption official arrested after police find $123 million in cash at his home," *The Independent*, 12 September 2016, http://www.independent.co.uk/news/world/europe/senior-russian-anti-corruption-official-arrested-after-police-find-123-million-in-cash-at-his-home-a7239041.html.

45. Transparency International's Russian site has some great links for following corruption in Russia: http://transparency.org.ru/.

46. Galeotti, Mark, "STOLYPIN: Corruption in Russia remains Putin's biggest threat," *BNE Intellinews*, 27 March 2017, Retrieved 26 April 2017, http://www.intellinews.com/stolypin-corruption-in-russia-remains-putin-s-biggest-threat-118370/#.WNkYt3ndUMA.twitter.

47. "Russia Won't Sit Still for Additional U.S. Sanctions," *Stratfor*, 28 December 2017, Retrieved 30 December 2017, https://worldview.stratfor.com/article/russia-wont-sit-still-additional-us-sanctions.

SEVEN

Conclusions

INTRODUCTION

Russians are smart and can think for themselves, of this I have no doubt. Anyone who says different knows nothing of Russia. Indeed, as I've argued, ordinary Russians, within the five aspects (Idea, Respect, Skill, Ally, and Money) to which I have dedicated a chapter each over the course of this book and the three themes (Eternal Russia, Unique Russia, and Independent Russia) that permeate each aspect/chapter, are intelligent and distinctly separate from the Putin regime, though they may vote for Putin and his lackeys on occasion.

Here I consider the findings of this book. Among the many other questions, the central focus of this book was: as distributed into the five important aspects, what do Russians think about Russia, how they see or imagine Russia, what do they consider important about their country in the past, present, and future, and where do they see Russia going in the future? Appropriate answers to these questions have been covered but will be summarized in the final sections here, though perhaps firstly it is more efficient now to see what this research has understood overall.

On several points, I considered how Russians and the Putin regime are not synonymous within the context of what must be understood as Russia. One on-going question was on differentiating ordinary Russians from the Putin regime, how they run parallel, how they can sometimes agree, and how they are different.

This is a very important array of points, because, while ordinary Russians simply desire abstracts of a proud idea, a country worthy of respect, good friends, and a strong economy, Putin (and his regime) wants to distort these desires for their own mostly financial gains and into something that smells of empire, and in turn this diversion makes other countries and peoples essentially feel the need to fear Russia.

As it is one of the most powerful undercurrents in Russian society, much like in other former imperial powers, Putin's usual rhetoric is inherently and ultimately based on Russian pride. These strictures, as encouraged by Putin and his syndicate,[1] are entirely responsible for greater instability, quite probably the ultimate disestablishment of Russia's internal integrity in future, and likely will spark further conflict at some point.

We learned over the course of this book that the Russian people are an exceedingly complex people and set of personages to examine. Throughout history, they have been bombarded by outside empires wanting to carve out a niche for themselves, but Russia, not to sound jingoistic like their propaganda, maintained itself. Nevertheless, the Russian people are far from a unified whole as well, which is a point that I have painstakingly tried to emphasize over the course of this book. I have nothing but respect for all these concepts, and the reasonable continuation of the same.

Still, the twenty-first century is different. Objectively-speaking, if Russia is to improve, the Putin regime must soon enter a final phase (which it may currently be doing), thus moving to the side, or must be overtaken by events led by some opposition; one that is capable and that can create an alternate version of Great Russia, and one that can be more open to civil society and dissent. The Russian people, to the extent covered by the whole of this book as differentiating from Putin's antagonistic rule as President, must at some point return and be a part of the "family of nations" again.

The system of "groupthink" as suggested from the introduction is not unbreakable. I wholeheartedly agree with Vladimir Gel'man when he wrote in his book, Authoritarian Russia, that: "the situation in Russia is likely to change over time due to the benefits of learning from the recent past and the effects of generational change."[2]

As a people, Russians consider themselves, and perhaps quite normally so, to be in the correct modality of life, given the pride and respect demanded. As such, considering Russian public opinion in some ways, the Earth revolves around the notional Russian "you," and perhaps your neighbor (if you like him or her), and perhaps your nation and country. This is not so strange, most every American is from birth preached such material, and especially for a nation with roots from imperialist times.

On one hand, ordinary Russians recognize, and oftentimes *like*, the authority of President Vladimir Putin, and they ask why they should put up with the myriad of problems of the Yeltsin era which are now almost mythologized (i.e., the normalized contrast with the 1990s decade), and it is, it must be said, a good question. No one should rightly live with chaos. On the other hand, this mythology of the past can easily be used by an authoritarian-minded leadership to become aggressive and self-righteous, as the Putin regime has done in Ukraine, Georgia, and places even farther away.

Over the course of the chapters here, we have seen and analyzed Russian views of themselves, their country, and the foreign world from five perspectives. Each approach offered a unique view on which to regard Russian society and how the constituents of that society view themselves.

WHAT WE KNOW

In the second chapter, I studied the Idea of Russia. It is a concept that cannot be avoided; it is an idealized vision, and one which even Western analysts should not overlook. The Idea of Russia for many ordinary Russians is a special thing; for them it is one which cannot and will not dismissed outright. As is understandable, many, if not most, Russian people love Russia. I've seen as much through own experiences and with my own eyes. That however has elements of insufficiency. Russian people want to see progress, and they want to see it for themselves. Briefly, I covered the difficulties of Russian language and the Russian Orthodox Church in coexisting alongside other native languages and burgeoning faiths within Russia itself.

By extension, possible expansion of the Idea of Russia is always a difficult subject. The problem of spreading the Idea of Russia to cover all Russians, that is, nationalism as vaunted by some Russian nationalists mentioned before in this book, including those who profess the Eurasianist mindset, is not so prominent unless the regime of Putin makes it so and chooses that path. While Crimea and other territories carry many problems where ethnic Russians are some substantive percentage, they do serve the political purposes of a regime that desires to stay in power, and as such, addressing the political question concerning Russians outside Russia will be a continuing security headache for both Russia's neighbors and for world powers and alliances.

The question is made worst by the manipulations of Putin regime, as Putin has used it as a pretext to have a more aggressive foreign policy. It will also be a question for whoever replaces Putin one day, as, by its very nature, the issue causes ill will among Russia's neighbors and those that fear Russian aggression.

Again, it is also true, I posit, that the Idea of Russia could exist independent of Putin and could be at harmony with all the other ideas of the peoples of the world. This must be in general as well as specific. A political settlement for Crimea must be reached at some point in the future, and that future settlement quite probably may mean that Crimea will have to be given back to Ukraine.

In home policy, the political climate of Russia today did not have to be; it was not inevitable. Only the opportunistic paradigms of the regime and political elite that is in charge today has brought the current climate to bear.

It must also be kept in mind that while NATO enlargement and lack of forethought considering the Russian ideal in the immediate post-Soviet period did not necessarily bring about the Putin era, those were easily manipulated as problems to bring the current internal Russian political situation to develop.

The West is an easy enemy to be portrayed as such to ordinary Russians in support of those in the Putin regime. How best to address the current situation is however of issue, especially concerning the Idea of Russia. As argued in the second chapter, given continued Russian aggression, only careful confrontation and determination by the Western powers, with detailed explanation and attempts at Russia-hindering aggressive counter-policies, can encumber the spreading of the Russian polity to take advantage of all the extraterritorial ethnic Russians outside what we consider to be Russia today (including Crimea, or not . . .).

In the third chapter, I studied the Respect of Russia. I posited that, like all peoples, the Russian people like, want, and deserve respect from other peoples of the world. Over the course of that chapter, I examined how ordinary Russians promoted their own country, and in surveys demanded respect from other peoples of the world, but at the same time mainly concerned themselves with eking out a livable existence. I also studied how the respect of Russia has been used and abused by political elements who think that not only Russia should be respected, but it should also predominate and gain respect from those who are not Russian and who are not inclined towards a simple respect for the Russian ideal.

So, the ultimate question is: does Russia command respect? It does *not* in the form of how the Soviet Union commanded respect, because Russia is not a superpower, or even a power worthy of emulation, despite what many Russophiles might seek to portray as such. Russia does, and should however command normalized respect as a strong power among powers with a strong people among other peoples; I have not but said this all along.

The second question here is: does Russia command a "sphere of influence?" as has been desired by the Russian political elite headed by Putin.

To answer this in part: Russia does have a sphere of influence, if only by the fact that Russia continues to regard its immediate neighbors as part of its realm, or responsibility, or imperial collective, or what not. One cannot overlook the realist argument, though it is abhorrent to many.

As much as those same neighbors would desire not to be part of any Russian sphere of influence, if Moscow continues as an antagonistic partner towards them, Moscow must be regarded as, effectively, a new Russian empire. This is unfortunate, but as the Putin regime is reliant on this concept politically, it cannot be easily escaped. Short of a third world war, we cannot escape what some might consider a backward concept in the twenty-first century, yet the simple fact that at least one empire as such remains.

In that chapter, I also talked about Respect+, that is, the expectation of respect from outside sources and, furthermore, the requirement that Russia be respected by those not inclined to do so. The Putin regime demands that Respect+ be tolerated.

However, Respect+ does not have to be granted, and, I advise, it should be fought against through whatever means necessary, including containment.

In the fourth chapter, I examined the skills of Russia. The question predominating this chapter was that, given how the Russian people are some of the most highly educated in the world but at the same time with lagging Soviet legacy technologies, what possibilities are open for the Russian people in the future? With the Putin regime's antagonistic outlook towards the West and with sanctions disrupting the attainment and maintenance of new technologies and skill-sets for the Russia people, I found that Russia's future is profoundly, but not inescapably, deterred by the current geopolitical climate.

Yet, the Russian people are proud of their skills and technologies and how they have maintained at least some semblance of parity with other developed countries in significant accomplishments and research.

Politically, Putin attempts to hide Russian weaknesses in research and development by constantly professing that Russia can generate the same technologies domestically. This is largely a false premise; Russia is unlikely to create reliable substituting structures for the unending need to expand the economy, in specific tapping new deep-cold climate petroleum prospects. Weapons sales, as a principal production, are far from the most viable of economic expansion, although they can be a reliable small crutch in hard times.

However, I add that this relative isolation is not inescapable, as Russia could and likely will pursue new technological capabilities through alternative sources, and perhaps even, one day, through some rapprochement with Western countries and companies. Yet, for now as of the mid-2010s decade, prospects seem more bleak than hopeful.

In the fifth chapter, I considered the friends and alliances of Russia and of the Russian people. I considered on how profoundly necessary it is to regard the Putin regime as differentiated from the Russian people. The Russian people are not the Putin regime, and vice versa.

Most importantly, the Russian people, I have found, are enemies with no one and with no other peoples, except for the usual extremist elements which do exist in Russian society.

Briefly, I looked at this in view of ethnic Russians and of non-ethnic Russians. As such I covered briefly the discrimination and racism which is ever present in Russian society in favor of ethnic Russians at the expense of a growing Muslim population and populations both within Russia and originating from the Caucasus and Central Asia. Also, as is politically expedient, the Putin regime is the relative enemy of a great many foreign government and foreign/domestic elite elements, not to mention including the Western democracies, and is the friend of only a select handful of governments who are either conducive to Russian leadership or sympathetic to Putin's aims.

The Putin regime can count, weakly, among its allies the Belarusian leadership of Alyaksandr Lukashenka, if Putin doesn't threaten Lukashenka's position. Lukashenka, by the way, will not last forever, and Putin no doubt has an alternative in mind already. With Putin's willingness to interfere in elections as far away as America, it is absolutely assured that his computer hackers and influence campaigners will be directed towards Belarus during the next presidential election (due in 2020). Given the history of Russia and Belarus, at least as of the late 2010s decade, there seems to be little that can be done to bring about a more pro-Western government to Belarus unless there is a change in situation.

Also, the Putin regime can count on pro-Russian leaderships in eastern Ukraine and in separatist sections of Georgia who are wholly dependent on Putin's assistance. The list of allies for the Putin regime is short indeed, and but should not be forgotten.

In the sixth chapter, I covered the money of Russia and the Russian people's relationship to money as befitting a post-Soviet capitalist country. The Russian people have been and continue to be somewhat reliant on the theory of a social contract with the Russian government, in that, in exchange for being non-political, the people are given guarantees of economic and health-related protections.

These social "contract" protections have however been weakening in the face of budget cuts and rent-seeking by the Putin regime, and this might be one of the things that brings about the end of the Putin regime or its successor, if it follows the same path, one day.

Given the Putin's regime's troubles, as I addressed in chapter 6, the people who strongly oppose the Putin regime are feeling less restricted by the general will that supported and supports the Putin regime. Hence, continuing from the March 2017 anti-corruption protests nominally against Prime Minister Dmitry Medvedev, there are signs of life in the opposition movement.

Yet, I venture to say that these protests, at least in and of themselves, do not yet represent the deathblow against the regime, or even the beginning of the deathblow against the regime. Rather, they help to motivate and support the morale of those who support the opposition, right now most prominently, Alexei Navalny, but they also give reasons to be hopeful when confronting the Putin regime in many facets of Russian government polity. We'll see how it goes, but until the next significant event happens, I remain skeptical.

As such, in these chapters, I explored and examined each of the ways that the Russian people popularly regard their own country. As I stated before, it is my belief that the Russian peoples' opinions are of more importance than the actions of the Putin regime. Yet, in the next section, I wish to examine broader implications of what has been explored in each chapter up to this point.

FINAL VIEWS

Having been through the chapters, each concerning an aspect by which the Russian people, duly separated into five here considered, view the overall concept of Russia, the average observer in some ways cannot but avoid coming back to a consideration of "democracy" and what that concept means. Most importantly, their attempts to rebuild their "house" notwithstanding, Russians have faced the difficulties of building a democracy in the post-Soviet era and suffer from the Putin regime's hostile takeover of the "structure."

Revisiting the *groupthink* mentioned in the introductory chapter, throughout my studies for this book, I have found that Russia's "motion" is slowly and steadily dipping down towards chaos after attempting stability in 1990s to 2000s decade in Russia. As of this writing, there has been no event or protest yet signifying adequate change or shock factor where the motion would be halted in favor of another potential model of interest, although the anti-corruption protests and "truckers" protest of early 2017 provide some suggestion that an alternate future could be on the horizon.

To some extent, democracy continues to be a social experiment in Russia (as perhaps everywhere), though some analysts consider building democracy almost at the level of a simple stepping stone approach. Many times, in these last two decades, I've heard the phrase "free and fair elections," and the absolute requirement of that practice. I've also heard the phrase, "open civil society" and that requirement for a functioning democracy. I agree with those conceptions as well, in that these ideals are mandatory for establishing what we understand as a democratic form of government. Almost every day on social media, I find a new armchair analyst who says that Russia failed to do this, or failed to do that, sniping at the methodology of Russia's attempt at democracy.

It is true and clear that Russia has failed to form both requirements. However, this escapes the fact that, given the unique traditions and circumstances of every country, particularly former imperial countries, Russia included, there is no single guidebook or magically-available master plan towards attaining those concepts. All democracies had and have continuous problems with democratic development, some of which have lasted until today. As concerning electioneering and civil development, the bare implementation of some elements of those concepts will not work if in the end there is disinterest among elites or failure to follow through towards the ultimate democratic goal.

Russia is expected to invent and perfect democracy in a hostile climate and tradition in the thirty years since the fall of the Soviet Union. While some including myself bemoan Putin's aggregate leadership, at some point one must look at Russian democracy objectively and look for ways insofar as improving it while keeping the most important thing, the Russian people, in mind.

THREE THEMES REVISITED

In analyzing Russian society through the five concepts I have studied in this book, I've found that the failure of the culmination of the admirable goals of civil society and fair elections has been, in Russian public opinion, juxtaposed with cultural themes that permeate society and which, in some ways, both help and hinder Russian democracy. These will represent my final thoughts on the investigations that I have endeavored to follow here.

The first theme was that of Eternal Russia. The second theme was that of Independent Russia. The third theme was that of Unique Russia. Each theme tells us something about the past, present, and future of Russia, Russians, and the Russian Putin state.

The concept of Eternal Russia can be understood to tell us much about the Russian people and the state under which they persistently profess support for and live under.

Russia has always had an often-overstated tradition for authoritarianism. This is well-known; everyone and their grandmother is familiar with the trope that Russia has been, is, and always will be, authoritarian in some sense. It doesn't really tell us as much in the modern era, though.

Beyond Putin and his ilk, Eternal Russia is what grounds Russia in the past, but does provide some hope for the present and future. Eternal Russia tells us that Russia can survive its current difficulties, and it can survive the age of Putin.

On a grander scale, Eternal Russia provides that Russia can survive great changes very quickly, is resilient, and will not be destroyed by rapid revolution, as may become necessary for Putin and/or his successors to ever be dislodged from power.

As a parallel consequence perhaps at odds with Eternal Russia, some observers inside and outside of Russia believe that gradual reform, according to individual issue or broader abstract, can take place. Those who think this must know that there are no rules by which the current regime is restrained in undoing anything unfamiliar or unkind to their politik. As Lilia Shevtsova comments on this:

> One also can be but amazed at the naivety or idealism of those who continue to believe in "gradual" reform (step by step). Supporters of the "gradual" path, for instance, assert that reform should begin, say, first in selected areas, for instance, in education, healthcare, and agriculture, and only then spread further. But how do you reform these sectors without de-monopolizing them and opening them to competition, and without the rule of law and independent courts? Anyway, the authorities' continued monopoly on power and its rejection of competition makes any real reform impossible, even in just these limited sectors.[3]

Such gradual reformers worry too much about the Russian peoples' ability to weather the storm. Eternal Russia changes very slowly and can survive much. The Eternal Russia concept is something of much pride in Russian society. Russia will survive those who seek to inhibit it, including Putin and his regime.

Independent Russia is a Russia which is reliant on no outside influences, including allies to an extent. Russia can fend for itself, or so I've been told, especially after a few such Russians had more than five shots of vodka. As evident, this oftentimes suggests a strong nationalist Russia. While other countries talk about being part of international law, or a "family of nations," or what-have-you, many Russians who believe in an Independent Russia buy into the regime's rhetoric and contemplate that Russia can survive international isolation. Second only to being told about Eternal Russia, I've been told that Russia can live regardless of anyone, including without the technologies of other nations and countries and possibly without the friendship of all other global actors.

Independent Russia as portrayed by radicals in competition with the global community is not a pretty thing. Those who obsess on an Independent Russia can often be reliant on the messianic idea that Russia must go down fighting. Russia for Russians, and so on.

Those who study and deal with Russia should know that this theme will never disappear and must be dealt with head-on. While the ultranationalist side of this theme must be opposed always, I am not convinced that the theme of Independent Russia cannot co-exist with good relations. An Independent Russia does not have to be alone in the world, and, as a concept, could be no more scary or intransigent than any other country that relies on pride or patriotism. Independent Russia does not have to be overtly-nationalistic, but it can be independent and proud.

Thirdly, Unique Russia is the idea that Russia is a leader of a Slavic world (or some other construct) that is unique, that is separate, and is (sometimes) apart from the problems of Europe, yet is most often, without a deepening explanation, inevitably a part of Europe. Multiple times in this book, I have talked about how Russia feels indebted to Europe yet feels separate from it in a variety of ways.

Many Western countries and elites are very annoyed with the concept of Unique Russia. Unique Russia suggests, as with other formerly imperial nations, that Russia is special in some ways. It isn't, but the feeling often remains in Russian society. Some Western societies, especially former empires, feel the same; it is not a revolutionary concept. Yet Russia adheres to this concept when considering policies on the global stage. We are different, we are the alternative to X, etc. etc. As with the themes of Eternal Russia and Independent Russia, those who study and deal with Russia can come to an understanding in dealing with Unique Russia, if simply by acknowledging the theme as an issue.

These themes also form disconnects within Russian society. How can the Russian people address these disconnects? As I would answer: not easily.

Until Russia's political actors are held accountable to the people, many other things are unreachable.

The opposition can and must get its act together, must find a strong unified leadership, and find a way to consistently "move" the people towards a greater ideal, using their intellects when possible, using their emotions and actions when necessary.

Hence, as I've discussed, perhaps Russia can be eternal, independent, and unique. As such, it fits the setting unusually well and it fits the research provided here. These themes sometimes conflict with one another as well, almost as often as they co-exist.

According to particularly ethnic Russians, we love Russia, we hope for the best, and we expect the worst. What else can we say? It is all relative in the end, as I am sure that even Putin would venture if he was sitting here next to me when I was typing this.

In the end, the Russian people are the most important factor.

If they should tire of Putin, or if he should fail a test of governance, or if he should significantly damage the "social contract" covered briefly over the course of this book, or if he should make a minority angry enough to start a *sustained* protest, or if he should fail to find a successor, then his regime will not last very long at all. If the Russian people are satisfied not to protest too loudly in the streets, then for the Putin regime, all is well, and the status quo cannot help but continue.

The future of Russia belongs to the Russian people, of that I have no doubt.

As a side note, as far as the West is concerned, and as the reader might have noticed, I advocate for no quick fix to separating the Russian people from the Putin regime and its allies, although I again strongly argue that the two are separate. My recommendations would be to continue targeted sanctions against the Putin regime, but do the best possible not to target the ordinary citizenry. Do not grant the Putin regime "Respect+," or respect beyond normalized international law. Stand up to Putin's aggressions outside of Russia's borders. Plan for a time when the Putin regime no longer exists. This includes supporting Russia's opposition, even when they spout nationalist concepts. Leave open the possibility of dropping sanctions if the regime falls. Above all, be flexible.

Beyond those points, it will be up to the Russian people as to the fate of the Putin regime, as I believe it always has been.

NOTES

1. It is indeed difficult to subjectively avoid Mafioso terms when talking about Putin and his regime in this context, even when one is trying to dodge grandiose characterizations of the same. This is a pitfall that some of my fellow analysts have fallen into, but, on rare occasion such as this one, I sadly admit, I too think such defining terms are applicable.

2. G el'man, Vladimir, *Authoritarian Russia: Analyzing Post-Soviet Regime Changes*, University of Pittsburgh Press, Pittsburgh PA, 2015, p. 153.

3. Shevtsova, Lilia, "Russia Under Putin: Titanic Looking for an Iceberg?" *Communist and Post-Communist Studies*, Volume 45, 2012, p. 122 (pp. 209–16).

Select Bibliography

NEWSPAPERS, TELEVISION, AND MEDIA SOURCES

Among the many television stations, newspapers, think tank publications, internet, and news sources of the past 17 years which have been researched, reviewed, and used in this study, these have been of interest.

Agence France-Presse (www.afp.com), *American Thinker, The Atlantic, Atlantic Council* (www.atlanticcouncil.org), *Associated Press* (www.ap.org), *BBC News* (www.bbc.com/news/), *The Bell, Bloomberg, CBS News, Christian Science Monitor, CNN, The Diplomat, EastView, The Economist, Financial Times, Fontanka* (St. Petersburg news, fontanka.ru), *Forbes* (Russia and otherwise) magazine, *Foreign Policy, Geopolitical Weekly, International Centre of Journalists, Institute for the Study of War, Institute of War and Peace Reporting* (IWPR), *Intersection project, Itar-Tass, Intersection, United Press International* (www.upi.com), *Izvestia, Johnson's Russia List, JSTOR, Kommersant-daily* (www.kommersant.ru/daily), *Le Monde* (www.lemonde.fr), *Life News* (www.lifenews.ru), *Meduza* (https://meduza.io/), *MN News, Moskovskye novostei, National Post, NBC News, New Times, New York Times, NEWSru.com, Newsweek, Nezavisimaya gazeta, Novaya Gazeta* (www.novayagazeta.ru/), *Novye izvestia, Obshchaia gazeta, Paul Goble's Blog* [Window on Eurasia Blog] (https://russianmilitaryanalysis.wordpress.com/), *Psychology Today, Pravda* (www.pravda.ru), *Radio Free Europe/Radio Liberty* (RFE/RL), *Radio Netherlands, Radio Svoboda, Reuters* (www.reuters.com), *Riddle* (ridl.io), *RIA Novostei* (www.rian.ru), *Rossiiskaia gazeta, Rossiiskiie vesti, Rossiya 1, Russia/Caucasus Update, Russia Journal, Russia Today* (www.rt.com), *Russian Military Analysis Blog* (https://russianmilitaryanalysis.wordpress.com/), *Segodnia, Slate magazine* (www.slate.com), *SOVA Centre, Sputnik, Stratfor, Telekanal DOZHD* (www.tvrain.ru), *The Baltic Times, The Local* (Sweden), *The Voice of Russia, The Moscow Times* (www.themoscowtimes.com), *The Saint Petersburg Times, TIME Magazine, Transition, Trud, TV Tsentre, Vatican Radio, Vedimosti, Vremia MN, Vremia novostei, Washington Post, Yeshednevny zhurnal* (www.ej.ru/?a=inner#).

ONLINE PUBLIC OPINION DATABASE SOURCES (MAINLY IN RUSSIAN LANGUAGE)

Yuri Levada/Levada Center: http://www.levada.ru
VTsIOM: http://www.wciom.com/

Public Opinion Foundation: www.fom.ru
ROMIR polling data: www.romir.ru

BOOKS AND JOURNAL ARTICLES

Alexseev, Mikhail, and Henry Hale. "A New Wave of Russian Nationalism? What Really Changed in Public Opinion after Crimea." PONARS Eurasia, PONARS Eurasia Policy Memo No. 362, May 2015.

Andrew, Christopher, and Visili Mitrokhin. *The Sword and the Shield: The Mitrokhin Archive and the Secret History of the KGB, 1st ed.* Basic Books, 1999.

Aron, Leon. "Russia Between Revolution and Democracy." *Post-Soviet Affairs*, Vol. 11, No. 4, Oct.–Dec. 2005, pp. 305–39.

Belin, Laura. "The Russian Media in the 1990s." *Russia After Communism*, (eds.) Rick Fawn and Stephen White. Frank Cass, London, 2002.

Belokurova, Elena. "NGOs and Politics." *The Politics of Sub-National Authoritarianism in Russia*, ed. Vladimir Gel'man and Cameron Ross. Ashgate Publishing, Surrey, UK, 2010, pp. 107–22.

Buckley, Mary. "Public Opinion in Russia on the Politics of Human Trafficking." *Europe-Asia Studies*, Vol. 61, No. 2, March 2009, pp. 213–48.

Burrett, Tina. *Television and Presidential Power in Putin's Russia*. Routledge, London, 2011.

Carnaghan, Ellen. *Out of Order: Russian Political Views in an Imperfect World*. Pennsylvania State University Press, University Park, PA, 2007.

Christensen, Paul T. "Russia as Semi-periphery: Political Economy, the State, and Society in the Contemporary World System." *The Political Economy of Russia*, ed. Neil Robinson. Rowman & Littlefield, Inc., Lanham, MD, 2013, pp. 169–90.

Clowes, Edith W. *Russia on the Edge: Imagined Geographies and Post-Soviet Identities*. Cornell University Press, Ithaca, NY and London, 2011.

Clunan, Anne L. *The Social Construction of Russia's Resurgence: Aspirations, Identity, and Security Interests*. The Johns Hopkins University Press, 2009.

Conquest, Robert. *The Harvest of Sorrow: Soviet Collectivization and the Terror-Famine*. Oxford University Press, Oxford, UK, 1987.

Cornell, Svante E., and S. Frederick Starr, eds. *The Guns of August 2008: Russia's War in Georgia*. M.E. Sharpe, New York and London, 2009.

Dahl, Robert A. *Democracy and Its Critics*. Yale University Press, New Haven, CT and London, 1989.

Dawisha, Karen. *Putin's Kleptocracy: Who Owns Russia?* Simon and Schuster, New York, 2015.

DeBardeleben, Joan, and Mikhail Zherebstsova. "'Managerial Patronage' and the 'Power Vertical.'" *The Politics of Sub-National Authoritarianism in Russia*, ed. Vladimir Gel'man and Cameron Ross. Ashgate Publishing, Surrey, UK, 2010, pp. 85–106.

Duncan, Peter J. S. *Russian Messianism*. Routledge, London and New York, 2000.

Galeotti, Mark. *The Vory*. Yale University Press, New Haven, CT, 2018.

Gel'man, Vladimir. *Authoritarian Russia*. University of Pittsburgh Press, Pittsburgh, PA, 2015.

German, Tracey C. *Russia's Chechen War*. RoutledgeCurzon, London and New York, 2003.

Gessen, Masha. *The Future is History*. Riverhead Books, New York, 2017.

———. *A Man Without a Face*. Riverhead Books/Penguin, New York, 2013.

Hale, Henry E. "The Myth of Mass Authoritarianism in Russia: Public Opinion Foundations of a Hybrid Regime." The National Council for Eurasian and East European Research. University of Washington and George Washington University, Seattle, WA, 2009, pp. 19–20.

Harding, Luke. *Mafia State: Spies, Surveillance and Russia's Secret Wars*. Guardian, London, 2012.

Hoffman, David E. *The Oligarchs*. BBS PublicAffairs, New York, 2002.
Jack, Andrew. *Inside Putin's Russia*. Granta Books, London, 2004.
Jowett, Garth S., and Victoria O'Donnell. *Propaganda and Persuasion*, 3rd ed. Sage Publications, London, 1999.
Kagarlitsky, Boris. *Russia Under Yeltsin and Putin*. Pluto Press, London, 2002.
Ledeneva, Alena. *Can Russia Modernize?* Power Networks and Informal Governance. Cambridge University Press, London, 2013.
———. *How Russia Really Works*. Cornell University Press, Ithaca, NY and London, 2006.
———. "Organized Crime in Russia Today." *Russian and Post-Soviet Organized Crime, (ed.)* Mark Galeotti. Ashgate Publishing, Keele, UK, 2002.
McFaul, Michael. *Russia's Unfinished Revolution: Political Change from Gorbachev to Putin*. Cornell University Press, Ithaca, NY and London, 2001.
Mearsheimer, John J. *When Leaders Lie*. Oxford University Press, Oxford, UK, 2011.
Nemtsov, Boris. *Provintsial*. Vagrius, Moscow, 1997.
Ostrovsky, Arkady. *The Invention of Russia: The Journey from Gorbachev's Freedom to Putin's War*. Atlantic Books, London, 2015.
Petrov, Nikolay, Maria Lipman & Henry E. Hale. "Three Dilemmas of Hybrid Regime Governance: Russia from Putin to Putin." *Post-Soviet Affairs*, Volume 30, Issue 1, 2014, p. 3, pp. 1–26.
Rantanen, Terhi. *The Global and the National*. Rowman and Littlefield Publishers Inc., Lanham, MD and Boulder, CO, 2002.
Richmond, Yale. *From Nyet to Da*. Intercultural Press, Yarmouth, ME, 2003.
Richters, Katja. *The Post-Soviet Orthodox Church*. Routledge, London, 2014.
Edited by Robinson, Neil. The Political Economy of Russia. Rowman & Littlefield, Lanham, MD, 2013.
Rose, Richard, William Mishler and Neil Munro. *Russia Transformed*. Cambridge University Press, Cambridge, UK, 2006.
———. *Popular Support for an Undemocratic Regime: The Changing Views of Russians*. Cambridge University Press, Cambridge, UK, 2011.
Rousselet, Kathy. "Constructing Moralities Around the Tsarist Family." *Multiple Moralities and Religions in Post-Soviet Russia*, Ed. by Jarrett Zigon, Berghahn Books, 2011.
Sakwa, Richard. *Frontline Ukraine: Crisis in the Borderlands*. IB Tauris Publishing, London and New York, 2015.
———. *Russian Politics and Society, 4th edition*. Routledge, New York, 2008.
Shevtsova, Lilia. *Putin's Russia*. Carnegie Endowment for International Peace, Washington, DC, 2005.
Shlapentokh, Vladimir, and Anna Arutunyan. *Freedom, Repression, and Private Property in Russia*. Cambridge University Press, Cambridge, UK, September 2013.
Skillen, Daphne. *Freedom of Speech in Russia: Politics and Media from Gorbachev to Putin*. Routledge, London and New York, 2017.
Trepanier, Lee. *Political Symbols in Russian History: Church, State, and the Quest for Order and Justice*. Lexington Books, Lanham, MD, 2007.
Tsygankov, Andrei P. *The Strong State in Russia: Development and Crisis*. Oxford University Press, Oxford and New York, 2014.
Vaughn, Jason. *A Socio-Political Model of Lies in Russia*. University Press of America, Lanham, MD, 2016.
Wilson, Andrew. 'The Crimean Tatar Question: A Prism for Changing Nationalisms and Rival Versions of Eurasianism." *Journal of Soviet and Post-Soviet Politics and Society*, Vol. 3, No. 2, 2017.
———. *Ukraine Crisis: What It Means for the West*. Yale University Press, New Haven, CT, 2014.
———. *Virtual Politics*. Yale University Press, New Haven, CT and London, 2005.
———. *The Ukrainians: Unexpected Nation*. Yale University Press, New Haven, CT and London, 2000.

Zlobin, Nikolai, and Vladimir Solov'ev. Russkii Virazh. EKSMO, Moscow, 2014.

Index

About the Author

Jason C. Vaughn has studied Russia and Russian public opinion for the past seventeen years. Over the years, he's worked as an intelligence analyst for the U.S. government, as a researcher, as an English teacher across Russia, as a journalist with myriad publications, and as an independent scholar. He holds a Master of Arts degree in 'Politics, Security, and Integration' and a Master of Philosophy research degree in Russian Politics from University College London. His first book, *A Socio-Political Model of Lies in Russia: Putin against the Personal,* was published by University Press of America in April 2016.